Sexy Girls, Heroes and Funny Losers

# Sexy Girls, Heroes and Funny Losers

## Gender Representations in Children's TV around the World

Edited by Maya Götz
and Dafna Lemish

PETER LANG

Frankfurt am Main · Berlin · Bern · Bruxelles · New York · Oxford · Wien

**Bibliographic Information published by the Deutsche Nationalbibliothek**
The Deutsche Nationalbibliothek lists this publication in the Deutsche Nationalbibliografie; detailed bibliographic data is available in the internet at http://dnb.d-nb.de.

ISBN 978-3-631-63319-9

© Peter Lang GmbH
Internationaler Verlag der Wissenschaften
Frankfurt am Main 2012
All rights reserved.

www.peterlang.de

# Contents

# Preface – How It All Began...

"Gender representation inequalities in children's TV. What? That's still an issue?"

"We have many strong girl characters, more than boy characters."

Both of these statements are typical responses by children's television executives and producers when gender representation issues are raised. Yet, from research as well as social perspectives, gender representation is definitely "still" an issue as, unfortunately, both equality as well as diversity "still" need to be worked on intensely in children's television, as well as in societies, worldwide, in general.

Interestingly, gender representation is an area with substantial potential for collaboration between researchers and TV-executives. As part of a public broadcasting service, the International Central Institute for Youth and Educational Television (IZI) at the Bavarian Broadcasting Cooperation in Germany is well-placed to advance realization of this collaborative potential since the IZI mission is to promote quality in children's, youth and educational television. One very concrete point for such collaboration is to foster sensitive, critical examination of the representations of gender in children's television. In addition, IZI has long realized that with an increasingly globalized media industry, such a pursuit can only be productive in the long run if it takes place within an international context.

One outstanding opportunity to combine research with praxis, in order to promote social change, is provided by the PRIX JEUNESSE INTERNATIONAL; a biannual festival and workshop with over 450 experts and decision makers of children's TV from over 60 countries who come together for six days to share their work, to learn, and to discuss such issues. The central theme of the 2008 gathering of the PRIX JEUNESSE, was "Boys, Girls and Television, the Role of Gender". The 2010 theme was "Celebrating Diversity". Together, these provided us with a rare opportunity to make a difference with our research results in children's television.

With this goal in mind, we began to seek research partners in the winter of 2006/2007 by activating our network of colleagues. In the end, researchers in 24 countries agreed to record and code "routine, everyday" television broadcasts for children and to systematically analyze the content. The result of this process is the largest international media analysis of children's television worldwide performed to date.

The cooperation of the Geena Davis Institute on Gender and Media, with the aid of a generous grant from the Ford Foundation, made it possible for 35 participating researchers to meet in Los Angeles in January 2008. Together with the Geena Davis Institute we organized the Research Round Table on Gender and Media, and also had an opportunity to work closely and constructively with producers.

When the initial results of this global study were presented in June 2008 at the PRIX JEUNESSE INTERNATIONAL, the television executives present were, to put it mildly, humbled. Gender-sensitive materials produced for television executives have since been part of 40 to 60 workshops that the PRIX JEUNESSE network runs every year worldwide. In this way, academic work and excellent collaboration within a large international team has actively contributed to the improvement of children's television across the world. We would like to take this opportunity once again to explicitly express our thanks to this committed group.

From an academic point of view it would almost have been a "sin" to interpret and assess this rich sample of children's television from 24 countries by solely conducting general quantitative content analysis and one special analysis that focused on the measures of body images. Accordingly, the next step was to undertake analyses of additional themes, such as the image of the family, the construction of femininity in dramaturgy, the construction of masculinity in successful series, and consumer behavior and themes in the specific genre of anime. Therefore this second phase of the project – *Children's Television Worldwide: Gender Representations* – sought to delve significantly deeper into the investigation of the construction of gender and to share it with over 450 producers at the PRIX JEUNESSE 2010. This book now presents results from both phases of the media analysis.

The entire project would have been unthinkable without the dedication of many people and the international collaboration of partners in 24 countries. We offer our sincere thanks to the leaders of the national teams and their participating members. The compilation of the large data set on over 26,000 TV characters and the statistical analysis that followed would not have been possible without the skill and diligence of Dr. Ole Hofmann and Sebastian Scheer.

Such a project required extensive and efficient administrative organization undertaken by Rosemarie Hagemeister and Birgit Kinateder. Evelyn Reiter did a wonderful job paying exceptional attention to detail and patience in dealing with very busy people and in assembling all the chapters together into a book. The professional editing for language and clarity, in particular of the non-native English contributions, was done by the skillful and dedicated work of Dr. Peter Lemish. We are deeply grateful to all of these professionals.

Finally, we are particularly grateful not only to individual people, but also to the institutions of the IZI and PRIX JEUNESSE FOUNDATION, as well as to the people who have made such institutions a thriving reality for nearly 50 years. These institutions offer the unique possibility of organizing and conducting ongoing research outside of the conventional routes of academic and industry research, as well as sharing the results with television professionals worldwide. Today, when children's media is dominated by the forces of the market and the maximization of profit, these are the institutions that can really make a difference, for the benefit not only of the media world, but for our societies at large.

*Maya Götz and Dafna Lemish*

# Introduction

## *Maya Götz* and *Dafna Lemish*

Television not only continues to be the most dominant medium for children around the world but it is a growing, blossoming global market. Over fifty years of research on the many roles of television in children's lives suggest that it is one of the most central storytellers and socializers of our times (e.g., Lemish, 2007; Pecora, Murray, & Wartella, 2007). More specifically, studies of the influence of gender images on television suggest they play a significant role in children's development of their gender identity. Children learn what are considered to be appropriate gendered norms of behavior and personality characteristics, and internalize expectations regarding gender roles; such as the range of professions available to them, aspirations regarding romance, management of intimate relationships, marriage and family life; and so forth (Lemish, 2010).

In this regard, the various roles played by television characters in children's lives are of particular interest, since children identify with characters, enter into forms of para-social interactions with them, imitate their behavior, and measure themselves against them. Television characters also play a major role in children's make-believe worlds and fantasy play (Götz, Lemish, Aidman, & Moon, 2005). Furthermore, these characters are a major influence and source of motivation for children's program preferences. Children also employ characters abstracted from media content in a variety of ways in their everyday life. They might adopt a character's personality in its entirety or incorporate specific traits such as abilities, appearance, names, or costumes. Identifying with a character allows the child to participate in the character's experiences, to a certain degree, and can be understood as the child's wish to be like or to behave like the character that is the subject of identification. Therefore, it is of utmost importance to examine the kind of characters offered children on television screens as they are resources for role modeling and identification.

Given this background, we submit that it is pertinent to advance investigations of the gender portrayals offered in children's television. While many studies examined specific programs and popular children's movies, no recent, systematic analyses of gender portrayals on children's television have been undertaken that map television offerings to children around the world. The foundations of the major endeavor reported in this book was a focused study conducted in 2003 by the International Central Institute for Youth and Educational Television (IZI) in

Munich. This study was initiated with a view to analyzing the main characters in the leading roles in the narratives on children's television from a gender perspective. In an attempt to avoid retaining dichotomous gender constructions in this research (Butler, 1990), a gender sensitized approach was applied to all main characters regardless of gender identity. The research question in this study focused on the character's role in the narrative: How does the character deal with the main conflict of the episode?

This 2003 study analyzed 40 programs[1] with 90 female and male protagonists selected from a representative sample of German's children's TV, comprised of locally produced (27%) and imported (73%) programs for children ages three to 13. Characters were analyzed in relation to the main research question by a mixed gender group of eight researchers. In addition, a detailed qualitative description was produced, with special attention devoted to the character's external appearance, body language, and behavior. In the second stage of the analysis, coders looked for typical patterns of dealing with the main conflict with limited consideration of gender issues. Finally, a quantitative analysis of a sample of 179 programs with 412 protagonists was conducted from a representative sample of German children's television programs. The research question and code book developed in this initial study were adopted, later, in developing the *Global Children's TV Study* reported in detail in this book. Here, in this introductory chapter, we report some of the main findings of the 2003 initial investigation (Götz, 2006).

### What Kinds of Protagonists Are Offered in Children's TV?

There was great variation in the characters and the specific ways with which they dealt with conflict. Six types of roles employed in narratives were identified, along with several sub-patterns. We referred to the first group of characters as "egocentrics". These characters staged conflicts or actively sought them out. If they solved problems, they did so entirely according to their own needs. Some characters demonstrated "reflective" capabilities and their attitude and individuality developed during the course of the program. *Pepper Ann* (Disney, USA) is a prototype for this group: A self-confident, self-reliant teenager, she employs many ideas as she advances her journey to finding her own individuality. Another sub-group of the "egocentrics" tries to make their environment conform to their own needs, such as *SpongeBob* (Nickelodeon, USA).

"Communicators", the second group of characters, serve as mediators in conflicts that emerge with partners and friends. They also inform by communicating knowledge about the world. The *Bear in the Big Blue House* (Jim Henson & Co, USA) is a model case: An adult friend who acts as arbiter in disputes, who invites on adventures and who offers explanatory remarks.

The third group of main characters acts as the "responsible" ones in the story. They initiate contact with conflict on their own initiative and demonstrate a sense of responsibility for others and/or care for the problem itself. Bob the Builder or Tintin (from *The Adventures of Tintin*) are such main characters, as they become involved in events intelligently, inquisitively, proactively and use individual initiative.

A related, fourth character – the "resistant" one – is close to this type, but adds a little twist. These characters resist problems and threaten their environment in a single-minded and responsible way. While Tintin (*The Adventures of Tintin*) identifies problems in his surroundings and then solves the crime, Batman, as a "resistant" prototype, is only moved to act when he feels threatened by the crimes of others.

While the main characters described so far are capable of functioning in their situation, the "clueless" characters, the fifth group, are overwhelmed and do not develop a sensible plan to solve the problem. Yet, they usually remain relatively relaxed and, somehow, ultimately survive their escapade. *Darkwing Duck* (Disney, USA), a prototype of this character is a rather foolish busybody who totally overestimates his abilities and still manages to master situations thanks to numerous technical devices.

The "helpless", the sixth type of main character, is the one who has to be rescued from real danger. This is due to the fact that they are either totally passive or helpless, or else despite their own ability to take the initiative, they find themselves in a situation from which they cannot extradite themselves. Wendy from the series *Peter Pan* (Nippon Animation, Japan) is a typical example.

Based on these group characterizations, the main characters were categorized and counted in the quantitative analysis of the representative sample. "Resistant" and "clueless" characters appeared most frequently (24.2% and 25.2% respectively); "egocentrics" composed about a fifth of the characters (19.7%); "communicators" and the "responsible" did not appear as frequently (around 12%); "helpless" characters appeared in only 6.6% of the shows as a main, but never the central character role.

In conclusion: The analysis demonstrated that there is a broad variety of characters in children's programming. While both male and female characters appear in all six categories, there are also clear quantitative differences. Overall, there was a general imbalance: 74.3% of the characters in the sample were male and 25.7% were female characters.

In addition, there were clear gender differences in character categorizations. Males were dominant in the "responsible" and "clueless" characters with over

80% male characters, mainly told by boy characters; while females comprised a significant portion of the "resistant" (32.3%) and especially the "helpless" (44%). So while the study demonstrates that there is a variety of main characters on children's television, it also presents a clear imbalance in their gender distribution across character types (see Figure 1).

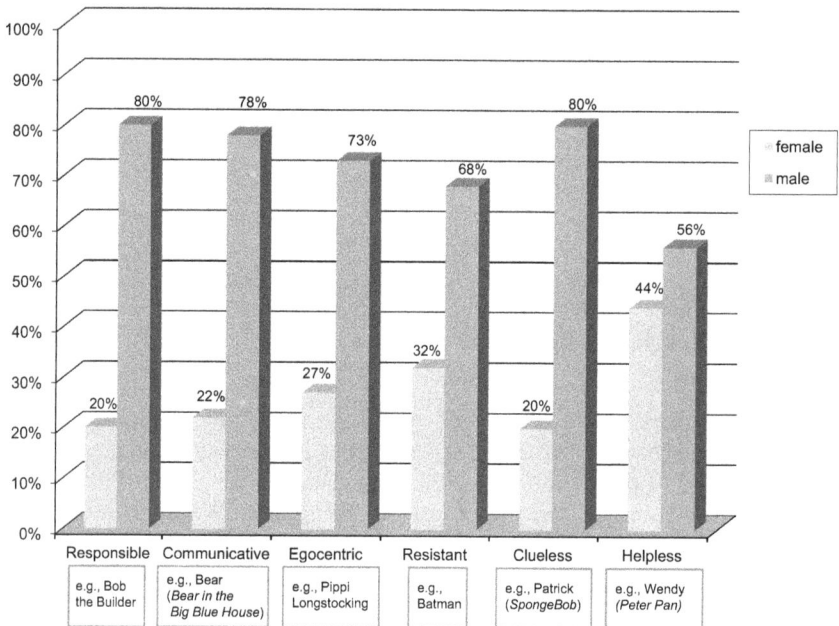

**Figure 1**
Types of main characters

## What Do Producers Say?

These initial findings were very striking, since producers of children's television often expressed the view that the programs they are producing are gender balanced, include many strong girl characters, and that, if anything, they may have neglected boy-characters. The findings demonstrated first, that the producers are mistaken; and, second, there is an urgent need for a systematic, reliable study that will provide an accurate and extensive gender mapping of children's programs.

The motivation for such a study was also reinforced by a different study that focused on the views of producers of quality television programming for children (Lemish, 2010). 135 producers from 65 countries around the world were interviewed about images of gender in children's television. While contextualizing their views, critiques of commercial television, and visions for change, they nevertheless shared their deep concerns for the need to look closely at gender portrayals as they interact with other variables, particularly those of ethnicity and class.

This second foundation of the studies reported in this book involved interviewing producers from around the world and provided unique insights into the location of different societies in their stance toward feminist ideas, as well as their struggles for gender equality. Risking over-generalization, Lemish located the discourse offered by the interviewees from various societies on a continuum following very much the development of feminist thought and activism in the second half of the 20th century. At one end of the continuum are interviewees in *pre-feminist awareness*, as a few producers glossed the issue of gender inequality in their societies as a whole, and in television for children more specifically. This is a form of ideological "gender blindness" characterized by discounting the obvious differences in the lives of boys and girls and the ways they are portrayed on television in those various societies. The second position identified is referred to *numerical equality*: Here, advocates explained that the most basic and obvious effort needed to deal with gender inequality on television was to make girls and boys visible to the same extent, in all genres, and for all ages. These producers argued that, traditionally, girls were usually excluded from many television programs and appeared as a "token" small minority in many others. This conveyed a message of their marginality and lower social status. Yet, their mere visibility on the screen raises consciousness, gives girls a possible voice and calls our attention to their place in society. In many countries, the expectation for presentation of equal numbers of boys and girls in children's programming was taken for granted, but in many others it was still an unattainable goal.

The *role-reversal* position offered is a more advanced stage of gender awareness. Most of these interviewees were very much aware of and able to discuss the gender inequalities pervasive in their cultures. In doing so, they employed liberal feminist arguments as they described attempts to offer viewers role-reversals on television: On the one hand, women and girls portrayed on television assume roles usually reserved for males; and, on the other hand, men and boys do anything traditionally associated with females.

The fourth position is referred to as *different but equal*: Interviewees from several countries expressed a need to go one step further in their attempt to challenge gendered societal norms and expectations. Rather than being concerned with girls' capability to do anything boys can do, and vice versa, they emphasized recognition of the inherent differences between boys and girls, and recommended that these be respected and celebrated in television for children.

Finally, some producers expressed *post-feminist sentiments* in which they argued that since gender equality seems to them to have been mainstreamed and accepted as a given in some societies, feminism has aged and become irrelevant. Such views were particularly evident among some producers in Western countries who believed that their television fare offers a fair portrayal of gender equality and that they were ready to move on to other concerns, mainly those of cultural and racial diversity (Lemish, 2010).

In conclusion, these *foundational* studies demonstrate that, from a global perspective, gender differences and visions for gender equity cannot be viewed in a monolithic manner. Second, no uniform treatment or single form of intervention is appropriate. Yet, basic studies of equity through such devices as numerical representations and distribution of appearances, personality traits and possibilities offer a starting point that can be ascertained and agreed upon, above and beyond cultural differences.

It is with this research background that we set out to plan and execute a study that aimed to move the discussion of gender equity in children's television worldwide away from a state of either lack of awareness and/or concern, as well as from ill-informed illusions that gender equity on the screen has been achieved and the work of feminism completed (Douglas, 2010). The research reported in this book presents findings from such a comprehensive project.

## Outline of the Book

The first chapter of the book (Götz & Lemish, chapter 1) presents the quantitative analysis of the research project – "Children's TV around the World". The main findings map gender representations on TV screens of 24 countries. The results of this extensive content-analysis-based project point to striking imbalances in the presentation of gender, despite a common sense feeling among many producers that this is not the case. This quantitative study led us to engage in in-depth, focused qualitative analyses of several of the main themes that emerged in the content analysis study. In particular, we felt that a closer, more extensive investigation needed to be devoted to girls, due to their consistent under-representation worldwide as well as the prevalence of stereotypical portrayals.

One overriding theme that emerged in the qualitative study was the girl characters' appearances; more specifically, the sexualization of girls, regardless of their roles in the narratives and their other characteristics. Accordingly, we devote a chapter to general body appearances of girls and boys (Götz & Herche, chapter 2). The findings presented demonstrate that unrealistic, unattainable and unhealthy popular body shapes are presented to children. Following this general analysis, Prinsloo (chapter 3) presents a close reading of selected examples of highly popular sexualized animated female characters traveling around the world that target pre-pubertian girls with prescriptions for expected appearance and behavior. The final chapter in this section, written by Spry (chapter 4) presents his investigation of the strong influence of Japanese animation styles on the construction of sexualized female characters in the most popular animation. While contextualized in historical and cultural fantasies designed originally for adult males, Spry demonstrates how these portrayals are now being imposed on children.

Discussion in the book of "sexy girls" then shifts to an analysis of boys as "heroes and funny losers" (Götz, Neubauer, & Winter, chapter 5). In contrast to the unified theme of sexuality for all girls, Götz et. al. map the diverse types of boys found on children's television. Given that ethnicity and gender are so closely intertwined, Scholte (chapter 6) examines the ethnic diversity of superheroines. She documents the continuing dominance of Caucasian characters and suggests that the introduction of some diversity into children's TV relies on commonly accepted stereotypes and does not offer truly new roles and empowering stories for girls with different ethnicities.

In addition to the construction of femininity and masculinity, Lemish (chapter 7) presents an in-depth analysis of the portrayals of families in children's television, as the central site of gender construction and division of labor. The chapter examines the presence and types of families in children's television and models offered to children.

Chan (chapter 8) presents a general understanding of consumerism as it relates to gender, by suggesting that while both genders are targeted with consumption values, the products advertised to them vary greatly.

In conclusion, we submit that this collection, while comprehensive, leaves many unanswered questions and opens up new realms of study for further investigation. Thus, we conclude the book with one such direction by sharing a totally different perspective – "viewers as experts". Given the gendered world presented to children on their television screens, as documented, analyzed, and criticized by researchers throughout this book, Götz & Herche (chapter 9) enable us to listen to the voices of children, and in doing so to gain a sense of what children around the world think of these images and the main themes identified in our studies.

## REFERENCES

Butler, J. (1990). *Gender Trouble*. New York, NY: Routledge.

Douglas, S. J. (2010). *Enlightened Sexism: The Seductive Message that Feminism's Work Is Done*. New York, NY: Times Books.

Götz, M. (2006). Die Hauptfiguren im deutschen Kinderfernsehen [Main characters in German children's television]. *TelevIZIon, 19*(1), 4-7.

Götz, M., Lemish, D., Aidman, A., & Moon, H. (2005). *Media and the Make-Believe Worlds of Children: When Harry Potter Meets Pokémon in Disneyland*. Mahwah, NJ: Erlbaum.

Lemish, D. (2007). *Children and Television: A Global Perspective*. Oxford, UK: Blackwell.

Lemish, D. (2010). *Screening Gender on Children's Television: The View of Producers Around the World*. New York, NY: Routledge.

Pecora, N., Murray, J. P., & Wartella, E. (Eds.). (2007). *Children and Television: Fifty Years of Research*. Mahwah, NJ: Lawrence Erlbaum.

---

[1] Ten programs have female and ten have male names in the title; for example, *Bibi Blocksberg* (ZDF, Germany) and *Spongebob* (Nickelodeon, USA); another ten include the name of the group in the title, such as *Totally Spies!* (Marathon, France); and the final ten link a location or species or more general name, such as *Pokémon* (OLM, Japan).

# 1

# GENDER REPRESENTATIONS IN CHILDREN'S TELEVISION WORLDWIDE: A COMPARATIVE STUDY OF 24 COUNTRIES

*Maya Götz* and *Dafna Lemish*

Children's television functions as a storyteller, providing the basic materials of fantasies and images of the world beyond viewers' immediate environment. Complimentary learning from storytelling occurs when viewing images or ideas, as viewers learn what it means to be a girl or boy, a man or woman. While children's identities and performance of gender are shaped, primarily, through children's experiences in their direct social environment, the media – and particularly the most influential medium, television – supply important images and perspectives that can make a strong impression and influence children's imagination, particularly in regard to gender-oriented learning (Götz, Lemish, Aidman, & Moon, 2005). Yet a closer look at the images broadcast on television reveals a major social imbalance in the way children's programs construct femininity and masculinity:

> On the whole, like adult males, boys are identified with "doing" in the public sphere that is associated with characteristics such as action, rationality, forcefulness, aggressiveness, independence, ambitiousness, competitiveness, achievement, higher social status, and humor. Girls, like adult women, are associated with "being" in the private sphere and are characterized, generally, as passive, emotional, caregiving, childish, sexy, subordinate to males, and of lower social status. (Lemish, 2010, pp. 1/2)

Girlhood is also constructed in a manner closely related to beautification and consumerism. Many girl characters, such as the Bratz dolls, seem to have mainly one desire that defines them; namely, a "passion for fashion" (McAllister, 2007).

An analysis of children's and family films produced for the cinema in the US found that only 28% of all characters who speak were female (Smith & Cook, 2008). Within the context of the United States, gender-specific content analyses have been conducted primarily on animated formats (Aubrey & Harrison, 2004; Baker & Raney, 2004; Barcus, 1983; Levinson, 1975; Sternglanz & Serbin, 1974; Streicher, 1974; Thompson & Zerbinos, 1995). The findings from these studies affirm the following tendencies: In comparison with male characters, female characters are less active, less loud, less likely to be in positions of responsibility and more likely to behave immaturely. They show more emotions, are presented more in the context of their relationships to others, are both more helpful and they more frequently ask for help and for protection. Male characters behave more aggressively, loudly and are more frequently rewarded within the storyline. They demonstrate more ingenuity, ask more questions, are more frequently presented through their particular abilities and talents, laugh more often, are more insulting and threaten others more frequently.

For example, Luther & Legg (2010) examined the kinds of aggression exhibited by animated cartoon characters in 147 half-hour animated shows. They found a clear difference between the sexes: Physical aggression was used more by male characters (48.1%) and by female characters (34% of the cases); forms of social aggression, such as slander, were used much more frequently by female characters (30.6% compared to 9.5% for males).

Studies of the images of gender find that there are strong, interesting female main characters in children's television and feature films. A qualitative analysis traced the narrative context of 13 film heroines in highly successful Hollywood films for children between 1937 and 2006, such as *Snow White and the Seven Dwarfs* (Disney, USA), *The Princess Diaries* (Disney, USA), *The Wizard of Oz* (MGM, USA), *Mulan* (Disney, USA) and so on (Smith & Cook, 2008). These films tell the stories of heroines who, for example, usually have to overcome great trials and save friends and family. In only a few exceptional cases are they victims of circumstance ("damsels in distress"), as in the case of Snow White. Nearly all characters were famed for their looks or undergoing a striking change, presenting them as a beauty desired by all – as in the case of *The Princess Diaries*. Thus, beauty is represented as the most important and most valued aspect of female personality in these texts.

In addition, female characters are driven by a range of different motivations. Some are daydreamers who lack a clear goal, while others are led astray or lose their way. There are also the daredevils who have a relevant goal in mind that drives them on. In nearly all of the films analyzed, the female character longs for true love; for example, she experiences love at first sight, love that has to overcome intrigue, love that is saved through communication. So, the researchers concluded that the main focus of the female roles is always: beauty, approval, and true love (Smith & Cook, 2008).

Another study examined the gender representation of 70 female and male superheroes featured on 160 hours of programs shown in 2004 (Baker & Raney, 2007). All of the characters in the corpus accomplished missions by fighting evil superpowers, in programs such as *Kim Possible* (Disney, USA), *Beyblade* (Madhouse, Japan), *The Powerpuff Girls* (Cartoon Network, USA) and *Totally*

*Spies!* (Marathon, France). The analysis found that in the case of superheroes, there were more male than female protagonists (65.7% male versus 34.3%). When there were heroines, they were more likely to react emotionally, especially in critical situations, and were given an unmistakably attractive outward appearance. Heroines were more likely to be superficial and more concerned with their looks than heroes, were more likely to ask questions than use threats, and usually work as a team (87.5%). In addition, twice as many heroines as heroes had a mentor, who was nearly always a man. While there are positive exceptions of programs where girls and their point of view take center stage, researchers found clear gender stereotyping even in the sometimes ultra-modern superheroes. Heroines were more concerned about their appearance, and tended to overreact in critical situations more than male protagonists. Girl heroines, on the whole, displayed more communicative abilities, were more frequently team players, and more likely to ask questions. In contrast, male heroes were more likely to issue threats through use of violence (Baker & Raney, 2007).

## The Outward Appearance of TV Heroes in Children's Television

The main characters in children's television are represented with certain outward features. Fictional formats, in particular, make conscious use of details such as skin or hair color, and body shape. Referred to as "hypersexualization" in scholarship and public debates (e.g., Durham, 2008; Levine & Kilbourne, 2008), this trend was also identified in an analysis of 4,000 characters in 400 successful children's and family films in the United States by Smith & Cook (2008). The researchers found that extreme thinness and provocative, sexy clothing was five times as common in female as in male characters. The percentage of hypersexualized girl and women characters grows even higher in animation, especially in regard to the hypersexualization of the body and "wasp waists" (i.e., a very small waist with curvy hips below). In summary, women and girl characters were hypersexualized five times as often as boy or men characters. They may no longer play helpless victims, but no matter what role they are assigned, they are always flawlessly beautiful and longing for true love (Smith & Cook, 2008).

Studies in Germany of media texts produced in Germany and the United States found that common stereotypes, such as the helpless blonde or the cheeky redhead, are repeated in children's television (Götz, 2006). The only current international comparative study on gender representation in a part of children's television analyzed several variables in adult advertisement in the United Kingdom and Poland (Furnham & Saar, 2005). The two studies found that there were more males as central figures. Although the difference between the two countries is not a huge one, the Polish advertisements are slightly more gender role stereotypical. Aside from the "Media Monitoring Project" (GMMP, 2010) examination of gender representations in news programs around the world, we lack broadly conceived, global, comparative studies of gender in children's television.

The "Children's Television Worldwide: Gender Representations" reported in this book was initiated as an effort to contribute to correcting this lacunae. The study collected a sample of children's television in 24 countries in May-July 2007, and then analyzed the texts in cooperation with colleagues across the globe. Functioning under the general research question – what is children's television really like? – we focused the quantitative content analysis on the following secondary questions:

- Who are the main protagonists in these programs?
- What role do the protagonists play in the storyline?
- What differences can be seen between male and female characters?
- Is there variation in the gender differences when comparing public service or state channels and private, commercial providers, as well as between domestic and international productions?

The main focus of the study reported here focused on fiction genres in children's television and on the construction of gender as presented to children on television screens around the world.

## Method

### The Sample

A sample, representative of the relevant children's television, with a share of at least five percent of the market, was selected in each of the 24 participating countries. Depending on the transmitting system, public service or state channels and commercial providers were included. The country-specific aim was to record between 100 and 200 hours of programs representative of week, day, and weekend options, respectively.[1] Admittedly, the sample was smaller due to limited number and variety of programs offered in some countries. In some countries, the size of the sample lay below 35 hours.[2] The recordings took place between 2 May 2007 and 1 July 2007.[3]

All individual samples were analyzed centrally in Munich (at the International Central Institute for Youth and Educational Television, IZI), both on a national level and as a complete aggregated sample.[4]

## Coding

A codebook was developed guided by the research questions. A first draft was drawn up in Germany, and the revision included the feedback and suggestions proposed by international colleagues. The second draft was accepted by all partners.

The code book included general variables, such as genre of the program, place of production, language, as well as, character-specific variables such as gender, age, ethnicity, body size, hair color, disability, role in the narrative, and context in which the character appears. Each variable was tested by different coding groups. Coders in every country were trained by jointly coding at least 20 programs. Sampling and coding were the responsibility of each research partner. Consolidation and the original interpretation of the data was organized centrally in Munich and confirmed in consultation with partners from the respective countries who also supplemented the study with specific interpretations of texts.

Due to the fact that the study was undertaken in 24 countries and in different languages, reliability pre-tests with all coders involved was impossible to organize. Each country ensured that training of coders was undertaken and internal reliability measures secured.

An additional post research reliability of the coding of the characters was tested following Lienert and Raatz (1989), by determining the share of the mainstream coding of the respective character for each variable. At this stage, all the characters coded in a minimum of two countries were included. The reliability of the coding of these 16,907 characters ranged between 80.6% and 99.8% for most variables.[5]

"Leadership" was the weakest reliability value (73.9%). Our explanation for this result is that different episodes of the same program were coded. The same could be the case for the 80.6% reliability result of the variable of "constellation of main character/s" (i.e., leader, follower, etc.), as it too could differ from episode to episode.

## Results

The worldwide sample consisted of 2,402 hours of television aimed explicitly at children, and contained 20,452 individual program elements. The main analytic focus during this first stage of the study was on fictional programs. Thus, the 6,375 programs with fictional content (1,654 hours) and 26,342 main characters formed the data base for analysis. Some of the coding was applied only to human characters (n=14,959).

The main results of the worldwide survey are summarized in the following pages (see Table 1.1).

## Table 1.1.
Participating countries and samples

| Country | Broadcaster | Hours of record | Hours of show-fiction | Fictional pro-grams | All char-acters | Human char-acters |
|---|---|---|---|---|---|---|
| Argentina | Canal 13, Canal 7, Canal 9, Telefe | 24:56 | 20:15 | 34 | 110 | 50 |
| Australia | ABC TV, Channel 10, Channel 7, Channel 9 | 111:25 | 76:43 | 282 | 878 | 516 |
| Austria | ORF1, ARD, KI.KA, Nick, RTL2, Super RTL, ZDF | 171:07 | 111:27 | 497 | 2,120 | 1,128 |
| Belgium | Ka2, Ketnet, La Deux, VT4, VTM | 117:54 | 86:35 | 445 | 1,803 | 1,032 |
| Brazil | Disney Channel, Globo, Nickelodeon, Record, RedeTV, SBT, TV Cultura | 30:49 | 22:29 | 95 | 693 | 408 |
| Canada | CBC, CTV, SRC, Teletoon/Télétoon, TQc, TQS, VRAK, YTV | 92:26 | 79:05 | 147 | 1,015 | 609 |
| China | BTV, CCTV | 182:03 | 57:05 | 277 | 1,015 | 596 |
| Cuba | Cubavisión, Tele Rebelde | 85:31 | 69:05 | 290 | 838 | 243 |
| Egypt | Art, Channel 1, Channel 2, Al Jazeera, Family & Children, MBC 3, Space Toon | 73:30 | 46:01 | 191 | 894 | 624 |
| Germany | ARD, KI.KA, Nick, RTL2, Super RTL, ZDF | 154:57 | 99:07 | 457 | 2,011 | 1,095 |
| Hong Kong | ATV Home, ATV World, TVB Jade, TVB Pearl | 123:31 | 88:24 | 169 | 447 | 277 |
| Hungary | Cartoon Network, Duna, Jetix, M2, minimax, minimax/A+, RTL Klub, TV2 | 22:09 | 17:13 | 281 | 910 | 468 |
| India | Animax, Australia Network, Cartoon Network, Chandana, Disney, Doordarshan, etv, jaya tv, Nick, Nick Jr., Pogo, Sony, Star one, Star plus, sun tv, surya, zee kannada | 101:54 | 50:10 | 158 | 877 | 439 |

| | | | | | |
|---|---|---|---|---|---|
| Israel | Cartoon, Channel 6, Hop!, Jetix, Nickelodeon, Yes Sababa | 172:34 | 148:19 | 360 | 1,041 | 690 |
| Kenya | Citizen Television, Family TV, KBC Television, Kenya Television Network, Nation Television, Television Network | 67:37 | 35:36 | 149 | 781 | 601 |
| Malaysia | Astro Ceria, RTM 1, RTM 2, TV 9 | 13:00 | 3:36 | 29 | 173 | 126 |
| Netherlands | Jetix, Nederland 3, Nickelodeon | 114:40 | 87:45 | 370 | 1,447 | 938 |
| New Zealand | Cartoon Network, Disney, Nickelodeon, Playhouse, tv2 | 103:07 | 62:16 | 382 | 1,619 | 970 |
| Norway | Disney Channel, NRK, TV2 | 25:09 | 20:56 | 78 | 364 | 215 |
| Slovenia | Cartoon Network, Kanal A, POP TV, TV 3, TV Slovenija 1 | 122:53 | 107:16 | 566 | 2,156 | 1,517 |
| South Africa | ETV, SABC | 83:07 | 66:13 | 204 | 1,123 | 820 |
| Syria | Al Jazeera Children, MBC 3 Children, Syrian 1st TV Channel, Syrian Satellite Channel | 11:38 | 6:28 | 31 | 134 | 84 |
| UK | CBBC, CBeebies, CITV | 102:28 | 91:06 | 260 | 1,178 | 588 |
| USA | ABC Family, Cartoon Network, Discovery Kids, Disney, Fox, Nickelodeon, Nicktoons, Noggin/The N; PBS, PBS/Digital Kids, Playhouse Disney, Toon Disney, Jetix, WLIW/PBS, WNET/PBS, WPIX/CW, CBS, CW, ION, NBC, TLC, Toon Disney, nick jr, sprout | 293:49 | 201:11 | 623 | 2,715 | 925 |
| **Total** | | **2,402:14** | **1,654:21** | **6,375** | **26,342** | **14,959** |

## 1. Children's Television Broadcast across the Globe

### Television Aimed Explicitly at Children Is Dominated by Fiction Programs

The sample analyzed consisted of 20,452 program elements and was initially coded according to the type of show. Each program was categorized as fiction, non-fiction, a combination of different formats, school television, documentary, or game show. Advertisements and trailers were coded as one block. This analysis identified 9,207 programs as follows: fictional content – 69.2% (n=6,375 programs); non-fiction programs – 17.1% (n=1,570 programs) categorized as documentary or school television; and combination of formats – 7.4% (n=678 programs). The percentage of non-fiction programs was significantly higher across the globe for public service channels (see Figure 1.1).

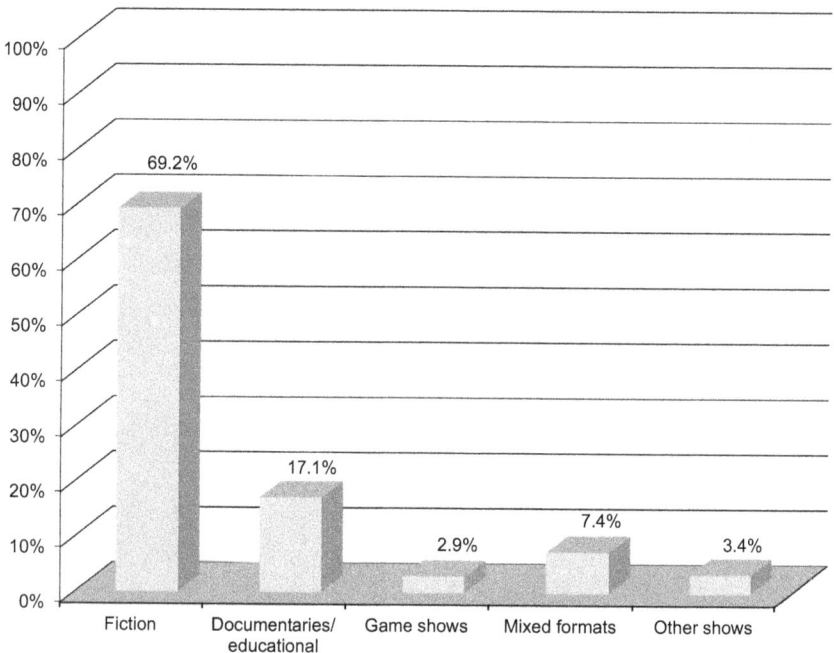

IZI – Children's Television Worldwide 2007; basis: all countries

**Figure 1.1.**
Overall genres of children's TV

## Children's Television Is Made up Primarily of Animation

Animated programs comprise by far the highest percentage of fictional programs worldwide (84%, n=5,345). The number of live action formats is far lower (9%, n=567). This is also the case for mixed formats (5%, n=290) and puppet formats (2%, n=152). The percentage of animation in television broadcasts for children is particularly high in Slovenia, China, Canada, and Egypt; and particularly low in Belgium and the United Kingdom. Colleagues in Belgium and the United Kingdom see their strong public service broadcasters, whose main emphasis lies on fiction programs with real actors (live action), as the reason for their comparatively low percentage of animation. The international comparison revealed that the percentage of public service channels with animation lies below that of commercial providers by a marginal, but nonetheless significant amount (80.7% to 85.5%). Thus, it seems that it depends on the individual profile of the public service channel whether or not other aesthetic forms besides animation constitute an important percentage of their broadcasts for children.

## Children's Television Consists Primarily of Imported Programs

In 77% of cases, the fictional programs of the international sample were created by production companies whose main base was not in the country where the programs were broadcast; that is, only 23% of the programs were produced or co-produced domestically. While the United States, Central China and Canada have the highest percentage of domestic productions, Kenya, New Zealand, Hong Kong and Austria have the lowest percentage of domestic productions (see Figure 1.2). Out of the public broadcasters, the United Kingdom and United States have the highest percentages of domestic productions in their broadcast schedule, while Austria and New Zealand have the lowest.

The often repeated claim that there is a globalization of children's television asserts television programs produced in few countries in the world travel to other countries (Pecora, 1998; Steemer, 2004). The explanation for this phenomenon is that it is much less expensive and simpler to acquire ready-made programs from a supplier than to produce one's own local production (Bryant, 2007).

In studying the origins of programs in our sample, we found that the biggest export region in children's television is North America with about 60% of domestically produced or co-produced programs, followed by Europe with 27.9% and Asia with 9.3%. The United States is the major "seller" of children's TV (48.5% of all programs) followed by Canada with 12.2% (775) of all shows coded in the sample (see Table 1.2).

**Table 1.2.**
Country of origin of children's TV traveling around the world

| Country | No. of Programs | % of Programs |
|---|---|---|
| USA | 3,092 | 48.5% |
| Canada | 775 | 12.2% |
| UK | 726 | 11.4% |
| France | 386 | 6.1% |
| Japan | 330 | 5.2% |
| Germany | 235 | 3.7% |
| Belgium | 196 | 3.1% |
| China | 152 | 2.4% |
| Australia | 96 | 1.5% |
| Netherlands | 89 | 1.4% |
| Spain | 74 | 1.2% |
| Other | 484 | 7.6% |
| Unknown | 399 | 6.3% |

We also found there to be a dominance of animation in children's television, because this is a genre that travels easily as it can be made less cultural specific (e.g., skin color of characters; imaginary creatures and settings).

The ensuing problems with program content are self-evident: Most children in the world grow up with the images, stories and worldviews of other, mostly Western, cultures. Thus, there are limited chances for them to learn about their own life world and hear stories from their own cultural repertoire. On the one hand, the global transfer of programs make it possible for viewers to discover and recognize people and life worlds similar to their own, and creates a sense of value and appreciation. On the other hand, a diet of program viewing consisting almost exclusively of stories from and representations of another culture runs the risk of creating alienation and implicit devaluation of local traditions and values.

While most countries have to deal with this import phenomenon, it is exactly the opposite in the United States where 82.7% of the programs broadcast are produced or co-produced by North American production companies. Thus, the United States is 60% above the world average. 9% of productions broadcast in the United States come from Canada, 4% from France, 1% from the United Kingdom, and marginal percentages from other countries. Thus 91.7% of the television programs broadcast to American children originated in North America. This creates a different range of problems, for here the chance to learn about other countries' cultures, everyday life, stories and traditions and so on is lost. This could well mean that young American viewers live in cultural isolation, and they may well lack wider awareness and open-mindedness toward the rest of the world.

Furthermore, in the United States promotion of quality programs is very different from the rest of the world. Commercial providers (e.g., ABC, CBS, Nick Jr., TLC and WPX) broadcast only programs produced in the United States. The Public Broadcasting System (PBS) offers a higher percentage of international productions. Discovery Kids has the highest percentage of non-US productions, as their company is based in Toronto (Nelvana), where they are obliged to offer a high percentage of Canadian productions.

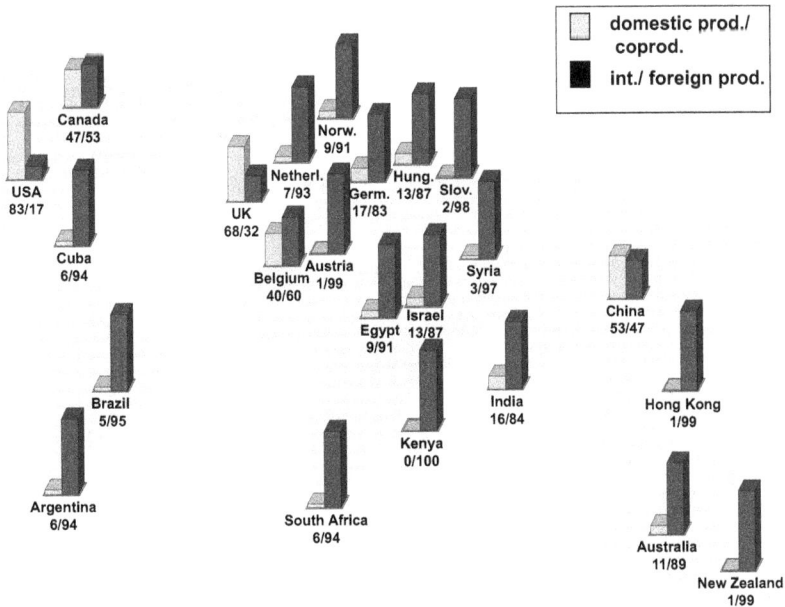

**Figure 1.2.**
Children's TV consists mainly of "imported" programs

## Programs Are Broadcast in the Country's Official Language in over 80% of the Cases

6,375 fictional programs in the worldwide sample are broadcast in the respective countries' main language (or official language) comprising 81.8% of cases. This means that the programs are dubbed in most countries. However, certain countries share the same language; this is particularly the case in the English-speaking world (i.e., in the United States, United Kingdom, New Zealand, and Australia).

Only one language is spoken in 95.9% of the programs. Two languages are intentionally combined for pedagogical reasons in some programs, such as *Dora the Explorer* (Nickelodeon, USA) or *Die Sendung mit dem Elefanten* (i.e., *The Show with the Elephant*) (WDR, Germany). In some countries, such as Slovenia, Belgium, Brazil, Israel, or the Netherlands, viewers are accustomed to reading subtitles of programs broadcast in a foreign language. This occurred in 6.8% of programs in the worldwide sample. Countries or language areas with more than one main language present a special case. In other countries with many languages, such as India or South Africa, some of the programs are dubbed in regional languages, which to a certain extent is cheaper than subtitling in for each of the low-resource countries such as India.

Most public service providers broadcast in their national language and most do not subtitle at all. While Syria subtitles 100% of its programs, public broadcasters in Belgium, the Netherlands and Slovenia use subtitles in some cases. Proportionally, as expected, the national language can be observed in domestic productions significantly more often than in international programs.

## 2. The Main Characters in Children's Television

### The Gender of the Main Characters: Male Characters Are Twice as Common as Female Characters

The programs' main characters were analyzed in the next step of the research. Main characters were defined as those on screen for at least 50% of the viewing time. The character's gender was coded based on the character's grammatical designation (he or she), the name of the character, the voice, and clear gender-specific characteristics.

The results are as follows: Of the 26,342 main characters of the fictional programs in the worldwide sample, 32% were girls or women and 68% boys or men. Numerically speaking, children's television clearly does not represent humanity's real proportion of 51% females and 49% males. In children's television, there were at least two male main characters for every female main character. The percentage of heroines was 34.0% in programs produced domestically, and somewhat higher in the imported programs (31.6% on world average).

Comparing individual countries, the United Kingdom (37% to 63%) and Israel (37% to 63%) were the countries with the highest percentage of female main characters, and Cuba (20% to 80%) had the lowest percentage of female characters (see Figure 1.3).

A surprising trend can be observed across the globe: Public service providers, with 31% female main characters, lie below the private, commercial providers by a small but significant 2%. One possible reason for this finding is that public service channels traditionally reach more girls, and are trying to become more attractive to boys by over-representing male characters. Market logic may be another mechanism at work here: Namely, private and commercial channels have a systematic, built-in orientation toward viewer demands. Channels with the highest percentage of female main characters are providers that aim to be attractive to girls, such as the Disney channel, while others target boys, such as Cartoon Network.

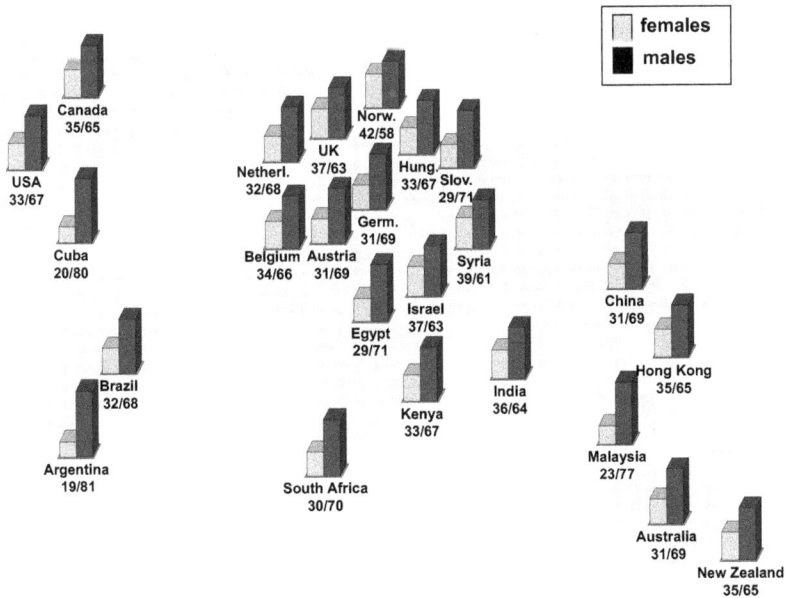

**Figure 1.3.**
Sex of the main characters

## Female Characters Are Most Likely to Be Humans,
## Far Less Likely to Be Animals or Other Beings

The main characters of children's television, worldwide, are humans (59%), animals (26%) along with some monsters, mythical creatures, plants, robots, or machines. From a gender-specific perspective, the under-represented ratio of female to male characters is as follows: humans (37% to 63%), animals (25% to 75%), monsters (21% to 79%), robots (16% to 84%) and other made-up creatures (13% to 87%) (see Figure 1.4).

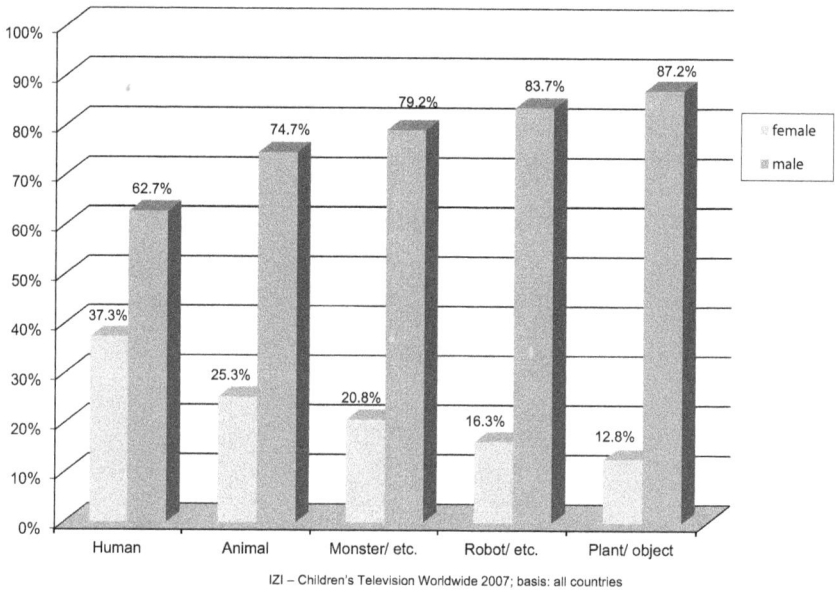

IZI – Children's Television Worldwide 2007; basis: all countries

**Figure 1.4.**
Type of characters

The extent of this unfair bias becomes even clearer when looking closely at the types of protagonists. If the stories are about humans, then girls (or women) make up nearly a third of characters. But if animals are at the center of the story, 87.1% of the main characters are males, while only 12.9% are female. One possible reason for this finding is that animated characters or animal main characters are pure constructions. In animation, whether an animal is given a female or male name or characteristics depends not on reality, but only on the wishes of the producers. As the genitals of animal actors are normally not visible, the decision to call the dolphin Flipper is left solely up to those in charge. One might conclude that the higher the degree of creative construction, the worse the ratio of the sexes. This is the phenomenon referred to by Simone de Beauvoir in *The Second Sex* (1949/2009): Those holding the power to define determine what is normal, by assuming, perhaps unconsciously, that their own values are shared by others. As many cartoon animators and authors are men, and many storytelling traditions are dominated by men, characters are naturally first conceived of as male and constructed accordingly. Characters are conceived of as girls only when the task is to tell a different kind of story, to be attractive to girls (e.g., Götz, 1999b), or to present girls as attractive for boys' pleasure.

## Whose Voiceover Is Heard?

A voiceover guides viewers through the story and comments on the events in several children's programs. Therefore, each program was coded according to whether there was a narrative voice and whether this voice was that of a man/boy or a woman/girl. There is no narrative voiceover in 75.6% of the programs. However, if one was present, it is on average 14.6% male and 6.1% female, worldwide. In 3.5% of programs there is both a male and a female voiceover. If a voiceover comments on events in children's television programs, then it is twice as frequent for a man or boy to provide the explanation. The countries with the highest percentage of male narrative voices are Cuba, Brazil, United Kingdom, and Egypt. There are no female narrative voices in China or Hong Kong. Female voiceovers are more common in Belgium (16.9%).

## 3. Constructing the Narrative in Children's Television Worldwide

Fictional programs tell stories that are a product of their authors' imagination, as realized by the production team. Nothing about their basic conception is "coincidental". It is presented purposefully – even if their thought is unconscious or preconscious. Following Berger and Luckmann (1965), when fantasy becomes objective reality, people (must) then deal with it. This understanding is fundamental to the research questions guiding this study: How are main roles distributed between the sexes? What part does gender play in the story?

Using the worldwide sample of children's television, we sought to answer these research questions using quantitative content analysis as far as possible. In doing so, we sought to determine the male to female ratio among the main characters of fictional television programs aimed explicitly at children; their social position in the story; their relationships; and the voiceover that was employed to frame the story in some programs.

## The Characters' Predisposition: Who Is the "Baddie"?
## Men and Boys Are the Wicked Characters

Regarding the social position of a character, the primary concern is to determine
whether the persona is a positive character (protagonist) or negative character
(antagonist) within the context of the story. The coding showed that most main
characters in children's TV are positive characters. However, 14% are presented
as obvious "baddies". The United Kingdom and Australia were the two main
countries in which many stories employed antagonists; 28.8% and 27.3% of the
main characters, respectfully, are wicked. Antagonists are rarely found in Israel
(4.5%), Belgium (6.4%) and Hong Kong (6.5%). We can only guess at the extent
to which this difference is cultural. For example, there is a strong tradition of ironic
comedy programs produced in the United Kingdom and Australia. In contrast,
Israeli television programs emphasize positive role models due, perhaps, to this
country's particular history of conflict and heightened sensitivity towards any forms
of glorification of people wishing to harm society. In addition, women are much
less likely to be antagonists in children's television throughout the world (10%),
whereas at least 15% of all male characters are antagonists.

### Social Relations: Female Characters Are More Commonly Part of a Team

Main characters are often shown in children's TV worldwide as members of a
group, and act within that group. Indeed, over half of the main characters (57%)
were found to be part of a larger team. Main characters that move through the story
as lone fighters or part of a team of two make up around 20% of characters. While
in Brazil, many stories feature loners, main characters who are members of a team
are featured in China, United States, Belgium, and Syria.

From a gender-specific perspective, female characters throughout the world
are significantly more common as members of groups than male characters (60%
to 54%) and they are less likely to be loners (18% to 22%) (see Figure 1.5). This
finding complements feminist theories that claim that the individualist and hierarchal
structure of male relationships is built on separation, in comparison to women's
horizontal networking that develops through togetherness and bonding (Chodorow,
1978). At the same time, this finding also reflects the Hollywood film tradition of
the strong, independent leader and the lonely "cowboy" who fights against evil and
does not trust anyone.

Girls, on the other hand, come in groups in popular culture (e.g., the *Spice
Girls, Charlie's Angels, The Powerpuff Girls,* the *Bratz*). This is such a common
phenomenon as to suggest that producers think that it requires a few female
characters to hold the narrative, in comparison with only one male figure. This is

particularly striking in light of the reality in which girls develop a friendship with "a best friend", while boys tend to associate in groups rather than function alone, creating a major discrepancy between reality and representations (Benson, 1990; Benenson, Apostoleris, & Parnass, 1997).

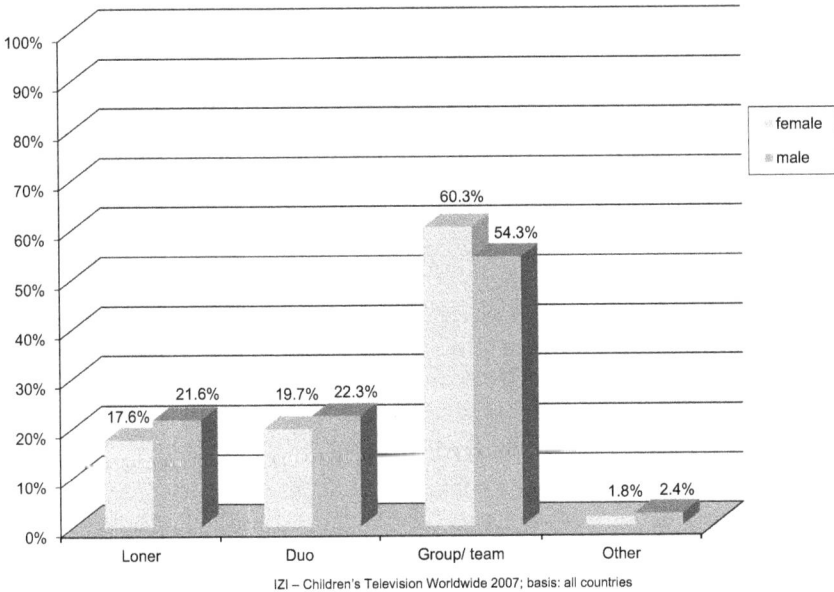

IZI – Children's Television Worldwide 2007; basis: all countries

**Figure 1.5.**
Relation of characters

Accordingly, it is important to examine more closely whether a character behaves in a particularly dominant mode in the course of a story, assumes a higher status or achieves greater importance in a given hierarchy, or whether they interact with others on an equal footing.21% of main characters in children's television worldwide are a kind of leader, in that they are involved in telling others what to do. In contrast, close to half (48%) interact with others on an equal footing within the story. 16% of the main characters were coded as *following others*. Taking a gender-sensitive viewpoint, female main characters are more frequently on an equal footing with their peers (53.2% of all characters) than are men or boy characters (45.6%). Yet, of all the characters analyzed, only 1,320 (16.9%) of the females held a leading position in the hierarchy, while this was the case for 3,736 male main characters (22.7%).

So, girl and women characters are presented more as members of groups and as equals than as holding hierarchically elevated positions where they act as the leaders of a group. The countries with the lowest percentage of female leaders are Hong Kong, the Netherlands, and Belgium. Countries where there are a comparatively high number of female leaders are India (40.5%) and Cuba (35.8%). However, Argentina and Cuba are the countries with the lowest percentage of female main characters (19% and 20% female characters versus 81% and 80% males as main characters). This finding merits further qualitative study; for example, investigations of those few programs that show girls and women in hierarchically elevated positions might determine if this is undertaken due to the gender imbalance or whether this is actually an indicator of further mechanisms devaluing strong women.

*Scene of First Appearance*

The question of the space within which a main character enters into the storyline is one way of positioning a character that has only seldom been subjected to explicit content analysis. Studying such a place lends insight in the context and is, as well, an implicit part of their characterization, since it points to the environment in which a character is frequently encountered (see Figure 1.6).

The most common places for introducing the main characters of children's TV across the globe are *private* spaces (44.1% of the spaces). 26.7% of characters first appear in public places or at professional workplaces. 17.2% of characters first appear in nature and 10.3% in school. Characters are more likely to have their first appearance in a nature environment in domestic productions; that is, a private or public environment is comparatively less often the first location of appearance.

There are far fewer gender differences in this analytical category than expected. Female main characters are introduced slightly more frequently in private spaces (46.4% females to 43% of the males). 28.4% of male characters are introduced in public spaces, but only 23.1% of the female characters. While not large, these differences remain in consonance with the general literature suggesting that throughout history masculinity has been associated with the public sphere of doing and action, while femininity is located in the private sphere of home, child rearing, emotions, and relationships (Criksena & Cuklanz, 1992). This relegation of genders to specific spheres restricts the possibilities offered to both boys and girls in all realms of human life, including, for example, the cultivation of child-caring aspirations for males, and public offices and leadership for females.

Interestingly, school settings were a place where more girls and women were introduced into the program (12.9% as opposed to 9% of male characters).

Once again, school settings, while outside of the realm of the private sphere, are nevertheless excellent backdrops for narratives evolving around relationships between friends, romantic encounters with the opposite sex, and conflicts with adult authority figures, all of which lend themselves easily to storylines that are favorites of girl audiences.

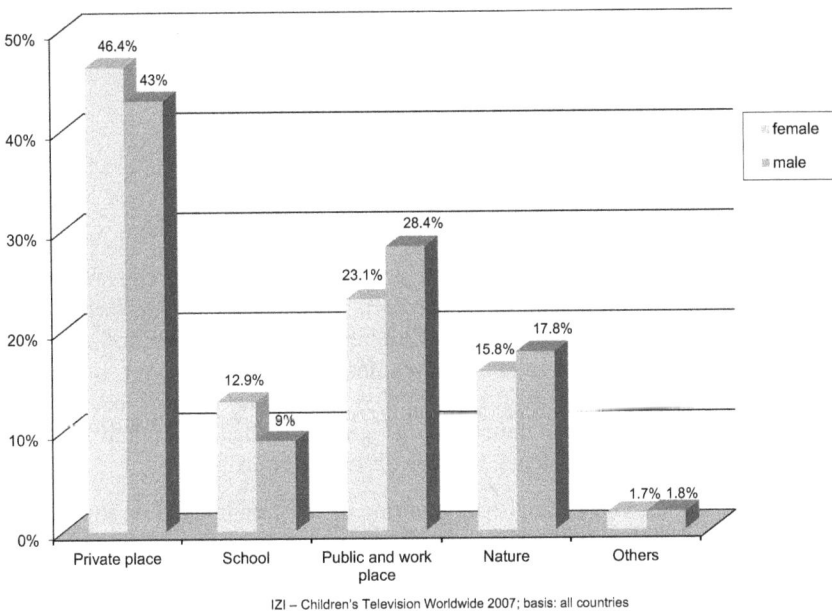

IZI – Children's Television Worldwide 2007; basis: all countries

**Figure 1.6.**
Place of introduction into the plot

## 4. Age and Appearance of the Main Human Characters

Casting of characters follows certain criteria in fictional programs. While drafting the story, authors already have certain visualizations in mind, which they then set down in words. In subsequent stages of the production process, character traits and possible casting are debated again and again, using live action format or visualization in the case of animation. Thus, in the final result, the main characters' appearance is purposefully staged. It is the outcome of both the production process and the team's collaborative efforts. Of course there are some moments of chance in this process, but on the whole choices are always made consciously – particularly where the outward appearance of characters is concerned. While the appearance of fictional characters – such as sponges, starfish or talking mice – is hard to determine, the representation of humans can be examined quantitatively according to characteristic features, and then be compared to reality.

Thus, the continuation of the present analysis focuses on the 14,959 human characters, and analyzes the color of the characters' hair and skin, age, and representations of chronic illness or disability. Each of these variables is examined from a gender-specific angle, in line with the research question.

## The Main Characters' Age

### Girls Are More Likely to Be Teenagers; Babies and Elderly People Hardly Appear at All in Children's TV

Human main characters were analyzed according to the age they are meant to represent. We found that three groups occur in relatively even distribution in children's television across the globe: Children comprised a third of the main characters (33.9%), besides adults (30.6%), and adolescents (29.3%). Babies are assigned hardly any of the main roles (1.6%) and elderly people, too, are also marginal (4.1%). Given the importance of grandparents for children in many nations, this last point in particular must be observed critically.

The countries with the highest proportion of children in children's television were Central China (52.5%) and New Zealand (49.2%). Hardly any children appeared in the main roles in Hungary (15.2%). The countries with the highest proportion of adults in children's TV were Brazil (54.9%) and Cuba (48.6%). The Netherlands (15.6%) and China (19.3%) have the lowest proportion of adults. The countries whose sample included the highest percentage of elderly people are Brazil (8.8%), Canada (7.1%), Kenya (5.7%), Slovenia (5.4%), and Egypt (5.0%), while they are unimportant in children's TV in New Zealand (0.4%), the United States (1.8%), and Hong Kong (1.8%).

Domestic productions tend to tell their stories more frequently with adult protagonists, while children and teenage characters are shown more frequently in international productions.

### Gender-Specific Perspective: Adults Were More Likely to Be Male, While Teenagers Were Female

Children's television worldwide shows only small gender differences in the distribution of age groups as far as children's characters are concerned. Male characters appear comparatively more frequently as children or as adults, but they are seldom teenagers. This finding is particularly clear when contrasting genders. While 36.8% of girl characters are depicted as teenagers, this is the case with only 25.2% of boys. Female characters are much less likely to be adults (24.1%) than are male characters (35%) (see Figure 1.7).

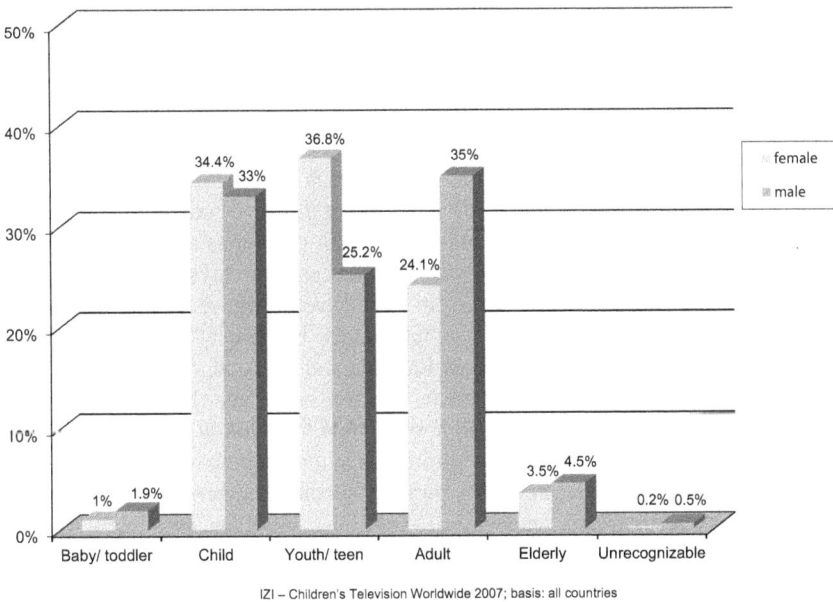

IZI – Children's Television Worldwide 2007; basis: all countries

**Figure 1.7.**
Age of the characters

The predominance of teenage girls in children's television is illuminating. Due to the patriarchal value assigned to women's appearance, it is in the adolescent years that possibilities for storytelling open up, and thus it is in casting teenagers or young adults looking like teenagers that focus is on beauty and sex appeal. The tendency to hyper-sexualize young girls moves the definition of adolescence (traditionally defined by the onset of puberty) to younger years. At the same time, the employment of older actresses to occupy roles of much younger teenagers than their real age also over inflates this age category (Lemish, 2010). Young-looking adult actresses can often be cheaper and more available for employment than real teenagers. Thanks to make-up and staging, they look like teenagers, even though the actresses are sometimes ten years older than their narrated roles.

Hungary is the country with the highest percentage of young girls (67% of all female characters are adolescents) followed by the Netherlands (61.6%), Australia (58.2%) and Israel (46.5%). The explanation for this finding may be that these countries have storytelling traditions that favor placing teenage girls at the center of their stories, and they do so frequently. Few young girls appear in main roles in Kenya (21.5%), and Egypt (22.6%), for example. We surmise that there may be a particular sensitivity to girls in sexualized scenarios due to the Islamic influence in these countries.

## Main Characters' Skin Color and Ethnic Background: The Dominant Skin Color Was Light/Caucasian

Determining the ethnic background of a character is not easy in practical research. The terminology itself is decidedly problematic, as it combines inherently controversial (e.g., colonial) concepts of race with categories such as culture and nationality, blending in a host of prior assumptions and stereotypes. There are some dominant characteristics such as "Asian" or "Black", whose coding implies an outward similarity that differs from other groups, but that becomes problematic in individual cases with codes such as Latino/a and characters of Arabic descent. This is particularly relevant in regard to live action formats that comprise seven percent of fictional children's television worldwide. In defining our coding system, we needed to consider the ethnic background of actors playing respective roles. We know that skin color is complicated by purposeful construction of ethnical hybridity and ambiguity as there is a tendency of "browning" of characters. Such "brown" characters speak to many races and travel successfully internationally (Valdivia, 2008, 2009).

While such vagueness exists, coding is important in terms of content, as it can reveal basic tendencies about the dominance of certain human categories. Thus, the international research team decided to undertake this coding, while bearing in mind the theoretical and practical difficulties. Practically, this meant that the program description was consulted when visual representation was ambiguous.

The coding of the 14,959 human characters revealed a very clear tendency, as can be seen in Figure 1.8: The majority (10,764 characters, 72%) were coded as light-skinned in the sense of having a Northern, Central or Eastern European background (covered internationally by the terms "White" or "Caucasian"), possibly intending to represent characters as of European or Anglo-American descent.

Asian body features comprise 12% (1,739) of the human characters. Such coding was defined within this project primarily by the shape of the eyes and the cultural background (in order to be able to include also anime characters with oversized eyes).

Six percent (961) of the main characters in children's TV worldwide can be clearly identified as "Black".

Three percent (383) were classified as Hispanic, and two percent (249) as South or Southeast Asian.

In spite of all the problems associated with this variable, the results of this analysis are very clear: The main characters in children's television are mostly light-skinned. Considering that only 15% of the world's population is estimated to be White, in some way (Fearon, 2003), they are clearly overrepresented with 70% presence in the sample.

Countries with the highest percentage of Black characters are the United Kingdom and the United States. There were no Black characters in Malaysia and Hong Kong – at least not in this sample. The highest percentage of White characters was found in Cuba and Argentina. South Africa has the "fourth-Whitest" children's TV screen with 81% of the main characters being White. This is particularly surprising, given that in reality only nine percent of the South African population is White (Statistics South Africa, 2007). So, clearly, the trend in children's television across the globe is towards presenting the central TV characters as persons from a White ethnic background. Such representations actually have very little to do with the actual reality of ethnic diversity in individual countries.

## Are Imported Programs Less Culturally or Ethnically Diverse?

The percentage of White main characters is higher, on an average worldwide, in programs that are not produced domestically. This is easy to understand, as the conception of a domestic production will always be oriented more closely towards the existing ethnic and cultural diversity.

When producing live action formats, in particular, people from the actual country itself are usually involved. Correspondingly, it seems obvious that programs not produced or co-produced domestically have a larger percentage of White characters, as these are imported programs produced with an eye on the international market and originate mainly in the United States and Canada. The likely conclusion would appear to be that the less diverse ethnic backgrounds of the main human characters on children's television around the world is a result of the dominance of these North American programs. Put differently: It is the North American programs that render the world of children's television so White.

On the other hand, it is important to note, that the programs broadcast in the United States are among the most diverse as regards skin color/ethnic background. It is true that White characters dominate with 67.8%, but this, too, places the United

States below the world average. The United States is nearly at the top of the table in regard to the representation of characters with an African ethnic background, with 112 main characters (12.2%). Considering the ratio of various ethnicities in the United States, Hispanic main characters are underrepresented with only 7.1% (in reality 12.5% of the population is Hispanic [Guzman, 2000]). Nonetheless, the programs shown in the United States demonstrate at least a quantitative sensitivity towards culturally diverse backgrounds.

At the same time, among the countries with a high proportion of children's television programs imported from the United States, such as Brazil where 80% of programs are produced in the United States, we found a high percentage of White main characters and particularly few Hispanic (4.4%) or Black (7.9%) characters.

What can be the explanation for this finding? After all, dominated as it is by North America, the children's television industry has a broad range of ethnicities to offer the rest of the world. Regardless of whether clients are regional channels or branches of a global network, they all have the opportunity to select from a broad pool of quite diverse programs. Thus, it is the job of individuals on the national level, who make the purchasing decisions for their respective channels, to make the selections that are eventually broadcast on the screens of that channel's programming schedule for children. So while the pool of programs is mainly from the United States, the results of this selection process in individual countries is quite diverse. The program schedule can be either more ethnically diverse, as in the case of New Zealand, or dominated more by light-skinned characters, as in the case of Brazil. It is striking that it is Brazil, a country with a population of around 191 million, whose dominant ethnic group is Hispanic, with a very visible Black population and various postcolonial ethnically heterogeneous groups, where programs with Hispanic or Black main characters are not selected.

### Ethnic Representation from the Perspective of Gender

White male main characters (73.8%) appeared significantly more often than other ethnicities in children's television worldwide, female characters were more often "other"; for example Asian (13.3% female to 10.8% male) or Black (7.2% to 6.0%). The double marginalization of female characters, both as a female as well as an ethnic minority, is thus reinforced, as producers find an easy way out by having both marginalized groups in one character (see Figure 1.8).

China and Hong Kong are countries with a high percentage of Asian girls and women as main characters. This is logical given this group's dominance in these countries' ethnic and cultural composition. Yet, incongruent with actual reality, hardly any Asian girls are found in British (2%) or Australian (2%) children's television. Yet, a surprising phenomenon can be observed in Kenya, where more Asian than Black girls and women feature in children's television (16% to 11%). In South Africa, the distribution of Black and Asian characters is equal, but on a low level (each 12%). However, this does not correspond to the population's varied ratio of skin colors.

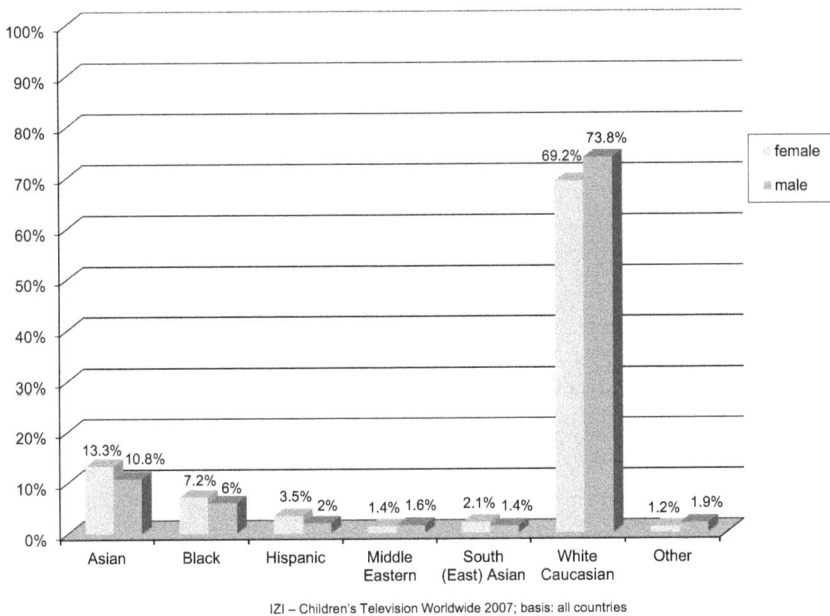

IZI – Children's Television Worldwide 2007; basis: all countries

**Figure 1.8.**
Skin color of the characters according to gender

## Characters' Physique

### What Is the Weight or Shape of the Main Characters?

We asked the coders to evaluate whether a character is in the normal weight range or shown as very thin or very overweight. Since most characters were coded as within the "normal range" (n=12,523; 83.5%), fewer were very thin (n=1,358; 9.1%) or very overweight (n=1,108; 7.4%). Adding a gender perspective to the analysis, we found that female characters were slightly but significantly more often very thin compared to males (14.8% to 5.8%), while males were nearly three times more likely to be characterized as overweight (8.8% males to 3.6% females; see Figure 1.9).

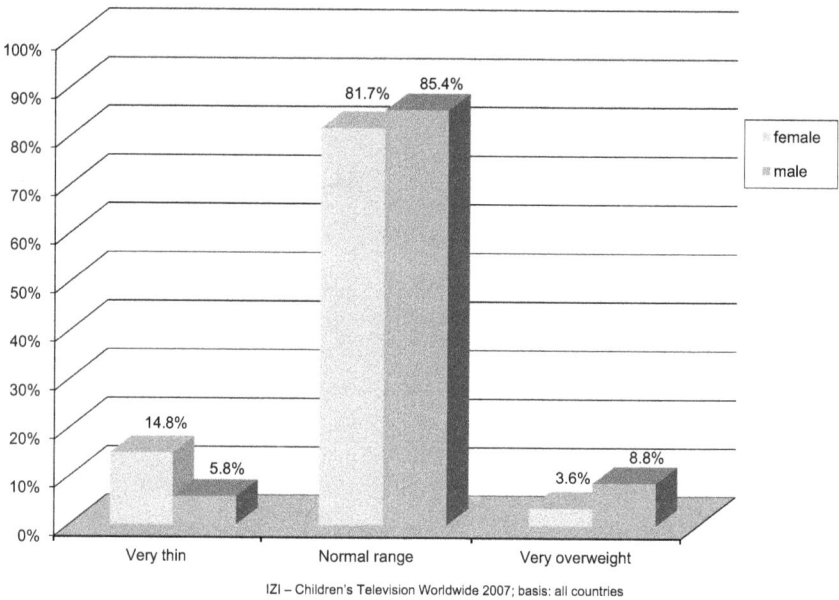

IZI – Children's Television Worldwide 2007; basis: all countries

**Figure 1.9.**
Physique of the characters by gender

The percentage of exceptionally slim characters was particularly notable in international productions. In reality, the shape of a body and its weight is influenced by many factors and differs greatly based on ethnic backgrounds and countries of origin. The statistical data regarding children's weight actually varies according to the individual country in question. Clearly, with the dramatic rise of obesity among children and youth in the world, the absence of overweight characters is quite striking. In the United States, for example, the prevalence of obesity among children and youth has tripled in the last 30 years and now stands around 17%, with substantial ethnic disparities: Hispanic boys and non-Hispanic black girls are disproportionately affected by obesity. Obesity is prevalent among older children and teens, with documentation of a clear trend that heavier boys are becoming even heavier (CDC, 2011).

Another important, related variable coded was presence of some kind of visible disability, an issue of particular concern for many cultures around the world. Surprisingly, we found only 1% of disability worldwide, with 0.6% among girls and 1.1% among boys. This is clearly not representative of the real prevalence of disability among children which while greatly varied in different countries, is still on the average around 10% (World Health Organization, 2010).

### The Main Characters' Appearance: Hair Color

The most common hair colors are black (30.1%), brown (22.7%) and blond (18.5%) in children's TV across the globe. Red-haired main characters occur 1,768 times in worldwide children's television (11.9%), white-haired characters (5.4%), and characters without hair 4.2% of main characters. Countries with many black-haired main characters are China (59.2%), India (50.7%), Syria (45.2%), and Egypt (42.9%). These findings are logical given the distribution of hair colors in their respective populations. Many blond characters appear in New Zealand (27.2%), Germany (26.6%), Austria (26.3%), and the Netherlands (23.2%), again, a finding that is appropriate for the population in these countries.

### Gender-Specific Perspective: Girls Are More Often Blonde or Red-Haired

A comparison of hair colors reveals a clear gender difference. Female main characters are significantly more likely to be blonde or red-haired (see Figure 1.10). This is particularly evident with girl characters: 23.3% of girl characters but only 15.8% of boy characters have blonde hair. The blonde stereotype's character is often constructed as helpless and sexy. The stereotype of the "dumb blonde" is deeply rooted in popular-culture. Numerous Hollywood film and television actresses have played the role of the fair-haired, intellectually-challenged and sexy women. Jokes about blondes have been popular for decades and are now in a renaissance in humorous texts circulated on the Internet (Shifman & Lemish, 2011). The two main characteristics assigned to this type of female – being stupid (and as a result, helpless and vulnerable), as well as being beautiful and sexy (and as a result, treated as a sex object) have been criticized for being a site of exaggerated misogynist sentiments. The fact that this stereotype is prevalent in children's television worldwide is an indication of the prevalence of these perceptions.

The country with the highest percentage of blonde girls is Australia, followed by the United Kingdom and, surprisingly, Syria. The high number of blonde girls on Australian television is not far from the reality of that country's ethnically diverse population, as large proportions of the country's population do have European and Anglo-American roots. Nonetheless we maintain that this is an overrepresentation and conflates an ideal of beauty with being blonde. The high percentage of blonde female characters in the Syrian sample is remarkable. While the population's hair color is definitely varied, black is nonetheless the most common. Looking at the images presented, for example, in a program where a mother and daughter are shown combing each other's blonde hair and singing, the question arises whether this does not represent an ideal of beauty far removed from everyday reality?

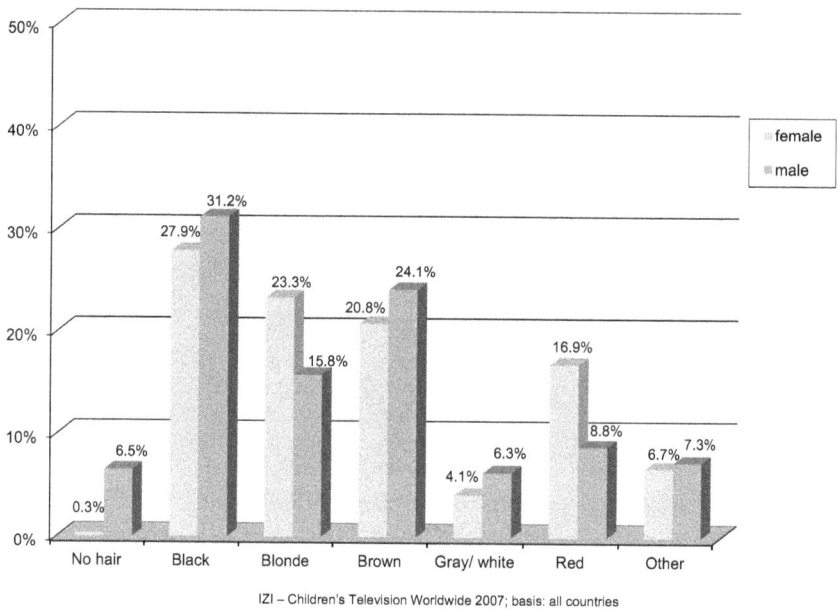

IZI – Children's Television Worldwide 2007; basis: all countries

**Figure 1.10.**
Hair color of the characters by gender

A marked difference between the sexes is evident in the case of main characters with red hair. Twice as many girl and women characters (16.9%) as men or boy characters (8.8%) are given red hair. Yet, this construction has no connection whatsoever with reality. We speculate that one possible underlying influence explaining such a construction could be the story of Pippi Longstocking, the foremother of the strong independent girl. But even here, Astrid Lindgren made use of a familiar stereotype: Girls with red hair are supposedly particularly stubborn, independent and "tomboy-ish".

The country with the highest percentage of red-haired girl characters is Slovenia (27%), followed by New Zealand, Germany, Austria, and Canada (each 22%). While red is a common hair color for male and female characters in Slovenia and Canada, in Germany only main characters who are girls have been constructed having red hair. In reality, only one of a hundred women in Germany is naturally red-haired (Henss, n.d.). Interestingly, the United Kingdom with four percent red-haired women and girls is only in 22nd place in the study's international ranking.

### A Case Study: The Phenomenon of Red-Haired Girls as the "Other" Other

Indeed, a marked gender difference is evident with red-haired characters. Analyzing this phenomenon in detail can serve as a case study in illuminating the constructed nature of television programming, and can thus be applied to other variables as well.

In German children's television, for example, red-haired girls constitute 22.5% of all female main characters and, thus, occur three times more often than red-haired boys (6.9%). Whether this is the KiKA in-house production *Chili das Schaf* (i.e., *Chili the Sheep* who appears in *Bernd das Brot* shows) or internationally marketed programs such as the anime version of Anne of Green Gables, Lilly the Witch, Tracey, Gloria Mitnixx or Pippi Longstocking; all these characters have fiery red hair and are the central characters of frequently eponymous shows. Children's television seems to have a strong liking for red-haired girls in main roles. The explanation for this phenomenon may be unconscious or preconscious mental images of TV decision-makers. For example, Claude Schmit, CEO at SUPER RTL stated that "it looks cheekier somehow".[6]

Schmit may not be alone in holding this opinion, as adults have certain associations with and assumptions about the characters of people, based significantly on the color of their hair. Young women with red hair are given more credit for emotional strength than young women with blonde hair. Viewers of images of women whose hair color had been altered in this respect think that the person depicted is less fearful, insecure, self-pitying, or oversensitive. They believe she is ready to take risks, enjoys experimenting, is adventurous, enterprising and creative – traits not assumed when the woman was shown with blonde hair. At the same time, redheads are thought to be less helpful, child-friendly, family-oriented and friendly – traits where blondes received higher scores (Rinck, 2002). Similar patterns are passed on in traditional children's stories, especially those written for strong girls. Red Zora always gets her own way and manages to save her friends through her inventiveness. Red-haired Pippi Longstocking is fearless, wild, adventurous, and breaks all the rules. In contrast, blonde Annika is a "proper girl": nice, caring, conscious of the rules, but also a bit timid and not very adventurous. Showing TV girls as redheads forges a link to existing adult stereotypes. Nonetheless, the linking of character traits to outward appearance as taken-for-granted has no basis in reality. Intrinsically, this is a form of inappropriate stereotyping.

In reality, as stated above, only one out of a hundred people is naturally red-haired in Germany (Henss, n.d.). This one percent of children is confronted with the clichéd assumption that they are adventurous, risk-loving, and creative, but also less helpful and friendly. Perhaps one or the other then appropriates the cliché and fulfills it, in the sense of a self-fulfilling prophecy. The question remains: Why should a girl with brown, blonde or black hair not be able to be adventurous or egocentric?

Producers and TV decision-makers use redheads when creating characters to symbolize a "special other". She is, admittedly, a girl, but nonetheless (at least) a very special one. This carries echoes of "just a girl", and implies that the attractiveness of "normal" girlhood is finite. In order to render her more attractive, she is given special traits and features. She is the "other Other", different not just from what counts as "normal" (i.e., boys and men), but also forming an exception among women.

The creation of the character ensemble for *Bernd das Brot* (i.e., *Bernd the Bread*) serves as an example. The producers decided that a female sheep with comic potential should appear:

> But that will stay boring if the sheep isn't special. "Being a girl" isn't enough on its own. Thus the sheep is turned yellow, given a crazy hairstyle and supplied with a biography. It is part of a circus family, is called Chili and is a stunt sheep. Cool stunts are somersaults on motorbikes and explosive leaps out of cannons. Little Miss Sheep needs a lot of courage to do that. Thinking about it would probably prevent her from doing these kinds of things. So Chili is naive, but not too much of a goody-goody. She's certainly not a conventional girl, but not too cheeky either; she's a Pippi Longstocking, lovable, stubborn, product of an anti-authoritarian upbringing, with some anarchist traits! (Lünenschloss, 2003)

Coming from an experienced editor, this testimony is very insightful. The character is not supposed to be a "conventional girl", not "just" a girl (see Figure 1.11). In order to achieve this goal, they designed a puppet with thick red plaits that stick out wildly – directly referencing Pippi Longstocking.

In summary, narrative traditions and the perspectives and images of editors led to a combination of features that recur again and again. While there is no direct connection to reality, nonetheless stereotypes have the potential to influence the mindscapes of children and teenagers, especially when they are reinforced repeatedly. Accordingly, it is important to point out these dominant stereotypes and, if possible, to challenge them, especially in quality television.

© KiKA/Christiane Pausch

**Figure 1.11.**
Chili the Sheep

## 5. Stereotyping through Common, Statistically Highly Significant Trait Combinations

In addition to statistically descriptive data, it is the volume of data that allows analysis of the extent to which certain traits appear in combination. For this purpose, contingency tables were developed in accordance with the main research questions in order to identify highly significant exceptional differences. Some of the main results are presented below.

## What Do Antagonists Look Like?
## Bitchy Blondes and Wicked Black-Haired Men

Antagonists, understood as a program's obvious negative characters, only comprise 14% of the sample's main characters. These characters are either loners or part of a group. Far fewer female characters are presented as wicked. If there is a female antagonist, she is most likely to be human (76% of antagonists). Among male antagonists, over half (59%) are human too, but their variety is greater. For example, male "baddies" can also be snowmen (Arktos in *Tabaluga*) or sharks (*The Pink Panther*). This construction is not surprising, given that female characters in children's television are statistically more likely to be human. In short, the more constructed a character is, the more likely it is to be male.

In our view, this finding means that when stereotypes of wicked female characters are constructed, they are posed as bad girls and women who look more realistic and less obviously imaginary creatures. Comparing the two sexes, these human female antagonists are more frequently children (23% girls to 16% boys), adolescents or teenagers (36% to 18%), and less commonly adults (36% to 56%). Typically they have blonde hair (27% of female compared to 8% of male antagonists) or red hair (14% of female compared to 7% of male antagonists).

Thus, wicked female characters are most often blonde or red-haired girls, and either children or teenagers. The assumption that the cliché of the "bitchy blonde", so popular in many television series (the one who is envious of other people's good fortune, tries to break up friendships and loving relationships, is totally engrossed with herself, her appearance and her belongings and has no concern for others) is confirmed by our empirical findings. Examples of these stereotypes retold afresh are Angelica (*All grown up*), Mitzi (*Winx Club*), Amy (*Generation Ninja*), Beautiful Gorgeous (*Jimmy Neutron*), Nanette Manoir (*Angela Anaconda*), or Burdine (*Bratz*). In contrast, male antagonists in children's TV are often dark-haired adult men (black hair 38%, brown hair 21%). Two percent of male antagonists suffer from disabilities or chronic illnesses (compared to 0.2% of female antagonists), a small but notable percentage, which is twice as large as with main characters in general.

So the wicked characters in children's television are most often dark-haired men. Prototypical clichéd antagonists who make the heroes' lives difficult include Count Falko (*Bibi und Tina*), Bluto (*Popeye*), Duke Sigmund Igthorn (*Adventures of the Gummi Bears*) or Randall (*Recess*).

## What Do Leaders and Followers Look Like? Light-Skinned, Red-Haired Girls as Leaders and Blond, Fat Boys as Followers

Leaders who tell groups what to do and what must happen are disproportionately light-skinned in children's television across the globe. If the leaders are girls, they are frequently red-haired, and male leaders are only seldom blond.

Consequently, followers are the "non-whites"[7] and disproportionately Asian or ethnic African. Furthermore, a high percentage (44%) of female followers has black hair (28% on an average) with a low percentage of redheads (14% compared to 23% altogether). In contrast, male followers are often blond and frequently overweight. The narrative stereotypes implied here are worth examining more closely.

## How Are Black, Hispanic, and Asian Characters Represented in Children's Television?

The majority of the 14,959 human characters in children's TV analyzed were White. Thus, it is all the more interesting to identify special trait combinations constructed for non-White characters. Black characters, for example, are much more often part of a team. This is particularly the case with Black male main characters: 74% in contrast to the 50% average of all characters. Teams of Black boys are presented as equal to those around them in 59% of the cases in comparison to 46% of all human male main characters. Here, the stereotype of "the" Black man who "always" forms part of a group of equals as gangs raiding the streets of urban centers is already being consolidated in children's television. In addition, similar to our discussion of the appearance of girls in groups, minorities, too, are hardly assumed to be able to lead the narrative on their own, and, thus, are presented as groups.

However, Black characters are not the only ones to be part of a team, as Hispanics and Asians also comprise an above average percentage of team members. One explanation for this finding lies in programs that present a group of children and teenagers from different ethnic backgrounds. The Bratz Dolls, for example, feature an Asian, a Black, a Hispanic and a light-skinned girl. While this may appear to be a good start toward including girls of diverse ethnic backgrounds, the question remains how different these characters really are under the general trend of "browning" all other ethnicities, as discussed above. Presumably these other characters were developed as part of a marketing plan concerned with successfully positioning the dolls in the global market (McAllister, 2007).

As stated above, the main characters of children's television are leaders who are disproportionately White. When leaders are girls, they are frequently red-haired, and male leaders are seldom blond. Those who follow others are mainly the "non-Whites" and they are disproportionately Asian or Black. While girls who follow others are likely to be dark-haired, male followers are likely to be blond and overweight – both qualities indicate femininity, feebleness, and vulnerability.

Significant tendencies become evident when non-White main characters form part of the story, as they are more commonly part of a team. This can be seen particularly in the case of Black male main characters, as they comprise three of four characters who are part of a team, mostly within an equal community.

Hispanic men are particularly often leaders, and Hispanic women are disproportionately presented as part of a duo.

The images of the Latin macho and the Hispanic girl who seem to be connected umbilically to her best friend are retold early on, and repeated over and over again. If girls with a Southeast Asian ethnic background appear, they are less frequently shown as equals and more often as followers (39% followers). In contrast, light-skinned girls are shown as followers much less frequently (11%).

## Summary of Results

### What Does Children's Television Look Like Across the Globe?

First, this study provides a good overview of what characterizes children's television across the globe. Children's TV is made up mainly of fictional programs, and most of these is animation. Furthermore, the fictional animated shows that shape children's television worldwide are usually not produced domestically, and a large percentage are imported from North America. Countries with a larger share of domestic productions include the United Kingdom, Central China, and Canada. Children in the United States watch only North American productions, across a number of channels.

Most programs are broadcast in the country's main language, meaning that non-domestic programs are dubbed. Subtitling is also used in children's television in some of the smaller countries and in some countries with several languages.

### The Main Characters in Children's Television

Viewed from a worldwide perspective, children's television shows a clear tendency: There are markedly more boy and men characters than girl or women characters in main roles. There are at least two male main characters for every female main character. The more purely imagined characters present (e.g., talking animals or magical creatures), the larger the proportion of males. In fact, there is a ratio of eight to one, males to females, in "non-human" characters.

Public service channels are even less balanced in their quantitative representation of gender. However, this does not mean, necessarily, that narrated girl characters are especially strong and interesting. This disproportion is also found to be the case with voiceovers, where males are employed three times more frequently than females.

### The Structure of Characters and Stories

Throughout the world, children's television tells lots of stories about equal groups, and some about loners and duos. In general, trends are relatively similar for both male and female characters. However, different tendencies can also be observed. Girls and women are more often members of an equal peer group. They only seldom appear as lone fighters or antagonists. Their introduction to the storyline occurs more frequently within the private sphere or in school.

### Age and Appearance of the Main Human Characters

Children, adolescents and adults comprise about a third each of the main characters analyzed in this global study. Babies and elderly people play only a marginal role as main characters. Male characters appear more frequently as children or adults, while girls are usually scripted to be adolescents.

In regards to appearance, the absolute majority of human main characters on children's television – 72% – are light-skinned (Caucasian). All other possibilities lag far behind, sometimes differing markedly from the reality of the populations in the countries in question. Boy/men characters are significantly more likely to be White, while girl/women characters more often than males have "other" skin colors. However, the sample includes twice as many Asian women as Asian men, but more characters of boys and men than of girls and women represent an ethnic African background.

The main characters' hair colors are most frequently black, brown, or blond.

A comparison reveals a clear difference between the sexes. The proportion of blondes and redheads is significantly higher in female characters.

### Recurrent Trait Combinations

Statistically, certain trait combinations occur frequently in the main characters of children's TV. Antagonists are more likely to be male than female. However, if we have a female antagonist, she is most often a blonde or red-haired girl, either a child or a teenager.

In contrast, male antagonists in children's TV are often adult dark-haired men. Even though this only occurs in a low percentage of cases, this particular group is most likely to have a disability.

When the main characters of children's television are leaders, they are disproportionately from the White population. When the leaders are girls, they are frequently red-haired, while male leaders are only seldom blond. Those who follow others are mainly the "non-Whites" and disproportionately Asian or Black. Girls who follow others are frequently dark-haired, while male followers are frequently blond and overweight.

Significant tendencies become evident when non-White main characters form part of the story. They are more commonly part of a team. This is particularly the case with Black male main characters, where three of four characters are part of a team, mostly within an equal community of peers. Hispanic men are particularly likely to be leaders, and Hispanic women are disproportionately presented as part of a duo. None of these trait combinations are realistic representations. Rather, they are the stereotypical constructions of the decision-makers.

In summary, the aim of the quantitative content analysis presented here is to present a descriptive overview of the children's television broadcast across the globe. The trends identified depend on the sample taken, and can only constitute a first step in which general tendencies are revealed.

Since quantitative analysis can obscure aesthetic and dramaturgical details, the main focus of the next stage of research is exploring these dimensions through use of focused content and other qualitative analyses.

Clearly, children's television varies throughout the world, with diverse national and regional trends that require further investigation. This renders the similarities all the more striking – particularly in regards to the ways in which gender is presented. Furthermore, the differences between domestic and international – mostly North American programs or public broadcasting programming in comparison to private, commercial providers are comparatively small in this regard. This finding supports our argument that gender on children's television around the world is constructed in similar ways, and as such it should be examined, criticized, and reconstructed in ways that are more reflective both of reality, as well as, supportive of the vision of increasing social equity.

## Acknowledgements

The authors wish to thank the researchers who conducted the data collection and coding in the various participating countries: Hans-Bernd Brosius, Cynthia Carter, Kara Chan, Stephanie Donald, JoEllen Fisherkeller, Micheline Frenette, Tone Kolbjønsen, Kati Lustyik, Divya McMillin, Juliette W. van der Molen, Norma Pecora, Martina Pestaj, Jeanne Prinsloo, Ana-Helena Mereilles Reis, Pablo Ramos Rivero, Frieda Saeys, Sebastian Scherr, Hongxia Zhang.

We also thank Ole Hofmann and Sebastian Scherr at the IZI in Munich who completed the data analysis.

## REFERENCES

Aubrey, J. S., & Harrison, K. (2004). The gender-role content of children's favorite television programs and its links to their gender-related perceptions. *Media psychology*, *6*(2), 111-146.

Baker, K., & Raney, A. A. (2007). Equally super?: Gender-role stereotyping of superheroes in children's animated programs. *Mass Communication and Society*, *10*(1), 25-41.

Barcus, E. F. (1983). *Images of Life on Children's Television: Sex Roles, Minorities and Families.* Westport, CT: Praeger Publishers.

Benenson, J.F. (1990). Gender differences in social networks. *The Journal of Early Adolescence*, *10*, 472-495.

Benenson, J. F., Apostoleris, N. H., & Parnass, J. (1997). Age and sex differences in dyadic and group integration. *Developmental Psychology*, *33*(3), 538-543.

Berger, P. L., & Luckmann, T. (1966). *The Social Construction of Reality. A Treatise in the Sociology of Knowledge.* Garden City, NY: Anchor Books.

Bryant, J. A. (2007). How has the kids' media industry evolved? In S. R. Mazzarella (Ed.), *20 questions about youth and the media* (pp. 13-28). New York, NY: Lang.

CDC. (2011). CDC grand roundtable: Childhood obesity in the United States. Available at http://www.cdc.gov/mmwr/preview/mmwrhtml/mm6002a2.htm

Chodorow, N. J. (1978). *The Reproduction of Mothering: Psychoanalysis and the Sociology of Gender.* Berkeley, CA: University of California Press.

Cirksena, K., & Cuklanz, L. (1992). Male is to female as ___ is to ___: A guided tour of five feminist frameworks for communication studies. In L. F. Rakow (Ed.), Women making meaning (pp. 18-44). New York, NY: Routledge.

de Beauvoir, S. (1949/2009). *The Second Sex.* New York, NY: Alfred A. Knopf.

Durham, M. G. (2008). *The Lolita Effect.* Woodstock & New York, NY: The Overlook Press.

Fearon, J. (2003). Ethnic and cultural diversity by country. *Journal of Economic Growth, 8,* 195-222.

Furnham, A., & Saar, A. (2005). Gender-role stereotyping in adult and children's television advertisements: A two-study comparison between Great Britain and Poland. *Communications, 30*(1), 73-90.

GMMP. (2010). Global Media Mentoring Project: Who makes the news? Available at http://www.whomakesthenews.org/images/stories/website/gmmp_reports/2010/global/gmmp_global_report_en.pdf

Götz, M. (1999). Von Heldinnen und Helden im Kinderfernsehen [Heroines and heroes in children's television]. *Forum, 3*(4), 28-35.

Götz, M. (2006). Die Hauptfiguren im deutschen Fernsehen [Main characters in German television]. *TelevIZIon, 19*(1), 4-7.

Götz, M., Lemish, D., Aidman, A., & Moon, H. (2005). *Media and the Make-Believe Worlds of Children: When Harry Potter Meets Pokémon in Disneyland.* Mahwah, NJ: Erlbaum.

Guzman, B. (2000). The Hispanic population: Census 2000 brief. Available at http://www.census.gov/prod/2001pubs/c2kbr01-3.pdf

Henss, R. (n.d.). Blond, braun, schwarz, rot: Häufigkeit von Haarfarben: Ergebnisse einer online Untersuchung [Blond, brown, black, red: Frequency of hair colors: Results of an online research]. http://www.haar-und psychologie.de/haarfarben/haarfarben_statistik_deutschland.html. Retrieved December 12, 2010.

Lemish, D. (2010). *Screening Gender on Children's Television: The View of producers around the World.* New York, NY: Routledge.

Levinson R. M. (1975). From Olive Oil to Sweet Poly Purebread: Sex-role stereotypes and televised cartoons. *Journal of Popular Culture, 9*(3), 561-572.

Levine, D. E., & Kilbourne, J. (2008). *So sexy so soon: The new sexualized childhood and what parents can do to protect their kids.* New York: Ballantine Books.

Lienert, G. A., & Raatz, U. (1989). *Textaufbau und Textanalyse* [Text structure and text analysis] Weinheim, Baden-Württemberg: Beltz.

Luther, C. A., & Legg, J. R. (2010). Gender differences in depictions of social and physical aggression in children's television cartoons in the US. *Journal of Children and Media, 4*(2), 191-205.

Lünenschloss, W. (2003). Am Anfang war das Schaf. Anmerkungen zum Sinn von Unsinn in der Serie CHILI TV vom Kinderkanal ARD/ZDF [At the beginning, there was the sheep. Annotations on the sense of nonsense in the series CHILI TV on children's program ARD/ZDF]. *TelevIZIon, 16*(1), 23-25.

McAllister, M. (2007). "Girls with a passion for fashion": The Bratz brand as integrated spectacular consumption. *Journal of Children and Media, 1*(3), 244-258.

Pecora, N. O. (1998). *The Business of Children's Entertainment.* New York, NY: Guilford Press.

Rinck, M. (2002). *Haarfarbe und Persönlichkeitseindruck* [Hair color and personality]. University of Saarbrücken: Unpublished dissertation.

Shifman, L., & Lemish, D. (2011). "Mars and Venus" in virtual space: Post-feminist humor and the internet. *Critical studies in media communication, 28*(3), 253-273.

Smith, S., & Cook, C. (2008). Gender stereotypes: An analysis of popular films and TV. Available at http://www.thegeenadavisinstitute.org/downloads/GDIGM_Gender_ Stereotypes.pdf.

Steemers, J. (2004). *Selling Television: British Television in the Global Marketplace*. London, UK: BFI.

Sternglanz, S. H., & Serbin, L. A. (1974). Sex role stereotyping in children's television programs. *Developmental Psychology, 10*(5), 710-715.

Statistics South Africa. (2007, July). Mid-year population estimates. Available at http://www. statssa.gov.za/publications/P0302/P03022007.pdf

Streicher, L. H., & Bonney, N. L. (1974). Children talk about television. *Journal of Communication, 24*(3), 54-61.

Thompson, T., & Zerbinos, E. (1995). Gender roles in animated cartoons. Has the picture changed in 20 years? *Sex roles, 32*(9/10), 651-673.

Valdivia, A. N. (2008). Mixed race on the Disney Channel: From Johnnie Tsunami through Lizzie McGuire and ending with the Cheetah Girls. In M. Beltrán & C. Fojas (Eds.), Mixed race Hollywood: Multiraciality in film and media culture (pp. 269-289). New York, NY: NYU Press.

Valdivia, A. N. (2009). Living in a hybrid material world. Girls, ethnicity and doll products. *Girlhood Studies, 2*(1), 73-79.

World Health Organization. (2010). World Report on Disability. Available at http://whqlibdoc. who.int/publications/2011/9789240685215_eng.pdf

---

[1] The sample selection and the inclusion or exclusion of one channel or the other is something that can be debated in individual cases. In the present study, the responsibility for the selection and coding of programs lay with local partners as the experts in their national programs.

[2] This affects Argentina, Norway, Brazil, Malaysia, and Syria. The reason for this partly have to do with the content, as the sample was intended to represent a program that is both freely accessible and explicitly aimed at children. In some countries this broadcast is simply very restricted. Nonetheless, some of the results must be viewed with caution with a sample of this size, as a sample of 31 programs with 134 characters in individual programs can easily distort the larger quantitative picture. This will be noted at relevant points in the following discussion. Therefore, a decision was made to include these countries in the overview data of the study, but to exclude them at the country level comparative analyses.

[3] In three cases, technical problems with the recording process meant that some additional sample recordings had to be made later, in November 2007. These recordings focused on similar programs.

[4] All reports are freely available at: www.childrens-tv-worldwide.de

[5] N varies according to the variables which were considered in the subcategories (e.g., human characters).

[6] Schmit on the program *Zapp* 2007 (NDR, North German Broadcasting), while commenting on the results of the study.

[7] Female followers are 17% Asian, 11% Black and 57% White; 69% of female main characters are White.

# 2

# "WASP WAISTS AND V-SHAPE TORSO"
# Measuring the Body of the "Global" Girl and Boy in Animated Children's Programs

*Maya Götz* and *Margit Herche*

Animated programs represent the largest proportion of fictional children's television worldwide – 84% in our global study (see Götz & Lemish, chapter 1). These are not filmic depictions of real people. Rather, graphic artists draw characters from their imagination, in consultation with the production team, including representatives of the broadcasters. Alongside numerous animals, magical beings and plants, 56% of these drawings represent humans. Figures designed in this way embody what the artist sees as essential traits. Then, computer technology is generally used to "breathe a soul" (anima in Latin) into them. Among the 22,541 animated protagonists analyzed in the worldwide study, 67% were male and 30% female characters.[1] Characters representing children and adolescents are particularly relevant for children. Children's favorite characters come from this pool (Götz, 2011) and reception studies found that while the media text may be polysemic, the physicality of television characters does make a precise impression on children's fantasies (Götz, Lemish, Aidman, & Moon, 2005). Thus, the body and representations have particular relevance for gender-sensitive analyses.

Accordingly, the research question that we sought to answer in the study reported in this chapter is: How are girls' and boys' bodies portrayed in animated programs?

## TV-Girls Are Slim and Beautiful

One of the variables coded in the "Children's TV worldwide" study described in chapter 1 was general body size. Coders were asked to evaluate the body shape of the human TV-characters in terms of whether it is in the normal range or shown as very thin or very overweight. The 10,153 globally marketed characters, examined in the reliability test regarding this variable, were categorized by junior researchers in the 24 countries in the same way in 93.9% of the cases. The main finding of this coding is that most of the characters were coded as within the "normal range" (83.5%). A small percentage was coded as very thin (9.1%). Employing a gender perspective produced highly significant differences: 4,189 analyzed female characters were less often "in the normal range" than the 7,401 male characters analyzed. Therefore, girls and women were more often "very thin" (14.8%) in comparison to the boys and men (5.8%), and the male characters were more often "very overweight" (8.8%) in comparison with female characters (3.6%) (see Figure 2.1).

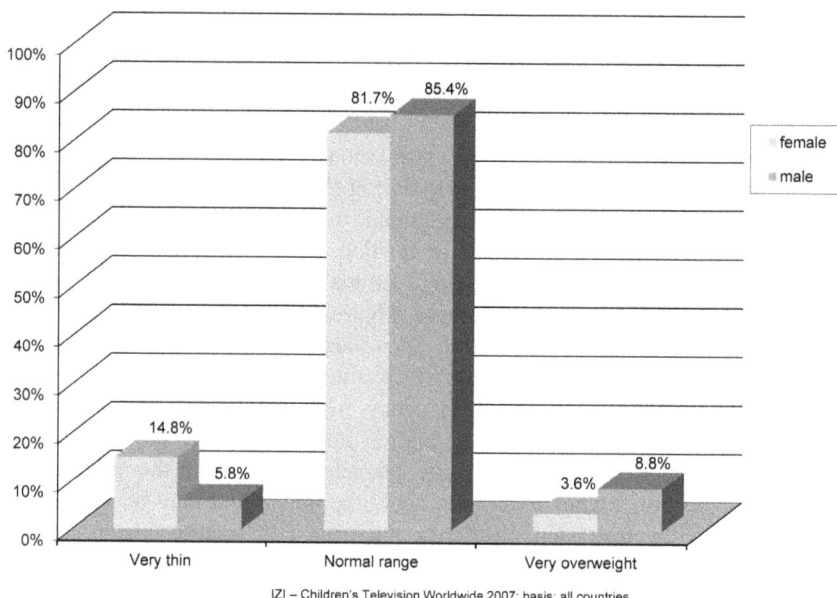

IZI – Children's Television Worldwide 2007; basis: all countries

**Figure 2.1.**

Physique of the characters according to the coding of the quantitative media analysis (see Götz & Lemish, chapter 2)

Therefore, portrayals of the human body depicted in children's TV seem clear: Most TV-characters are in the normal range when it comes to weight. However, if they are not so portrayed, then "normal" girls are shown more often as very slim and boys more often clearly overweight. As discussed in chapter 1, girls – at least a small percentage of them – are assessed primarily by their appearance and attractiveness, and therefore are portrayed in an underweight, beauty idealizing way.

These results caused us to reflect on the merits of concern solely with shape and weight. Fortunately, at the same time, our work on the depiction of luck in Disney classic movies from a gender perspective (Götz, 2009; Herche, 2007) led us to adopt what we consider to be a much more enlightening measurement: We sized the body in detail. Following some of the measurements of research on attractiveness, we measured the size of shoulder, hip, waist, upper body, and legs.

## Measuring the Female Body

Research on attractiveness employs an empirical/statistical approach that is now well established, particularly in Great Britain and the United States of America, to answer the question of what people find attractive about faces and physicality (e.g., Furnham, Petrides, & Constantinides, 2005; Little, Jones, & DeBruine, 2011). Drawing on research orientations such as the psychology of perception, cognitive psychology, and evolutionary psychology (cf. for example Zebrowitz, 2009), this line of research investigates such questions as the influence of hormones or alcohol on the perceived attractiveness of faces (n.b., see following sources for summaries of this line of research; e.g., DeBruine et al., 2010; Little, Penton-Voak, Burt, & Perrett, 2002; Welling et al., 2008).

For example, Singh (1993) developed the "Waist-to-Hip Ratio" (WHR) based on dividing the circumference of the waist (at the narrowest point around the torso below the iliac crest) by the circumference of the hips (at the point of greatest protrusion of the buttocks). Singh argues that the WHR is a reliable indicator of a female's reproductive age, sex hormone profile, parity and risk for various diseases. But, also, what males judge as attractive reliably signals youthfulness, healthiness, and fertility or female-mate value. His studies used cartoon images and later photographs (Singh, 1994a) of identical women who differed only in their WHR and overall body weight. White and Hispanic men in the US were asked to rank the figures in terms of attractiveness and healthiness, along with other variables (Singh, 1993). The 12 depictions ranged from 0.7 to 1.0 in three weight categories: underweight, normal, and overweight. This method produced the following results: The normal-weight figure with WHR 0.7 was judged to be the most attractive, healthy and with the greatest desire and capability for having children. Preferences did not differ, significantly, between White or Hispanic men (in the US) and were consistent across generations. Singh concluded that WHR and female attractiveness are neither culture-specific nor inculcated by fashion or media, but rather are genetically based (Singh, 1993).

While there has been much critical discussion of this approach and attempts have been made to limit these findings to Westernized societies (Marlowe & Wetsman, 2001; Yu & Shepard, 1998), the basic idea that there is a specific WHR of 0.7 preferred by adults has been largely confirmed (e.g., Connolly, Mealey, & Slaughter, 2000; Furnham, Tan, & McManus, 1997; Henss, 1995; Singh, 1994b; Singh & Luis, 1995; Singh & Young, 1995).

This research approach is regarded as problematic from the point of view of gender studies. Arguments include the need to question the assumption of the presumably natural, evolutionary and absolute bipolarity of the sexes. This assumption justifies hierarchies, at least implicitly, as genetic and caused by evolution. Thus, according to this approach, women and men are reduced to their physicality and presumably they are driven mainly by hormones and reproductive drives.

Though we may reject the entire approach, it is the case that some of the measurements have been proven to be a valid way to measure TV characters' bodies.

Initially, we studied animated characters since they appear in 82% of all fictional shows and are, therefore, the largest part of children's TV worldwide (see Götz & Lemish, chapter 1). We recall that these characters, as is the case in most animation, are constructed by TV producers. Therefore, we focused on how the producers constructed children and young people (6 to around 18 years of age). Our aim in this investigation was to analyze the body image of female and male animated characters. Our primary research question asked: Are there visible tendencies in media portrayals of the body as opposed to the real life children or teenagers? After a brief presentation of our research method, we will present findings from the analysis of female portrayals, followed by males.

## Sample: Stills of the "Global" Girls

The programs studied in this project came from the corpus of "Children's TV worldwide: Gender representation" described in Götz & Lemish, chapter 1. We selected programs that are fictional, animated, and portray human beings in the center of their story. Furthermore, the programs selected had to have been broadcast in at least three countries during the sampling period. This multi-level-selection process enabled us to develop a corpus of global programs that consisted of 59 shows, with 102 female characters representing girls and young women between the ages of six to 16.

## Method

The characters selected from this international resource were identified and a still photo was taken at the eye level of each character. When possible, characters wearing tight clothes were selected (without puffy-sleeves or loose-fitting clothing). Five lines were drawn on each photo: First, a line was drawn from shoulder to shoulder along the shoulder-bone line (shoulder-line); the second line was drawn at the slimmest part of the upper body (waist-line); the third line was drawn where the hipbones are constructed in the animation (hip-line); the fourth imaginary line was drawn where the ankles of the character were presumed (ankle-line); and, finally, a line from the shoulder-line to ankle-line (body-line). Three measures were then taken for each character at these points:

1. Waist-to-hip ratio (WHR)
2. Waist-to-shoulder ratio (WSR)
3. Upper body-to-lower body ratio (UB/LB)

Natural body                    Typical cartoon characters' body*

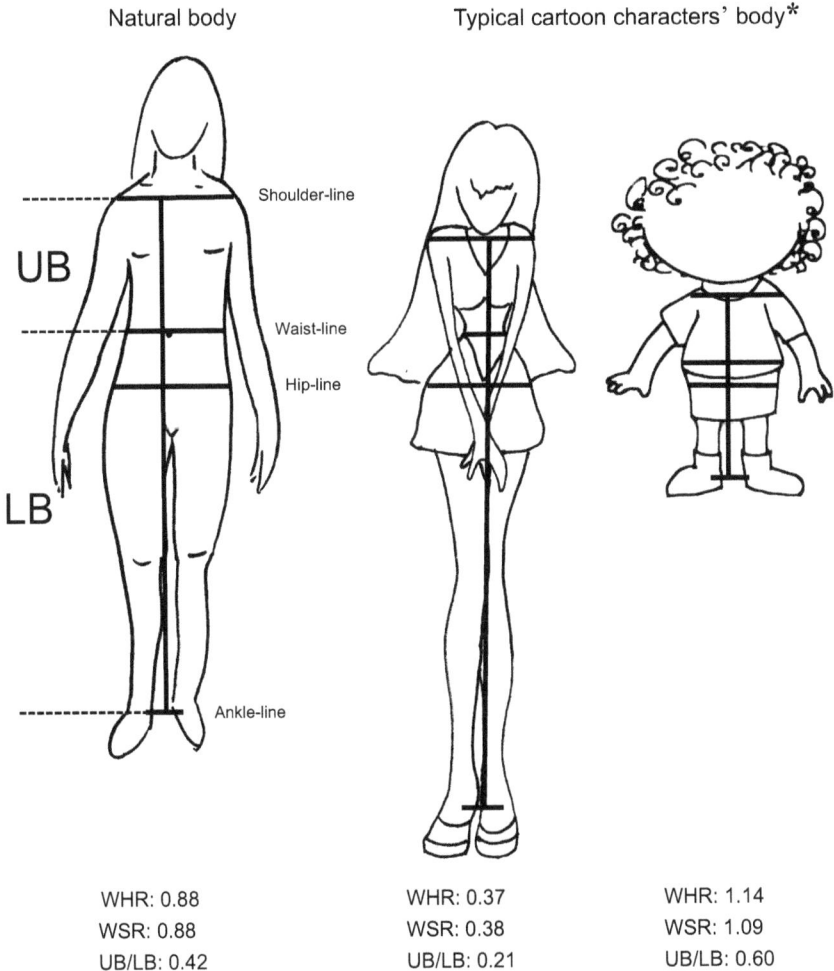

| | | |
|---|---|---|
| WHR: 0.88 | WHR: 0.37 | WHR: 1.14 |
| WSR: 0.88 | WSR: 0.38 | WSR: 1.09 |
| UB/LB: 0.42 | UB/LB: 0.21 | UB/LB: 0.60 |

**Figure 2.2.**
Measuring the body

*Due to copyright restrictions, we cannot include the original characters from children's TV in this book. To visualize the typical proportions of animated characters, Götz drew the body shapes with the corresponding lines.

Coding of the 204 characters was performed by five coders with a reliability of the waist-to-hip ratio at 79% and of the waist-to-shoulder ratio at 92% (see e.g., Figure 2.2). The character's clothing and movement often made the research difficult. Thus, it is clear to us that this study is but the first step in developing a way to measure the bodies of animated characters.

## Results

### Girl Characters with Wasp Waists and Feminine Curves: Waist-to-Hip Ratio (WHR) and Waist-to-Shoulder Ratio (WSR)

102 female characters were measured using this procedure. The lowest WHR we found was 0.26 (Marfa, *Jacob Two-Two*), followed by the girls from the *Winx Club* (Rainbow S.p.A., Italy). The highest WHR was Cindy from *The Adventures of Jimmy Neutron: Boy Genius* (O Entertainment & Co, USA) and Dora the Explorer with 1.26 and 1.3.

Employing the WHR of the animated girls-characters, we found there to be a variety of body shapes. According to the overview (see Figure 2.3), it is clear that very few characters are located at 1.0 and most are below 0.7. Characters constructed in this manner would have the naturally attainable WHR, idealized as the 90-60-90 proportions. There are some women in real life whose bodies do have a WHR of 0.69 or even, in very exceptional cases, as low as 0.67. Taking this as the potentially reachable number, 67% of all girl-characters in the corpus do not attain this ratio and are definitely not in the "normal range", according to the media analysis (see Götz & Lemish, chapter 1).

To categorize the characters further, the two ratios of WHR and WSR were determined for all 102 characters, and assigned one of three categories. The basis of comparison was the average ratio of the slender and healthy female body, no more than 0.67 and up (Henss, 2000; Singh, 1993; Thompson & Tantleff, 1992). Values below this average level were further divided into two categories: We distinguished on the one hand, characters that have an unnatural but still moderately low waist-to-hip ratio such as Barbie, from, on the other hand, those with an even lower ratio (see Figure 2.4). This distinction was based on the claim that though the classical Barbie is hypersexualized and heavily criticized (WHR of 0.6), she is still deemed to be a socially acceptable image of femininity (Brownell & Napolitano, 1995; Rogers, 1999).

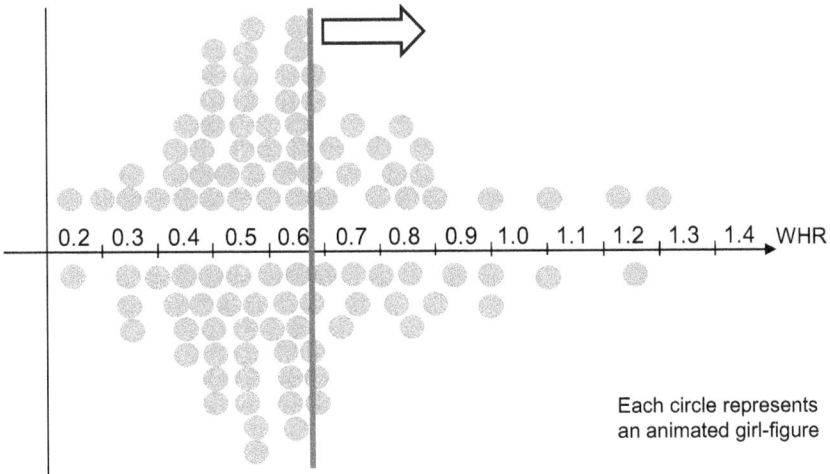

**Figure 2.3.**
N=102 "global girls": WHR and what is naturally reachable (line)

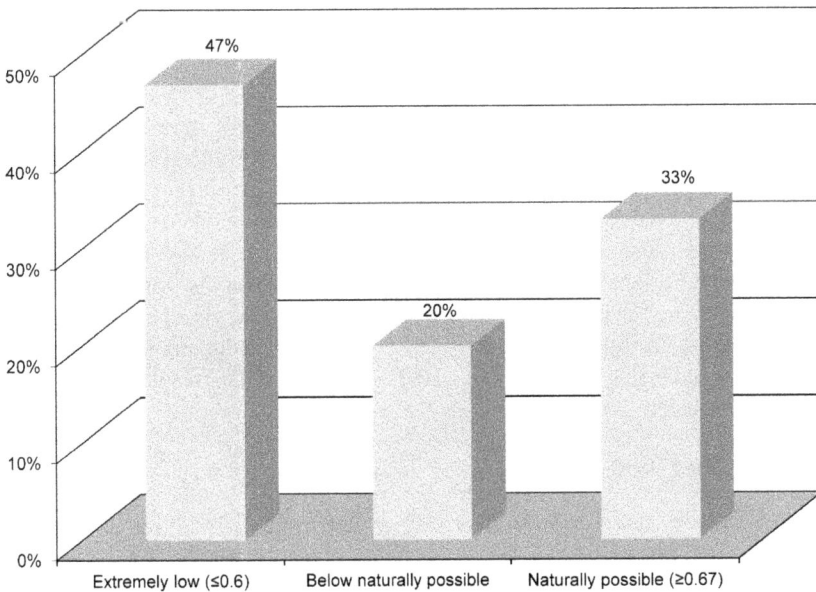

**Figure 2.4.**
Classification of female characters in 3 groups according to WHR

These results demonstrate that only a minority of female cartoon characters have the proportions of the normal range of female body proportions. To be as accurate as possible, we choose the low WHR of 0.67 as a number that though very rare, could be found in real life. But, even with this measure, over two-thirds of the characters were found to be below what is reachable in reality, as nearly half are below the "wasp waist" of the classical Barbie.

In fact, some of the "wasp waists" presented would hardly accommodate a spinal column. For example, Bloom is a 16-year-old girl from the show *Winx Club* (WHR: 0.34 and WSR: 0.37); Rose is a 16-year-old from *American Dragon: Jake Long* (Disney, USA) with a 0.42 WHR; the infamous secret agent *Kim Possible* (Disney, USA) is in her normal life a cheerleader but regularly protects against foreign antagonists, and has a 0.56 WHR. Even children's characters, such as 11-year-old Sarah from *Horseland* (DIC Entertainment, USA), are drawn with a 0.48 WHR.

Our finding becomes even more acute when the target audience is taken into account. Before puberty, boys and girls both have an average WHR of 1.0 (Ley, Lees, & Stevenson, 1992). This means that only a very small proportion of the target audience of girls sees its own body shape represented in a more or less realistic way. In summary, the results show that the majority of the characters (67%) have body proportions that are non-existent in reality for children, and all the more so for most adults.

Considering these results in relationship to critiques of Barbie doll measures (summarized in Brownell & Napolitano, 1995; Lord, 1994; Wanless, 2001) is particularly illuminating. In order to attain Barbie's figure (Classic edition), a woman would have to be between 6'2" and 7'4" tall or have one rib removed. In applying these results to the animated global girls measured in this study, we found a high percentage of characters have even lower ratios than Barbie's proportions. This finding raises serious concerns, but is even more alarming given the accumulated literature about the relationships between exposure to media and development of body image and eating disorders (e.g., Harrison, 2000, 2003; Westerberg-Jacobson, Edlund, & Ghaderi, 2010).

## Thin Body and Long Legs

While the above mentioned ratios clearly indicate the extreme curviness of the female body as presented in cartoons, the third ratio – measured between the torso and the lower body – presents us with the vertical characteristics of the bodies. We found in the sample 102 globally marketed girl characters with normal or even short legs; for example, the twins Mary and Susan from *Johnny Test* (Warner Bros. & Cookie Jar, USA) and Kim Possible. Others have legs nearly twice as long as is possible in real life; for example, Mordin from the *Bratz* (MGA Entertainment, USA) or Cornelia from the *W.I.T.C.H.* (Saban International Paris, France). So there is some variety in body shape, but clearly a lot of the TV-girls have unnaturally long legs.

Advancing our investigations one step further, we employed the two values as the basis to differentiate between the three categories. The first value represents the reachable proportions of children or young women (UB/LB of 0.32 and up). In assessing this value, we employed photographic images to measure the properties of bodies of children and young persons. This was deemed necessary due to the absence of findings from previous research that could serve as a referent. The second value used as a basis for comparison was the measurements of Barbie, with an upper-lower-body proportion of UB/LB: 0.26 (see Figure 2.5).

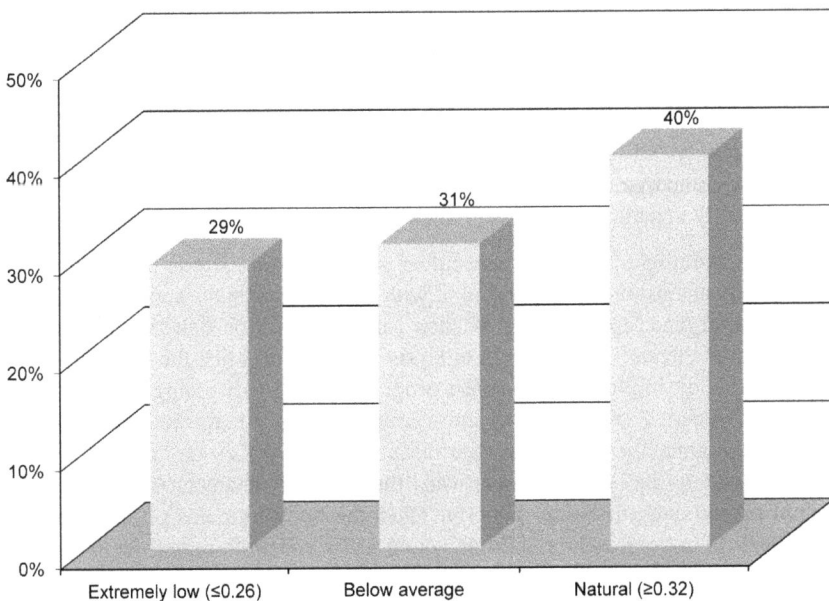

**Figure 2.5.**
Classification of female characters according to UB/LB proportion

These results present us with a very problematic picture: Only one out of three female characters measured in the analysis had the vertical proportions of average real life bodies. More than half of the female cartoon characters had legs longer than could be achieved naturally. Consequently, their bodies appear thinner and their legs longer in comparison with other body parts. Finally, nearly one in every three characters has legs longer than Barbie.

The most extreme example of this finding is DeeDee (*Dexter's Laboratory*), the 12-year-old sister of the hero Dexter, a boy genius with his own laboratory with a UB/LB of 0.14. This measurement explains clearly the extreme cartoon style of the show. Other images that try to link to the shape of the human body more directly do nevertheless have legs more than twice as long as is possible; for example, the teenage girl characters of the *Bratz* (0.21), *Totally Spies!* (Marathon, France) (0.23), or 10-year-old Misty from *Pokémon* (OLM, Japan) who has a proportion of 0.25.

## Summary: The Body of the "Global" Girl

The results of this study are unequivocal. Three out of four characters have bodies that are not attainable naturally and should by no means be presented as desirable examples that might serve as role models for young viewers.

Obviously, one could argue that while cartoon characters and Barbie bodies are constructed, their presentation is an artistic expression whose purpose is not to represent reality but to please audiences aesthetically. Furthermore, exaggeration is a highly important stylistic resource used by cartoonists that results in a predominantly unnatural body image in cartoons.

If so, we might ask: What sense does it make to pit cartoon portrayal of the female body against reality and to link it with negative attributes and effects? Truly, it could be argued, exaggeration as such cannot always be linked with negative attributes and effects. However, our analysis clearly shows that the presentation of the female body in globally broadcast programs is not only exaggerated but also clearly one-sided. These programs show young viewers a mainstream body image that is predominantly sexualized (see discussion in Götz & Lemish, chapter 1). Yet, it is exactly the lack of a wasp waist that typically characterizes the body of a child or a young girl before puberty. Thus, the body formulas of animated girl characters do not represent a child or young girl's body, but rather the sexualized bodies of little women. Female bodily attractiveness in cartoons is presented as sexy and unnaturally slender by accentuating extreme feminine curves and long, disproportional legs in unexpected measures.

So what about the boys' bodies?

## Measuring the "Global" Boys

### Sample – Unit of Analysis and Measurements

For purposes of comparison, we analyzed the bodies of 102 global boy and young men characters from 55 globally broadcast programs, included in the main study. The procedural method corresponded with the one used for female characters. However, the unit of analysis was, in this case, the individual male animated character. Only characters that appeared in programs broadcast in at least three countries were identified as global characters. Here, too, US productions were the majority of the programs (59%) identified as global.

The main objective of the analysis presented here was to find out whether there is a similar one-sided, exaggerated, presentation style of boy characters' bodies in cartoons, equivalent to girls' characteristics found above. If our findings lead us to conclude with an affirmative answer, then one could claim that the one-sided presentation form is, generally, a typical representation style used in cartoons.

Following the same guidelines applied in the investigations of animated portrayals of girls, photographic images of male characters were analyzed. Measurements were made at the hips, waist, shoulders, and height. Ratios were calculated using stills of frontal views, just as they were made for girls: waist-to-hip ratio (WHR), waist-to-shoulder ratio (WSR), upper body-lower body ratio (UB/LB).

While the WHR is considered as the critical variable of female bodily attractiveness, the WSR plays a similarly important role in judging male attractiveness (see Figure 2.6). Previous research demonstrated that a relatively low WSR (0.6-0.7) and a comparatively high WHR (0.8-0.9) create the "V-shaped torso" associated with high levels of male bodily attractiveness (Dixson, Halliwell, East, Wignarajah, & Anderson, 2003; Thompson & Tantleff, 1992). The WSR of the average male body in reality varies between 0.7 and 0.85 (Thompson & Tantleff, 1992). Finally, the ratio measured between the upper body and the lower body establishes the vertical properties of the body. Here, the lower the ratio the more stretched out the character's body appears. This results in a thin image of the male body, often characterized with unnaturally long legs.

### Results

### The Waist-to-Shoulder Ratio of the "Global" Boy in Animated Shows

Here, too, we found significant forms of stylization and sexualization in the 102 globally marketed boy and young men characters in the sample. Measuring the waist-to-shoulder ratio, we found characters with 0.24, like Kronk (*Emperor's New*

*School*) as the most extreme example, or Ty (*Grossology*) and Johnny (*Johnny Bravo*) with 0.36 and 0.38. Since there is no natural way to achieve such a WSR, our findings demonstrate that these characters are the exceptions (see Figure 2.7). The maximum WSR that could be reached with professional training would be around 0.5. Among the animated global boys, 5.9% of the characters are shown with ratio below this level; something that is unreachable naturally. For the sake of comparison, 67% of the portrayals of girls had such a ratio.

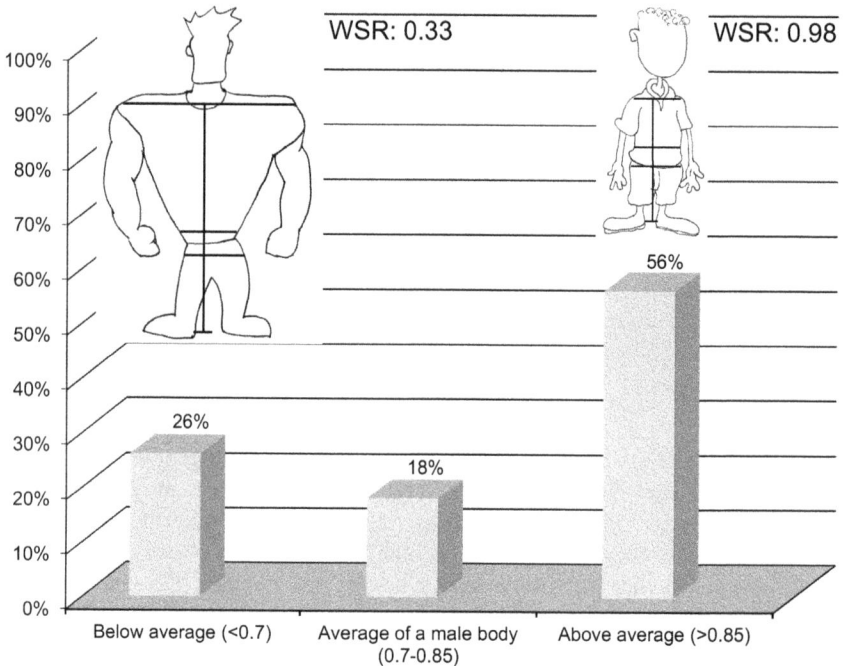

**Figure 2.6.**
Classification of male characters according to WSR

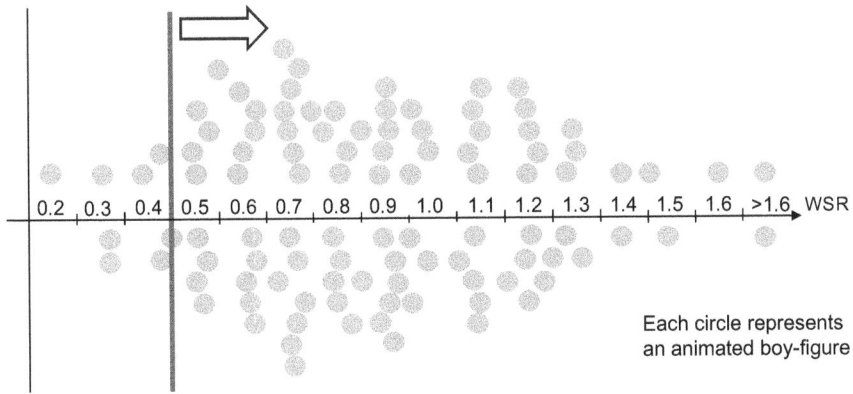

Each circle represents
an animated boy-figure

**Figure 2.7.**
N=102 "global boys": WSR and what is naturally reachable (line)

## The Waist-to-Hip Ratio of the "Global" Boy in Animated Shows

Measuring the WHR of boy-characters, we found examples like Odd Super (*Code Lyoko*) with a 0.73 and Kuririn (*Dragon Ball Z*) with a 0.81. Nearly half of these portrayals are above 0.95. This means that they are more or less straight and "not-waisted" in the way they are drawn. This can be interpreted as a tendency to avoid any kind of "waisting" which might look like a sexualized girl.

Another 40% of the animated portrayals are shaped in a way that lies between 0.95 and 0.85. Compared to reality, the WHR of healthy and slim men is between 0.85-0.95 (Dixson et al., 2003). For example, the average WHR for adult males ages 18 to 49 in the Australian population is 0.87 (Abernethy, Olds, Eden, Neill, & Baines, 1996). So, most of the boy TV-characters are in this natural shape or drawn by the animators with less hip size. Only 12% are below the 0.85 (e.g., Johnny of *Johnny Bravo* has 1.47 or Albert of *Fat Albert* with 1.32) (see Figure 2.8).

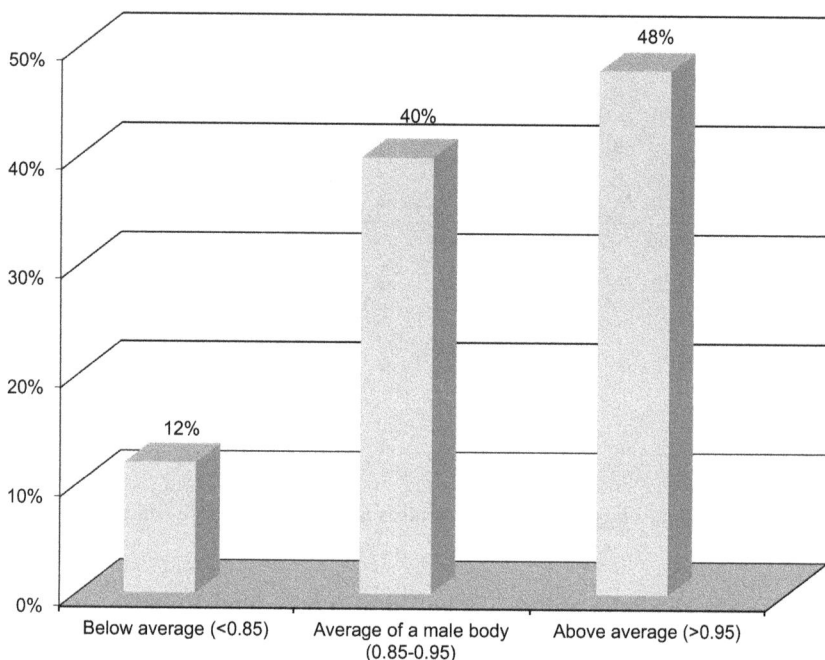

**Figure 2.8.**
Classification of male characters according to WHR

## The Upper-to-Lower Ratio of the "Global" Boy in Animated Shows

The analysis of the proportions of the torso to the lower part of the body of male characters shows that nearly one in two characters has an average ratio (see Figure 2.9).

Regarding the UB/LB, we found long-legged examples, such as Tristan Taylor (*Yu-Gi-Oh!*) at 0.18 or Lik (*What's With Andy?*) with a proportion of 0.27; and short-legged examples, such as Johnny (*Johnny Bravo*) at 1.25 and Clay (*Xiaolin Showdown*) with 0.97. Overall, then, the characteristically slender portrayal of the female body with unnaturally long legs is not found among boy characters. Thus, we have two opposing characterizations: While female characters are sexualized with overly long legs, male characters are sexualized by being portrayed with an enlongated upper body, which results in a shorter lower body. Additionally, a high number of characters are portrayed with ball shaped bodies, as overweight.

## Summary: The Body of the "Global" Boy

Our findings demonstrate that unnatural body images among male characters dominate the animation world. However, in comparison with female cartoon characters, the number of male characters with natural body proportions is comparatively higher than the number of female characters with natural body proportions. Furthermore, here, too, the sexualization of the body applies to male characters (26% of male characters are portrayed with V-shaped torsos which is the equivalent to female characters with low WHR). Thus, the portrayal of the male body in animated shows is not as one-sided as the portrayal of female bodies has been proved to be, as the range of physical features employed to depict male bodies is considerably wider than what is applied to female characters.

## Discussion

Even though this analysis is an initial step in analyzing the body of cartoon characters, the results show a clear direction: Globally broadcast cartoons show a tendency to depict girls and young women as unnaturally slender with great emphasis placed on feminine curves. More than 50% of "global" female characters in cartoons have an unnaturally curvy body with accentuated wasp-waists and unnaturally long legs. These are distinctive signs of an exaggerated and sexualized image of the female body. Such an image could hardly be attained even by means of medical surgery. While the classic Barbie is criticized as an unsuitable role model for young girls and teenagers (Brownell & Napolitano, 1995), such criticism applies even more to a large number of globally marketed cartoon girls and teenagers.

Certainly, it could be objected that both Barbie and cartoon characters are merely constructions whose presentation follows artistic forms of expression. Thus, so the argument goes, there is no intention that they represent reality and, consequently, should not be linked to reality. However, this study has shown that bodies of female and male characters are presented predominantly in unnatural ways. Furthermore, there are significant gender specific differences in portrayal of their unnaturalness. The range of physical features employed in depicting male bodies in cartoons is considerably wider than the range of features used in portrayal of female characters, and the female body of young girls and teenagers is overly sexualized in cartoons.

Considering men's dominance in the production of globally marketed animated programs, there is much to be said for the idea that they offer a masculine view of the female body. While the male body is presented in a wide variety of shapes, probably representing the physicality of the producers (as boys), the female body remains almost exclusively hypersexualized. As early as 1975, Laura Mulvey argued in her article "Visual pleasure and narrative cinema" (1975/1985) that "the determining male gaze projects its fantasy on to the female form which is styled accordingly" (Mulvey, 1985, p. 309). Here, years later and far removed from Hollywood cinema, we find further evidence of phenomena, which has received little attention to date, to support this argument.

This general trend having been noted, research presented in this volume does advance study of how *hypersexualization* is involved in movement, patterns of action, and narratives. Prinsloo, in chapter 3 of this volume, studied the extent to which hypersexualization is infused in the whole media text. Spry's study of Japanese anime is an example of investigations of hypersexualization in certain formats and styles (see Spry, chapter 4).

Certainly we are not presuming that there is a simple stimulus-response effect in play with young viewers, as we understand children to be active viewers and meaning-makers who are not likely to aspire exactly to the same physical look appearing in *Winx Club* or *Bratz*. Yet, it certainly can be the case that characters' physical appearance has meaning for children. Research on media effects on young audiences has proven that the media can have inevitable negative consequences on a viewer's body image and self-perception (Consumano & Thomson, 2001; Groesz, Levine, & Murnen, 2002; Hargreaves & Tiggemann, 2004). For example, Dohnt and Tiggerman (2006) showed that girls as young as six years of age believed that thinness is essential for beauty (the thin "ideal"). Other studies found that girls aged nine to twelve years of age share the concerns of adult women about body shape and weight. For example, Sands and Wardle (2003) argued that awareness of the thin ideal propagated on television influences young girls' feelings of dissatisfaction with their bodies. Furthermore, negative effects are even stronger if the thin ideal has become internalized. In a five-year longitudinal study, Westerberg-Jacobson, Edlund, & Ghaderi (2010) showed that the wish to be thinner was related to life style factors and girls were four times more likely to develop disturbed eating attitudes.

Other studies demonstrated that gender specific differences in media texts can have immediate negative effects on perceptions of body image, and that such negative effects are more normative for girls than for boys (Hargreaves & Tiggemann, 2004). Such negative effects may well mirror gender specific differences in the portrayal of girls/women and boys/men on TV. This study has demonstrated that portrayal in animated programs of the slender ideal of the female body, with accentuated feminine curves, is much more prevalent and normative than portrayals of the masculine muscular ideal.

Interestingly, the original coding of the worldwide study described by Götz & Lemish in chapter 1 in this volume found that 84% of the main characters fell within the normal range of body size. Yet, this study has demonstrated this finding to be incorrect for the boys, and even clearer in the case of the girls. Using the WHR measurement, we found that 67% of the characters are skinnier and constructed with wasp-like waist figures unachievable in reality. We believe that our explanation for such differences is insightful. We begin by noting that "normal" coding procedures were employed in analyzing the 10,153 main human characters. Each character was coded in at least two different countries, by two different coders. The overall reliability rating achieved was 93.9%. This means that different junior researchers, in different parts of the world, who studied the shows considered the shapes portrayed to be "in the normal range". This finding from the worldwide study is a clear comment on what seems to be the impact or certainly an adjustment to what is considered "normal" – or at least the normality of children's TV. This may also serve as a self-referential hint of a kind of cultivation effect (Gerbner, Gross, Morgan, Signorielli, & Shanahan, 2002) that includes the researchers themselves.

## REFERENCES

Abernethy, P., Olds, T., Eden, B., Neill, M., & Baines, L. (1996). *Anthropometry, Health and Body Composition*. Sydney, Australia: University of New South Wales Press.

Brownell, K. D., & Napolitano, M. A. (1995). Distorting reality for children: Body size proportions of Barbie and Ken dolls. *International Journal of Eating Disorders, 18*(3), 295-298.

Connolly, J. M., Slaughter, V., Mealey, L. (2000). The development of body shape preferences. *Perspectives in Human Biology, 5*, 19-29.

Cusumano, D. L., & Thompson, J. K. (2001). Media influence and body image in 8-11 year old boys and girls: A preliminary report on the Multidimensional Media Influence Scale. *International Journal of Eating Disorders, 29*, 37-44.

DeBruine, L., Jones, B. C., Frederick, D. A., Haselton, M. G., Penton-Voak, I. S., & Perrett, D. I. (2010). Evidence for menstrual cycle shifts in women's preferences for masculinity: A response to Harris (in press) "Menstrual cycle and facial preferences reconsidered". *Evolutionary Psychology, 8*(4), 768-775.

Dixson, A. F., Halliwell, G., East, R., Wignarajah, P., & Anderson, M. J. (2003). Masculine somatotype and hirsuteness as determinants of sexual attractiveness to women. *Archives of Sexual Behaviour, 32*, 29-39.

Dohnt, H., & Tiggemann, M. (2006). The contribution of peer and media influences to the development of body satisfaction and self-esteem in young girls: A prospective study. *Developmental Psychology, 42*(5), 929-936.

Furnham, A., Petrides, K. V., & Constantinides, A. (2005). The effects of body mass index and waist-to-hip ratio on ratings of female attractiveness, fecundity, and health. *Personality and Individual Differences, 38*(8), 1823-1834.

Furnham, A. ,Tan, T., & McManus, I. C. (1997). Waist-to-hip ratio and preferences for body shape: A replication and extension. *Personality and Individual Differences, 22*, 539-549.

Gerbner, G., Gross, L., Morgan, M., Signorielli, N., & Shanahan, J. (2002). Growing up with television: Cultivation processes. In J. Bryant (Ed.), *Media effects* (pp. 43-67). Mahwah, NJ: Erlbaum.

Götz, M. (2009). Macht Fernsehen unglückliche oder glückliche TagträumerInnen? [Does television make happy or unhappy daydreamers?]. In M. Schächter (Ed.), Wunschlos glücklich? Konzepte und Rahmenbedingungen einer glücklichen Kindheit [Perfectly happy? Concepts and basic conditions of a happy childhood] (pp. 57-61). Baden-Baden, Baden-Württemberg: Nomos.

Götz, M. (2011). What makes them so special? The utility value of children's favourite heroes and heroines. *TelevIZIon, 24*, 27-32.

Götz, M., Lemish, D., Aidman, A., & Moon, H. (2005). *Media and the Make-Believe Worlds of Children: When Harry Potter Meets Pokémon in Disneyland.* Mahwah, NJ: Erlbaum.

Groesz, L. M., Levine, M. P., & Murnen, S. K. (2002). The effect of experimental presentation of thin media images on body satisfaction: A meta-analytic review. *International Journal of Eating Disorders, 31*(1), 1-16.

Hargreaves, D. A., & Tiggemann, M. (2004). Idealized media images and adolescent body image: "Comparing" boys and girls. *Body Image, 1*(4), 351-361.

Harrison, K. (2000). Television viewing, fat stereotyping, body shape standards, and eating disorder symptomatology in grade school children. *Communication Research, 27*(5), 617-640.

Harrison, K. (2003). Television viewers' ideal body proportions: The case of the curvaceously thin woman. *Sex roles, 48*, 255-264.

Herche, M. (2007, September). Von der Bewahrung der Tugend und der Rettung der Welt. Darstellung des Glücks in Kindermedien [On the preservation of the virtue and the rescue of the world. Depiction of luck in children's media]. IZI: Unpublished research report.

Henss, R. (1995). Waist-to-hip ratio and attractiveness. Replication and extension. *Personality and Individual Differences, 19*, 479-488.

Henss, R. (2000). Waist-to-hip ratio and attractiveness of the female figure. Evidence from photographic stimuli and methodological considerations. *Personality and Individual Differences, 28*, 501-513.

Ley, C. J., Lees, B., & Stevenson, J. C. (1992). Sex- and menopause-associated changes in body-fat distribution. *American Journal of Clinical Nutrition, 55*, 950-954.

Little, A. C., Jones, B. C., & DeBruine, L. M. (2011). Facial attractiveness: Evolutionary based research. *Philosophical Transactions of the Royal Society B, 366*(1571), 1638-1659.

Little, A. C., Penton-Voak, I. S., Burt, D. M., & Perrett, D. I. (2002). Evolution and individual differences in the perception of attractiveness: How cyclic hormonal changes and self-perceived attractiveness influence female preferences for male faces. In G. Rhodes & L. A. Zebrowitz (Eds.), *Facial attractiveness: Evolutionary, cognitive and social perspectives* (pp. 59-90). Westport, CT: Ablex.

Lord, M. G. (1994). *Forever Barbie: The Unauthorized Biography of a Real Doll*. New York, NY: Walker & Company.

Marlowe, F., & Wetsman, A. (2001). Preferred waist-to-hip ratio and ecology. *Personality and Individual Differences, 30*(3), 481-489.

Mulvey, L. (1975/1985). Visual Pleasure and Narrative Cinema. In: B. Nichols (Ed.), *Movies and Methods Volume 2* (305-315). Berkeley, CA: University of California Press.

Rogers, M. F. (1999). *Barbie Culture*. London, England: Sage.

Sands, E. R., & Wardle, J. (2003). Internalization of ideal body shapes in 9-12 year-old girls. *International Journal of Eating Disorders, 33*(2), 193-204.

Singh, D. (1993). Adaptive significance of female physical attractiveness: Role of waist-to-hip ratio. *Journal of Personality and Social Psychology, 65*(2), 293-307.

Singh, D. (1994a). Waist-to-hip ratio and judgment of attractiveness and healthiness of female figures by male and female physicians. *International Journal of Obesity, 18*(11), 731-737.

Singh, D. (1994b). Is thin really beautiful and good? Relationship between waist-to-hip ratio (WHR) and female attractiveness. *Personality and Individual Differences, 16*(1), 123-132.

Singh, D., & Luis, S. (1995). Ethnic and gender consensus for the role of waist-to-hip ratio on judgment of women's attractiveness. *Human Nature, 6*, 51-65.

Singh, D., & Young, R. K. (1995). Body weight, waist-to-hip ratio, breasts and hips: Role in judgments of female attractiveness and desirability for relationships. *Ethology and Sociobiology, 16*, 483-507.

Thompson, J. K., & Tantleff, S. (1992). Female and male ratings of upper torso: Actual, ideal and stereotypical conceptions. *Journal of Social Behavior and Personality, 7*, 345-354.

Wanless, M. D. (2001). Barbie's body images. *Feminist Media Studies, 1*, 125-126.

Welling, L. L. M., Jones, B. C., DeBruine, L. M., Smith, F. G., Feinberg, D. R., Little, A. C., & Al-Dujaili, E. A. S. (2008). Men report stronger attraction to femininity in women's faces when their testosterone levels are high. *Hormones and Behavior, 54*(5), 703-708.

Westerberg-Jacobson, J., Edlund, B., & Ghaderi, A. (2010). A 5-year longitudinal study of the relationship between the wish to be thinner, lifestyle behaviours and disturbed eating in 9-20-year old girls. *European Eating Disorders Review, 18*(3), 207-219.

Yu, D. W., & Shepard, G. H. (1998). Is beauty in the eye of the beholder? *Nature, 396*, 321-322.

Zebrowitz, L. A. (2009). Attractiveness. In *The Oxford Companion to Emotion and the Affective Sciences* (p. 61). New York, NY: Oxford University Press.

---

[1] 3% could not be coded as clearly one or the other.

# 3

# SEDUCTIVE LITTLE GIRLS ON CHILDREN'S TV: SEXUALIZATION AND GENDER RELATIONS

*Jeanne Prinsloo*


Childhood – that golden time of innocence and becoming, of "trailing clouds of glory"[1], the precursor to the myriad of concerns and responsibilities of adulthood! Well, so we are told. And consistent with that construction, adults who are concerned about their children take care to ensure that their children's consumption of TV and other media forms is appropriate to this stage of life. Their concern with the media as unsuitable for children tends to revolve around two issues, namely exposure to sex and violence. To avoid this, adults direct their innocent lambs to kids' media, to keep them snug and safe. Well, one might indeed wonder about that!

Childhood has not been understood in this way always and in all places. This particular construction has its roots in Western discourse as far back as Rousseau's (1762/1979) exploration of childhood in his book about *Emile*. "Childhood" has retained and deepened its status as a space of difference to adulthood through the increasing specialization and diversification of goodies made for children. This includes all the media productions, the toys, and clothing produced for this charmed space (e.g., Disney products, Tesco who marketed the pole dancing kit as a toy for girls or other producers of discourse around children). What is notable is that in spite of the idea of childhood as neutral, it is a hugely gendered space where childhood is additionally mostly constructed as generically male (Prinsloo, 2003). The international research undertaken by IZI demonstrates the extent to which this is so, as the content analysis revealed that at least two thirds of the characters in the extensive global TV sample were male.

It can be argued that content analysis is a rather blunt, albeit important, instrument and that it is not only numbers that count but how the characters are represented. Indeed both reservations are true. Many of the girls listed in the research were identified as protagonists in the stories and could be argued therefore to defy the discourse of female subservience and serve as important role models in a patriarchal world. Yes, maybe. But accepting this argument requires that we look at those representations more carefully. In addition, the research did not and could not code for those concerns people have about children's exposure to adult media forms considered unsuitable for children, namely sex and violence. Ironically, these concerns are themselves implicitly gendered. We might speak about violence and explicit sex, but the unease is not really about girls becoming too violent, nor is there anxiety about boys being hypersexualized. Whether expressed in public debates or scholarly literature, the unease actually relates to violent boys and hyper-sexy girls while phrased as a concern with "childhood" or "children". In this paper the issue is taken up but confined to the constructions of girlhood within popular TV/film texts made for girls that they encounter frequently on TV. It is concerned with the nature of the sexualization of girl children and seeks to participate in the conversations that circulate both in the form of popular and of scholarly debate.

## Popular Debates

The content of popular debate varies but a recent online debate is sufficient to establish the different range of positions taken up. "Girls aged 5 sexualised by toys like Bratz dolls, MSP told" ran the headline in the online version of the *The Scotsman* (Maddox, *The Scotsman*, 3 December 2008). The headline represents the concern voiced by the SPCC[2] in Scotland in response to the merchandise for children that accompanies the Bratz media productions (MGA Entertainment, USA). The varied responses of the subsequent online debate that developed focused on the sexualization of girls through popular culture and were fairly predictable. On one hand, some protested that Bratz dolls and the associated media fare were no more than good clean fun. In contrast, they were seen as one aspect of broad cultural production; and the media, specifically TV, were identified as responsible for the problem. A concern was expressed about young girls being sexualized before they are physically or emotionally mature. Others rejected this focus on sexualization and argued that children's programs provide diverse and positive scripts for girls. And, finally, the interest in sexy dress, make-up, etc. that the merchandise encourages was constructed as charming in that it enables fantasy – girls will be girls was the kind of response.

## Scholarly Literature

If the report and online discussions indicate different takes on the sexualized representations and merchandise aimed at girls, the scholarly literature is also varied in its positions. When scholars have attempted to map the literature around the sexualization of girls in media texts produced for children, they quickly note that there is little research on the topic, that the phenomenon is prevalent, and that it should be of great concern. While the sexualization of girls in texts is not a new phenomenon, most feminist media studies have focused on adults and when attention has been given to sexuality and young people, it has been in relation to adolescent sexuality (e.g., McRobbie, 1991) or to concerns with socialization and sex roles which Walkerdine (1997) critiques.

More recently there have been a few comprehensive responses to the phenomenon, including a *Report of the APA Task Force on the Sexualization of Girls* by the American Psychological Association (APA, 2007), and two books informed by scholarly work but written to be accessible and popular reads; namely *The Lolita Effect* (Durham, 2008) and *So Sexy So Soon: The New Sexualized Childhood and What Parents Can Do to Protect Their Kids* (Levine & Kilbourne, 2008). All three tend to be concerned with what media *does* to their audiences, are framed as interventions, and were generated in the USA where most commercial children's TV and media are produced. The other significant contribution in this field in the Anglo-speaking world is in the works of Valerie Walkerdine and it differs from the three interventions mentioned in being more academic in intent and challenging of certain of their critiques. All these accounts are careful to distance themselves from conservative attitudes that disallow that children are indeed also sexual and they differentiate between sexuality and sexualization or the production of the "baby-faced nymphet" (Durham, 2008, p. 24).

M. Gigi Durham's book, *The Lolita Effect* (2008), is concerned with the sexualization of young girls. She spreads her net far wider than merely media made for children to include the contemporary media environment with its wide range of media products, marketing and associated merchandise that work to achieve the sexy little girl or, in her words, the Lolita effect. She identifies a range of responses to sexualized girls, not fundamentally different from those in the online debate cited above. Some take these sexualized performances at face value and view the girls as deliberately sexual – as wanton provocateurs or "little Lolitas". Others view sexualized performance on the part of young girls as a symbol of sexual empowerment or, alternatively, as an achievement in line with the prevailing beauty myth. These roles are celebrated as progressive or liberal rather than conservative. Durham disagrees and argues that the sexual imagery is neither progressive nor at odds with conservative politics. The kinds of bodies and behaviors positioned as sexual are consistent with the traditional male gaze and amounts to "a construction of sexuality that both exploits and limits sexual expression and agency, [...] deliberately focused on young girls" (2008, p. 34).

Durham identifies five "myths" that work to achieve the Lolita effect in contemporary American society (and by implication then, as broadly as the spread of American cultural products, that is globally). The myths relate to sexualization or the imperative to get and keep your man. The first myth proposes that "if you've got it, flaunt it" (2008, p. 63), and thus is an injunction to be "hot". Stylish clothing and the presentation of self in ways that attract boys' sexual interest are viewed as inherent prerequisites for "hotness" and consequently other aspects of their lives and personalities are devalued. The second "myth" identifies what counts as hot and this is the "anatomy of a sex goddess". The sex goddess (second cousin to Barbie) is slender, long-legged, fat-free, busty, wasp-waisted, long haired and White. "Myth" three, or "pretty babes", relates to the Lolita effect whereby little girls are seen as sexually appealing. Ads are considered as cultural spaces where very young girls are often sexualized. She cites the *Calvin Klein* jeans ad in which the girl models appear to be removing their clothes in a manner suggestive of sex work. This is the Lolita effect that Durham addresses – sexiness linked to youth and the younger the sexier!

"Violence is sexy" goes "myth" four and these scenarios occur most obviously in many horror and slasher movies and also in video games, music videos, wrestling programs, TV programs and billboards. The final "myth" exhorts girls to do what boys like. Teen magazines are loaded with advice to girls about how to keep that man, to learn to please boys to get their attention, and not have a sexual voice themselves. While asserting "girl power", they appear to exhort girls to be themselves, but this self must be complicit with this ideal Barbie femininity and traditional heterosexuality. In summary:

> If you've got it, flaunt it – but don't dare flaunt it unless you have the anatomy of a sex goddess; the younger you are, the better; make sure you're flaunting it so boys like it; and if you spice it up with a soupcon of violence, so much the better. (2008, pp. 179-180)

The critique of the media by Levine and Kilbourne's (2008) intervention is cast in the same mold but relates to both sexes. They argue as follows:

> Both girls and boys are routinely exposed to images of sexual behavior devoid of emotions, attachment or consequences. [...] They learn that sex is often linked to violence. And they learn to associate physical appearance and buying the right products not only with being sexy but also with being successful as a person. (Levine & Kilbourne, 2008, p. 2)

Similar concerns informed the APA task force (APA, 2007) that investigated the phenomenon of sexualization of girls and girlhood in US culture in response to expressions of public concern. Again the concern related to both the media representations and the products targeted at young girls; such as, the lacy thongs, t-shirts with suggestive and flirtatious slogans, and salacious toys. The authors differentiated between "healthy sexuality" and sexualization and described the sexualization of girls as a complex social phenomenon reinforced across three spheres; namely the cultural norms and values communicated through the media, interpersonal communication among family and peers and self-sexualization when girls recognize that sexualized behaviors receive approval and they "internalize these standards" (2007, p. 3). As this term and other references to the media as "socializing influences" (2007, p. 4) indicate, this report is framed primarily in a socialization paradigm.

The media is seen as delivering "messages" that "teach girls that women are sexual objects" (APA, 2007, p. 5). One study that relates to the focus of the report is Thompson and Zerbinos' discussion (1995) relating to child cartoons and animation. It finds that girls are primarily portrayed as "domestic, interested in boys, and concerned with their appearance" (APA, 2007, p. 8). The APA report notes that there was only anecdotal evidence that these representations may contain "sexualizing images of girls and women" (2007, p. 8), a further indication of the neglect of the topic.

Advertising is again singled out as the media form where the sexualization of women is particularly prominent and where women and girls might be depicted as sexual objects: (un)dressed in sexually provocative clothing, posed in submissive, sexually exploitative and violent positions. Three forms of sexualization of girlhood in media representations are listed: first, the occasional depiction of girls as "sexual objects or as counterparts to adult versions" (APA, 2007, p. 13); second, girls are dressed up to appear like adults and women dressed down to appear like children in what is described as both a trickle down and trickle up effect; and finally, youthful celebrities are presented in highly suggestive ways. It concludes that "girls exposed to sexualizing media are more prone to experiencing dissatisfaction, depression and low self esteem" (2007, p. 35), and to experience a sense of shame. They express concern that girls' sexual development may be affected as a result of being exposed to models of sexual passivity.

Lerum and Dworkin (2009) provide an important riposte to the APA report, both expanding and challenging a number of its claims with reference to a broader frame of feminist scholarship. They are critical of its review of literature that addresses only the negative consequences of the sexualization of girls and thus treats sexualized representations as exclusively and necessarily dangerous. Importantly they emphasize girls' sexual agency and resistance, thereby introducing the significance of desire.

Similarly Walkerdine (1990, 1997) presents a different take to those described above. She has been concerned with the interrelationship of cultural products and little girls' subjectification and written extensively in relation to education and popular culture. She argues that feminism has rarely addressed the issue of the girl child except in terms of socialization processes and sex-role stereotypes, and that such approaches assume a passive subject. She criticizes the cognitivist or rationalist approach (evident in the interventions of APA, 2007; Durham, 2008; Levine & Kilbourne, 2008) that is an adjunct to such work for it assumes that, if the girl had "the veil of distortion lifted from her eyes" (Walkerdine, 1990, p. 89), she would wish to engage in all those activities from which she had been precluded. Such approaches neglect the centrality of cultural practices in actually producing the forms of thought and positions for women (for they are constituted within powerful and naturalized patriarchal discourses) and consequently how desire is inscribed.

Thus, she adopts a Cultural Studies or Constructionist approach informed by Foucault's understandings of discourse and the formation of subjects through practices. The media texts, here those targeting girls, do not then distort or bias reality, but present practices and, through the meanings they propose, they create subject positions for the audience. These subject positions also do not exist merely in the texts, but relate to "existing social and psychic struggle" (Walkerdine, 1990, p. 89) and these psychic conflicts are then lived out in the fantasy situations and resolutions. Another important aspect of her position is her insistence on childhood as constructed. If childhood is normatively constructed as an unsullied space of innocence, popular culture is argued to insert sexuality, conceived of as adult, into that space. Children consequently encounter the contesting discourses of innocent versus sexualized childhood and these discourses both propose different subject positions as well as validate different practices. Walkerdine foregrounds how an erotic gaze is focused on little girls across media forms, even while disavowing it.

While her studies are wide ranging, she picks up on the repetitive theme of young working class girls and big daddies in fifties movies like *Annie* (Raster, USA) which began as a comic strip, *Gigi* (MGM, USA) and *My Fair Lady* (Warner Bros., USA), and *My Girl* (Imagine Entertainment, USA) in the 1990s. The narratives tell of the class transformations of the female protagonist from working to middle class through the patronage of an older man. The maternal or nurturant mother is written out of these scenarios – "pushed out or killed off" – and the older man/young girl relationship is suggestive of a pre-teen Lolita while "carefully avoiding any sexual reference" (Walkerdine, 1997, p. 140).

Beauty pageants and stardom on the television are again identified as a sexualized space for girls to transform themselves with sexy attire and suggestive performance to achieve fame. She describes her observations of little girls mimicking pop songs as though in talent contests and singing the words of *Mickey*, a popular and very sexually explicit song of the 1980s, including the words:

So come on and give it to me any way you can
Any way you wanna do it, I'll take it like a man.
(Walkerdine, 1997, p. 145).

The crucial point for Walkerdine, who constantly reflects on her own working class childhood, is that popular culture texts play a central role in constructing desire, particularly in relation to working class girls. It is they who tend to engage in talent and beauty contests as moments of fantasy, of escape and of transformation. For working class girls who want more than they have, these scenarios present alternative fantasies and desires that take a particular social and cultural form, but are exploitative. Paradoxically, popular cultural forms thus enable an escape from institutional constraints, but an escape that enacts a further subjectification this time as sexualized girls. The talent contest fantasy does not present the same escape route for middle class girls who are differently positioned.

Another aspect of popular culture Walkerdine considered was the representation of little girls in advertisements and the "fine soft pornographic line walked by such portrayals of little girls" and where "the look of advertisement and fashion shots is similar to child pornography" (1997, p. 165). Images of seductive little girls return the camera's gaze as though offering future sexualization. Thus, culture is seen to carry adult fantasies and the adult language and fantasies are projected onto the girl child. She conceives of this as a complex seduction of the girl child into the fantasies of adults, parents and culture. Consistent with her Cultural Studies position, she acknowledges that any text will receive multiple readings. Individual girls will draw on the range of discourses they have encountered and these will include class, race, and gendered dimensions.

While Walkerdine foregrounds the working class girl and issues of desire, a more celebratory approach to "tweens" engagement with popular culture co-exists. Sports and pop stars are argued to serve as cultural icons that are imitated, idealized and identified with. Boden (2006) sees "tweens" performances and stylizing of their looks as "safe play, controlled adventure, imagination and enchantment" (p. 297) that is created through "the market" that enables them hedonistically and even fleetingly to be one of their idols. While this focus on pleasure and desire is similar to Walkerdine's (1997) descriptions, Boden differs in that she offers no gender or class analysis and thus sidesteps the arguably more complex issues around the subjectivities of "precocious girls" or "violent boys" (Walkerdine, 1999). Popular culture, Walkerdine argues, introduces the young girl to the possibility of the seductress girl child and offers the script for its performance.

Walkerdine's understandings, like the analysis offered below, are informed by Foucauldian (Foucault, 1981) notions of discourse and power and their interrelationship with the body. Other feminist theorists (such as Bartky, 1990;

Butler, 2007; Connell, 1987; mentioned below) use Foucault's ideas as they enable them to both consider the practices by which people train and constrain themselves to become particular kinds of gendered subjects. Connell's conceptualizing (1987) of the gender order provides a framework for the analysis of media texts. He provides us with the idea of the gender order where centrality is attributed to "hegemonic masculinity", a socially endorsed, normative, heterosexual masculinity where men are characterized by physical strength, aggression, emotional control, and self-reliance. In contrast "emphasized femininities" (in the plural) complement hegemonic masculinity and include various subject positions such as the traditional nurturing mothering role, feminine attractiveness and sexual availability – all of which are oriented to the needs and interests of men. The structure of sexuality is one of the elements of any gender order and sexuality is understood as social; it is "enacted or conducted, it is not 'expressed'" (Connell, 1987, p. 111).

A crucial aspect of sexualizing women as objects of desire in relation to heterosexuality is the standardization of feminine appeal and this is what fashion enables. To be sexualized and sexy, the injunction is to be fashionable. In line with this, Judith Butler (2006) argues that gender is a performance. She considers bodily performance as a mode of address which may not be the same as the "meaning proffered by any given verbal utterance" (2006, p. 530). Textual analysis, then, needs to attend to what is both being said and what is being performed. Bartky's (1990) three groups of feminine disciplinary practices include those that aim to produce a body of a certain shape and size, practices that elicit a certain repertoire of gestures including restricted movements, limbs close to the body, shorter strides, etc; and practices that encourage bodily adornment including a focus on smooth and unblemished skin, hairlessness save the head, dress, fashion, and make-up.

In summary, then, this literature recognizes sexuality as being performed also through dress, merchandise and gesture or behaviors. These are aspects then that need to be scrutinized when analyzing media texts designed for little girls.

### Researching Bratz and Winx

The literature reviewed above raises important issues around childhood, its gendering and the sexualization of young girls in particular, without specifically focusing on how the media targeting girls are implicated in this process. This study undertook a qualitative textual analysis of how girl children are sexualized in children's television fiction. While the media often stand accused of doing so, the question remains: Do media texts made for girls in fact validate sexualized behaviors through their representations? And, if so, how do they do this?

## Sample

To consider this research question, this paper limits itself to two sets of programs, *Bratz* and *Winx Club (Winx)* (Rainbow S.p.A., Italy) which formed part of the sample of the international research undertaken by IZI. Both are very popular animation productions; both depict a group of young female characters; and both frequently stand accused of presenting and validating highly sexualized representations of and for girl children. (The furor around Bratz in the popular debate described earlier is indicative of this.) Bratz and Winx are chosen as more extreme examples which would present the strategies more obviously. These two titles form the focus of the investigation described in the rest of this chapter into if and how they constitute femininity in relation to sexualization.

The Bratz media products have been developed alongside and to promote Bratz dolls and the wide range of associated merchandise. They include the computer-animated television series and a series of films, and are produced by the United States based Mike Young Productions and MGA Entertainment. With an intended preteen target audience, *Bratz TV*, made up of 47 episodes, premiered on the Fox 4Kids TV in 2005, following on from the direct-to-DVD film, *Bratz Rock Angelz,* one of the films discussed below. The TV series and movies revolve around the lives of five close friends constantly billed as having "a passion for fashion" (see, for example, the DVD cover for *Bratz Genie Magic*). The *Bratz* sample used here consists of three *Bratz* films[3] available on DVD, namely *Bratz Fashion Pixiez, Bratz Rock Angelz,* and *Bratz Genie Magic* as reasonably representative.

The *Winx Club* refers to another group of five close friends who are students at Alfea College, a fairy school where, according to the official website, "teenage fairies from all over the Universe enrol to improve their super-natural powers" (Winx Club, n.d.). The *Winx Club* series is the creation of Italian based Iginio Straffi, founder and CEO of the animation studio, Rainbow S.p.A. It was first broadcast in 2004 ostensibly to a target audience of five to twelve year olds. To date it consists of three seasons of twenty-six episodes, each twenty-four minutes long. According to the official website, the series has been broadcast in more than one hundred countries (Winx Club, n.d.). For the purpose of analysis of *Winx,* the second season, *Battle for the Codex,* was accessed on DVD.

## Research Process

To investigate these texts, first *Bratz* and then *Winx* is analyzed in relation to the theme of sexualization. For both sets of texts, first a narratival analysis is undertaken in order to probe the nature and form of the narratives and the nature of the roles taken by the characters. This is supplemented by analysis informed by semiotic understandings and presented in relation to two broad concerns identified in the scholarly literature, namely the physical and facial appearances (hot bodies and faces of sex-goddesses), and gesture and dress (bodily movement and performance). These are linked generally to the preoccupations of the literature.

Narrative analysis is a productive analytic tool as it enables the researcher to undertake a structured analysis that provides empirical evidence in relation to the topic. Here I draw on two narrative models, namely those of Todorov (described in Wigston, 2001) and Propp (1968). Todorov's five-stage narrative structure provides an accessible model where narrative is understood as a transformation through five stages. The first stage of the model is a point of equilibrium or harmony. This state is usually disrupted fairly early in the process (stage two) as the result of some action on the part of another person, group of people, a creature or even a natural phenomenon. The course of the narrative is then caught up with the attempt to deal with the disruption and its effects. This is dependent on there being recognition that the disruption has occurred (stage three). At stage four, a consequent action or set of actions or a quest to address the disequilibrium is undertaken. By stage five or the conclusion of the narrative, this disequilibrium has been rectified and there is restoration to a new state of equilibrium. The nature of the transformation presented is what we are concerned about then, as after all the specific transformation validated in a text is one of many possible ways of framing. Therefore, we can ask what counts as the initial equilibrium, what counts as the disruption, what is the nature of the quest (stage four), and who is the hero/actor who recognizes and acts to resolve the disruption. As narratives can include complex workings of main and sub-plots, both are considered in the ensuing analysis.

In addition, this analysis draws on Propp's character functions. Propp (1968) established seven character functions: villain, donor, helper (to the hero or the villain), princess and father, dispatcher, hero or victim and, finally, false hero. A character function is defined in terms of their sphere of action in the narrative, rather than by their personal characteristics. A hero goes on a quest or a mission, a helper assists the hero. What is significant here is whether and to what extent the roles of female protagonists in *Bratz* and *Winx* reinforce emphasized and sexualized femininities. Clearly they are the protagonists of these narratives as was evident from the IZI content analysis. However, by looking at the nature of the quest and the character functions, it is possible to probe what constitutes the nature and object of the quest and consider whether these are sexual constructs.

The semiotic dimension of the analysis works through identifying the visual aspects and investigating their connotative and ideological dimensions. Choices as to the body shape and size, the gestures and bodily adornment as identified by Bartky (1990) inform this discussion. It is not possible within the scope of this paper to do more than identify certain trends and this is done in relation in particular to the sub-plots described below.

## Textual Analysis

### Story Lines: Bratz

What became evident through a narratival analysis using Todorov's (Wigston, 2001) model and Propp's (1968) character functions was that in spite of some bad press, the *Bratz* stories are constructed in line with traditional narrative conventions. Consider *Bratz Fashion Pixiez*. Here, the Bratz team is working with Cymbeline to organize the Magnolia Ball (stage one). Cymbeline however has been lured by the evil Lina (the villain) to Pixie world in order to undermine the power of her father, the king of the Pixiez (the disruption stage). Riana, Cymbeline's sister and two of the Bratz, Cloe and Yasmin, recognize that Cymbeline (the princess in Propp's character functions) is behaving oddly (stage three). Cloe and Yasmin follow her, but get caught up in the invisible world of pixies. It is Cymbeline's younger sister (the real hero) who involves the other two Bratz who work with her to fight the evil pixies (stage four), and rescue her sister. The evil Lina is finally defeated (stage five), thanks to the support of the Bratz team and harmony prevails.

In *Bratz Genie Magic*, the disruption (stage two) consists in the evil plot of Colin and Sal to gain power over the world. They are using Katia, a girl genie with the power to grant wishes, to help them gain world control through unsuspectingly granting wishes that cause massive climate change and devastation. Meanwhile the unsuspecting Katia is fed up with being confined and escapes to earth and meets the Bratz team who befriend her. A secret service agent, Byron, informs Katia and the Bratz of the nefarious plot causing them to recognize the disruption (stage three) and act (stage four) to restore harmony. Together they manage to overpower Colin and thus undo the devastation caused (stage five) – using genie magic on the way.

If these two narratives are set in worlds of fantasy where pixies and genies exist, the world of *Bratz Rock Angelz* is ground in the world of contemporary consumerism. The team starts up a magazine about teen styling which is in opposition to the older Burdine Maxwell's magazine. The disruption (stage two) occurs when Burdine tries to scoop them on their first assignment to cover a rock concert in London through nefarious means and steals their passes. The team recognizes the dilemma and acts (stage three/four) by setting themselves up as a rock band. They get in, wow the crowds, get their scoop (stage five), and become famous.

All three narratives present a team of girls who are active. In all instances they encounter a villainy and a set of villains – the evil pixie, the nefarious master minders bent on world control, and the older magazine editor rival with shocking fashion sense (she likes pink, for heaven's sake, and she has a long nose!). In their roles as heroes or helpers to the heroes, the Bratz team themselves are decidedly on the side of good. As such they can serve as powerful objects of identification for their audiences in negotiating their own worlds as strong active characters. Additionally, the teen girls operate as a team – best friends forever (BFF), where personal qualities of loyalty and empathy are validated. They are prepared, often, to act unselfishly or to readily apologize when they are self-interested. While commendable, these qualities of care, nurturing and selflessness constitute one form of emphasized femininities – qualities that validate and bolster the patriarchal project of dominant masculinity.

Importantly, it must be conceded that at this level of narrative construction the Bratz characters' active engagement in the world and empathetic relationships serve to legitimate the position that Bratz provide "positive" role models for girls that are not passive or domestic only, and that Bratz products discursively assert "girl power". However, before this sounds overly celebratory, there is more to the texts than the achievement of a quest in the primary narrative trajectory.

If one turns to *Bratz Rock Angelz* for a moment, they achieve success that is premised on their sexual appeal as rock stars. This Lolita allure constitutes the magical agent (in Propp's terms) that enables them to achieve success. Furthermore, the narratives are complex with a range of subplots. Indeed, to consider the discursive work around femininities and sexualization, an examination of the subplots is most productive. What the broad narrative analysis does not takes into account is precisely what else these narratives propose; arguably a particular sexualized sway of being feminine. The girl power identity I suggest is complicit with this ideal Barbie doll femininity and traditional heterosexuality. Therefore, below, I consider briefly the sub-plots.

*Bratz Fashion Pixies* opens with a romantic sub-plot about wanting and getting a man. Riana, the daughter of the pixie king, asks her sister Cymbeline about asking Dylan, who is in the same class as Cymbeline and the Bratz at school, to the Magnolia Ball. However, this sub-plot has its own disruption for in the Bratz classroom Dylan sees the sexy new girl, Lina, and makes his move on her. Her sex appeal clearly makes her "hot" and she is eminently desirable, consistent with Durham's Lolita myth number one outlined above. Her enticement of Dylan is explicitly sexual, too. In a scene in the forest, her gestures, words and tones are reminiscent of a call girl come-on. Touching him under his chin, she croons, "Come here, there's something I want to show you." When he demurs about a cooking class, she puts her fingers on his lips and touches his chest and responds seductively, "Sshh. You're not nervous are you? Follow me; I've got something to show you that's much more fun than cooking!" Her provocative body language that includes moving intimately up to Dylan, the touching, low sexy tones and sensual hip movements ensure this reads as a particularly sexualized encounter. However, by the conclusion Cymbeline's sister does get to the Magnolia Ball with Dylan, the sub-plot thereby ending with the happy finale. She gets her man.

Throughout these texts there is a preoccupation with style and fashion, one re-affirmed by the title – *Fashion Pixiez,* and reiterated on the DVD cover. The narrative image of the five wide-eyed, open-mouthed, large headed Bratz is anchored thus, "Fashionable Pixies make the coolest friends!" As Durham proposed, style and dress to attract boys' sexual curiosity are the prerequisites for "hotness", and it is this aspect of their lives that is constantly valued and foregrounded.

In *Bratz Genie Magic* the main narrative scenario outlined above is overshadowed by the secondary tale that depends on the bigger intrigue. This parallel or sub-plot complies with Todorov's (Wingston, 2001) five stages, too. Katia lives with her loving father, Sebastian, but the disruption to her life takes the form of her father's strict rules and her isolation from other young people. She wears gypsy style clothing and is not allowed to wear makeup, speaks in anachronistic formal language and simply is not hip or hot (the disruption). The quest exists in her recognition of her need for an "ordinary" life and the act of running off to Stylesville where she encounters the happening Bratz and their friend Bryce. During the course of her interactions, she learns about makeup and fashion, makes friends, has a date, and by the conclusion dresses in high-heeled boots and sexy tight-fitting clothes. Her transformation is from being a magical other-worldish girl to "normality", and that consists of wearing makeup and sexy clothing in order to be hot, and dating a boy. She is thus apprenticed to the world of sexualized fashion which here discursively guarantees popularity and "normality".

The romantic sub-plot in *Bratz Rock Angelz* involves blonde Cloe who falls for a self-opinionated upper-class British lord. She stands her friends up in order to date him and there is the expectation that, while it is irritating, boys and romance are more crucial than their BFFs. This constant sub-plot of heterosexual romance that is characteristic of adult genres centers around sexual attractiveness and appeal. It plays alongside the holding narrative and in effect it provides the vehicle for particular sexualized discourses which are as much the substance of the narratives as the primary story. The form that these heterosexual relationships take relies on the characters being hot and they achieve this through stylishness, continuous consumption, and hypersexualized gear and gesture.

The preferred form of leisure for these girls is mall shopping, in groups, and this activity is celebrated constantly. The discourse proposes that this is what "normal" girls do, and, as McAllister (2007) suggests, hanging out together in the mall is seen to "build solidarity and to lift group spirits" (2007, p. 253). Thus, shopping and consumption (in order to be hot) are built into each narrative. In *Bratz Genie Magic* one of the Bratz wants to use their magic wish for shopping. For the *Rock Angelz*, being in London entails a shopping spree and so on.

Finally, their relationship with boys and men is central to how they construct themselves and how they perform their subjectivities. Mention has already been made of the romantic sub-plots. It is also interesting is how in two of the three *Bratz* DVDs discussed here, single father figures are scripted in. The Pixie girls had a mysteriously vanished mother and the genie Katia has her strict father but no mother nor mention of her. This links to a cultural phenomenon of *the young girl older man coupling* that Walkerdine (1997) identified in popular films about young girls since the fifties that needs noting. It is curious and puzzling.

### Hot Bodies and Faces of Sex-Goddesses: Bratz

Having identified these narrative tendencies in the *Bratz* sample, our attention now moves to a semiotic analysis of the visual aspects of the representations in relation to the topic of sexualization. A single glance at the images of Bratz establishes the dis-proportionality of the physical representations. While acknowledging that caricaturing is generic as in all cartooning and animation, what is relevant here are the particular choices made and their gendered nature. The girls' heads are disproportionately large as they are as wide as the Bratz' shoulders, thereby emphasizing their facial features. The slender bodies have exaggerated hourglass waists and full breasts (in spite of their slenderness), both iconic signifiers of feminine sexiness across adult media and popular constructions. Their hands are tapered, arms are thin and there is no muscle definition at all. These coupled with the hairlessness of their bodies stand as signifiers of their emphasized femininity; one defined in contrast to dominant masculinity with its physical traits of muscular, definition, hirsuteness, and physical strength.

Their faces have very large anime-like eyes with long lashes beneath from which they peer seductively, and full (botox-type) lips often open as though in surprise. These eyes are highly sexualized by their size and the kind of vampish eye makeup they wear, while their noses are minimized to present as mere blips on their faces without any indication of nostrils. Their facial expressions are limited to eye movements, eye brows indicate the occasional frown, and mouths that can show surprised expressions. The mask-like faces lack any distinguishing marks or blemishes. Designed in this way, the Bratz girls are identical to each other and distinguishable only by their hair, eye and skin coloring. Their sleek long hair hangs below their bottoms and while reference has been made to their ambiguous ethnicity, this hair type rules them out as Afro anyway. In a sense, this sameness provides a discourse of what it is to be a hot teen and discursively normalizes this (bimbo) construct as a very desirable way to be.

### Body Movements and Performance: Bratz

The Bratz repertoire of body movements and gestures are contained – their hips sway seductively and their poses are formulaic and explicitly sexual. It is an entirely hyperfeminized adult look that is sassy and ever so sexy. Moreover, the animation tends to mimic soft-core camera framing that focuses in on bit of women's bodies. In several instances, the screen is filled with the swaying hips of the girls. Moreover, their body movements are constrained and their physical expressions of delight do not include leaping and stretching out their limbs, for even on these occasions the elbows are kept close to the body and the space they use is confined in line with the cultural norms of femininity (McLaren, 2002). They walk like ramp models with their torsos held motionless, even leaning slightly backwards while their hips sway in line with model conventions. Similarly, their dancing consists of erotic moves with a great deal of pelvic mobility.

The sexualization is extended through their dress and makeup and although their styles change constantly, it is consistently fashionable, sexy and revealing.[4] Their frequently exposed midriffs work to emphasize the tiny hourglass waists. Shoes become a fetish and the clothes are about looking "hot". Consistent with the merchandising intention of the producers, the Bratz slogan is "girls with a passion for fashion" (Bratz, n.d.). The focus on consuming fashion and its role in sexualizing female subjects within the gender order was established earlier. Here it reaches its zenith.

Using beauty products is constructed as indispensable. At one point in *Bratz Genie Magic* Katia mentions that her father does not allow her to wear makeup. This is simply inconceivable for the Bratz. One responds to Katia's leaving home in horror, for being a homeless person means, "No makeup! No showers! And you'll get smellier and smellier!" Wearing makeup is as essential to these girls as washing.

### Story Lines: Winx

I move to Winx, another set of very popular texts that rehearse similar form and substance. These similarities are significant for they point to tendencies and therefore justify a degree of generalization about these programs in terms of sexualized constructions. The Winx are fairies who live in another dimension or galaxy, and they each have their individual biographies that have led them to the fairy academy of Alfea. In the 14 episodes of *Battle for the Codex*, there is a broad larger narrative quest of epic proportions where the Winx engage with forces of darkness to prevent the evil Lord Darkor from getting control of the universe. These broader narratives are the conventional fare of adventure and action, and serve as moral tales that draw intertextually on science fiction. It is the quest for the four pieces of the codex by Darkor that is the narrative disruption and that gives the series a certain coherence. The Winx are portrayed as canny and they use their wits to resolve disruptions. Like Bratz, they achieve this by working together, but here also by dint of their magic and spells (their magical agents). In addition, the specialists or "boys" at the Alfea Academy accompany them on certain quests and provide romantic interest. However, having established the major plot (for there is not the space to present more empirical detail), as with Bratz, the sub-plots are frequently as dominant as the primary narrative. Indeed, there are several episodes that have nothing to do with this central quest to protect the codex. It is the minor episodes of their lives that provide the substance of what it is to be "hot", and the sub-plots rehearse particular feminized and highly sexualized ways of being in the world. Reference is made here to the sub-plots in relation to the topic of sexualization.

In the episode *Gangs of Gardenia*, Winx defy the rules of the academy, go to earth, and enter a club because they want to dance. Their dancing is highly sexualized and they finally have to be saved from a rough, sinister and physically threatening male gang. This scenario is reminiscent of adult movies where women's sexuality renders them vulnerable. They are not heroes within this scenario, but "princesses" in Proppian (Propp, 1968) terms that require rescue. Similarly, when they are sent to earth for a break in the episode *Trouble in Paradise*, the boys are ordered to accompany them for protection and stand watch at night. The Winx sense of fun relates in the first instance to socializing with the boys, something disallowed on this trip, and their conversations tend to be about appearance, their bathing costume styles, sun-block, hair conditioner and being alluring. They do have an adventure and narrowly escape from a failing ski-lift, but this is against the backdrop of what is validated as a holiday and central to this are boys and cool appearance.

Then, there is the constant refrain of heterosexual romance in the plots and sub-plots in Winx products that specifically target young girls. The "boys" at the academy are part of their lives and are represented in line with the hegemonic masculinity Connell (1987) proposed. They are large, muscular and have chiseled facial features. Their competences relate to martial arts and brawn, while the emphasized femininities incorporated in these scripts relate to the Winx being sexual (hot) and also in need of protection. The heterosexual romance theme operates in line with the five myths that Durham (2008) identified that constitute the Lolita effect with its imperative to get and keep your man. For example, the relationship between Bloom, one of the Winx, and Skye is foregrounded in the

*Battle for the Codex* series. Consider the *Wrong Righters* episode. While the central quest might be the rescue of Diaspora principally by Skye (Bloom's boyfriend), the episode begins and ends with Bloom being taken by her boyfriend Skye to meet his parents. She is anxious for their approval and in fact earns this through helping Skye to rescue his ex-fiancée. In later episodes, Bloom is kidnapped in order for Lord Darkor to achieve ultimate power and Bloom is depicted supine and helplessly in chains (and the line between this and S&M is slight). In the process, Darkor transforms Bloom to evil. It is only through Skye determinedly addressing Bloom and telling her "I love you" that the spell is broken and Bloom reverts to her true self and defeats Darkor's evil intent. However, this declaration of love is perhaps the culminating moment of the series for it simultaneously destroys Darkor's power and the "hot" sexy Bloom is recognized and gets her man.

The imperative to get your man by flaunting yourself sexually through style is a refrain through the narratives. Yet, as in Bratz, the narrative lines cannot be reduced to merely foregrounding sexualization and fashion at the narrative level. The way of being that is proposed is an active one. Coupled with a concern about fashion, the *Winx* series validates self-belief and a girl power discourse. The opening song on the DVDs that promotes the *Winx Club* goes:

> Close your eyes and open your heart
> Believe in yourself
> That's how it starts.
> Dreams will come true
> Just wait and see
> 'Cos the magic's in you
> And the magic's in me.

In addition, the script even occasionally mocks the obsessions it rehearses. In *The Wrong Righters*, a social justice group who ostensibly fight poverty, stop environmental degradation and uphold justice, have intervened and capture Diasporo. She is portrayed as a foolish and autocratic ruler who rules her realm in line with her superficial notions of style. She fines people for wearing chipped nail polish and views hair accessories as basic necessities and this constitutes the disruption that needs to be corrected. I mention these in order to foreground a plurality of discourses in *Winx*. However, while such several narrative lines occur, arguably it is precisely consumption in relation to fashion that Winx mostly validates.

## Hot Bodies and Faces of Sex-Goddesses: Winx

If the fairies of conventional tales, like Tinkerbell in *Peter Pan* (Disney, USA), are ephemeral and light, it is the corporality of Winx that is evident – for the visual emphasis is precisely on their physicality and these are some hyper-sexualized fairies. These fairies flaunt elongated slim bodies with tiny wasp waists, very long legs (with slim knees for extra definition) and slender arms. More so than Bratz, their breasts are very full and their skimpy drapes emphasize their voluptuousness. The eyes of all the fairies (good and bad) are large slanted ones with the requisite long lashes for batting their eyelids and they are frequently depicted giving seductive sideward glances. Their faces might all have the same shape that narrow to pointed chins, yet they sport a range of hairstyles from Tecna's short dark hair through all shades to blonde. Like Bratz their ethnicities are ambiguous as their skin shades vary but none are really very dark and certainly, once again, there is no evidence of Afro hair or styling into corn rows. Its repeated absence is significant and these representations consequently serve to endorse only a certain kind of beauty. While the Winx are not one-dimensional texts, there is little reason to be too celebratory for once again, their sexualization is enacted or performed in Butler's (2006) terms through the body.

## Body Movements and Performance: Winx

In order to discuss aspects of their physical performance, reference is made here to the images depicted on the DVD cover for *Battle for the Codex* for these are carefully selected to present the narrative image. Here the producers' choice is to present the characters in sexual poses as though for the male gaze, with chests thrust forwards provocatively while they make eye contact with their assumed audience. It links to the words in the second verse of the Winx song:

> We've got the style
> And we've got the flair.
> Look all you want
> But don't touch our hair.

All are depicted precisely as inviting the gaze of the voyeur. Musa seductively sticks out her chest and buttocks, while coyly holding her hand against her breast. Stella presents the viewer with a sexualized come-hither look over her shoulder and with hand demurely under her chin. Their clothing is reminiscent of erotic dancers. The darker skinned Layla, for example, wears a green strapless halter over her breasts and a narrow cloth seductively draped and tied around her hips. Ultra short shorts and skirts, body hugging gear, strapless dresses – this clothing is much skimpier than their Bratz contemporaries and more explicitly sexualized. While they ostensibly share Bratz obsession with fashion, their fairy outfits are the stuff of erotic night club dancers and what is on view is not their nakedness, but their nudity. For as Berger noted, "To be naked is to be oneself. To be nude is to be seen naked by others and yet not recognized for oneself" (1972, p. 54). The Winx are represented here as objects of the gaze – to appeal to male sexuality and not their own. Their expressions are full of vitality, but at the same time they are the expressions as though "of a woman responding with calculated charm to the man whom she imagines looking at her" (1972, p. 55). They are representations of feminine sexiness enacted within the dominant heterosexual frame of patriarchy.

The nature of their sexualized feminine construction is more evident when you hold these representations against those of the boyfriends and again the front image on the DVD cover illustrates this. Bloom's boyfriend, the blond Skye, is tall with very broad shoulders and a body that tapers consistent with the construct of hypermasculinity. In comparison with the girl characters, his eyes are much smaller, his chin square, his lips are not rosy and his nose is more defined. He has clear muscle definition and even in this single image, he is wielding a sword and his movements are depicted as broad and sweeping. In contrast, the coy image of his "girl", Bloom, shows her posing in a way that assumes a male gaze. She looks back at the viewer while Skye is caught in action. Even the fairy wings she dons do not necessarily signify magic or childlike innocence for it is coupled with her nude torso and come-hither expression.

### Conclusion

In the opening I mentioned that children's TV is assumed to be a safe and snug space for children, however, what the analysis presented here suggests is that the adult world of hypersexualization of girls also intrudes into this space. Thus, the question must be asked whether all this matters. After all, the analysis has demonstrated that these texts present complex narratives with active female protagonists and positive friendship relationships. While they do validate "girl power", this discussion has pointed out that is only part of the story. The sub-plots rehearse different scenarios that endorse particular sexualized ways of being that include hypersexualized bodily design, dress, and performance. Clearly, then, there are a range of different discourses within the narratives and different points of identification are possible.

Yes indeed! But, here comes the but. If I acknowledge that a girl child might identify with the active hero and wish to emulate her, then I must allow that she might as easily wish to emulate the wanton seductress, to enact those roles and value consumption highly for it promises to make her hot. Indeed, as Walkerdine

(1997) argues, such media texts introduce the young girl to the possibility of the seductress girl child and offer the script for its performance. And there is the rub. Why would I consider this benign just because there is a complex narrative? Why should this be the fare of girl children's media? The discourse of the sexy little girl is one that enacts the unequal power relations of the gender order. The "safe play [and] controlled adventure" (Boden, 2006, p. 297) is constrained within the violence that is patriarchy. Would playing slaves and masters be considered cute and safe? Would the performance of racism be reduced to or condoned as controlled adventure? Discourses are not immaterial for they depend constantly on the material aspects of desirability. This does not mean that all people are duped or harmed by such discourses that propose inequalities, but it does mean they exist, have power and therefore potential effects. It does mean that it proposes that construction of sexuality identified by Durham "that both exploits and limits sexual expression and agency, [...] deliberately focussed on young girls" (2008, p. 34).

The issue of the sexualization of little girls in these media texts should consequently be of serious concern. The potential scripts they offer need to be contextualized in relation also to the larger patriarchal project as they serve, in Foucauldian terms, as disciplinary procedures to normalize these unequal power relations. They validate the performances of little Lolitas (or "prosti-tots") where "presumed heterosexuality and its appearance [...] is now the routine obligation of every woman, be she a grandmother or a barely pubescent girl" (Bartky, 1990, p. 80). Moreover, it is evident that this seduction is now being persistently scripted into the prepubescent worlds of Bratz and Winx audiences.

## REFERENCES

APA – Task Force on the Sexualization of Girls. (2007). Report of the APA Task Force on the Sexualization of Girls. Washington, DC: American Psychological Association.

Bartky, S. (1990). *Femininity and Domination: Studies in the Phenomenology of Oppression.* New York, NY: Routledge.

Berger, J. (1972). *Ways of Seeing.* Harmondsworth, England: BBC/Penguin.

Boden, S. (2006). Dedicated followers of fashion? The influence of popular culture on children's social identities. *Media, Culture and Society, 28*(2), 289-298.

Bratz. (n.d.). Retrieved December 12, 2008, from http://www.bratz.com/

Butler, J. (2006). Response. *British Journal of Sociology of Education, 27*(4), 529-534.

Connell, R. (1987). *Gender and Power*. Cambridge, MA: Polity Press. University of Auckland, Aotearoa New Zealand.

Durham, M. G. (2008). *The Lolita Effect*. Woodstock & New York, NY: The Overlook Press.

Foucault, M. (1981). The Order of Discourse. In R. Young (Ed.), *Untying the text – A poststructuralist reader* (pp. 48-78). London, England: Routledge.

Lerum, K., & Dworkin, S. L. (2009). "Bad girls rule": An interdisciplinary feminist commentary on the Report of the APA Task Force on the Sexualization of Girls. *Journal of Sex Research, 46*(4), 250–63.

Levine, D. E., & Kilbourne, J. (2008). *So Sexy So Soon: The New Sexualized Childhood and What Parents Can Do to Protect Their Kids*. New York, NY: Ballantine Books.

Maddox, D. (2008, December 3). Girls aged 5 sexualised by toys like Bratz dolls, MSP told. *The Scotsman*, UK.

McAllister, M. (2007). "Girls with a passion for fashion" The Bratz Brand as integrated spectacular consumption. *Journal of Children and Media, 1*(3), 244-258.

McLaren, M. A. (2002). *Feminism, Foucault and Embodied Subjectivity*. Albany, NY: State University of New York Press.

McRobbie, A. (1991). *Feminism and Youth Culture: From "Jackie" to "Just Seventeen"*. Boston, MA: Unwin Hyman.

Prinsloo, J. (2003). Childish images: The gendered depiction of childhood in popular South African magazines. *Agenda, 56*, 26-37.

Propp, V. (1968). *Morphology of the Folktale*. Austin, TX: University of Texas Press.

Rousseau, J.-J. (1762/1979). *Emile: Or on Education*. New York, NY: Basic Books.

Thompson, T., & Zerbinos, E. (1995). Gender roles in animated cartoons. Has the picture changed in 20 years? *Sex Roles, 32*(9/10), 651-673.

Walkerdine, V. (1990). *Schoolgirl Fictions*. London, England: Verso.

Walkerdine, V. (1997). *Daddy's Girl. Young Girls and Popular Culture*. London, England: Macmillan Press.

Walkerdine, V. (1999). Violent boys and precocious girls: Regulating childhood at the end of the millenium. *Contemporary Issues in Early Childhood, 1*(1), 3-23.

Wigston, D. (2001). Narrative analysis. In P. Fourie (Ed.), Vol. 2, *Media studies: Content, audiences and production* (pp. 150-182). Lansdowne, South Africa: Juta Education.

Winx Club. (n.d.). Retrieved December 12, 2008, from http://www.rbw.it/winx.asp

[1] As Wordsworth's "Ode to the intimations of immortality" suggests.

[2] The National Society for the Prevention of Cruelty to Children (NSPCC) also referred to as the SPCC is a UK charity campaigning and working in the area of child protection in Great Britain.

[3] While the TV episodes of *Bratz* formed part of the IZI sample, these three films of approximately 70 minutes in length were selected for analysis for pragmatic reasons and as reasonably representative of the textual strategies, as was the case for the choice of *Winx* programs.

[4] It is noteworthy that Bratz was mentioned explicitly in the APA report discussed earlier where concern was expressed over sexuality and the Bratz dolls, the merchandise the animation programs shore up, allegedly portray:

> Bratz dolls come dressed in sexualized clothing such as miniskirts, fishnet stockings, and feather boas. Although these dolls may present no more sexualization of girls or women than is seen in MTV videos, it is worrisome when dolls designed specifically for 4- to 8-year-olds are associated with an objectified adult sexuality. (2007, p. 14)

# 4

# "MAKE HER SKINNIER, MAKE HER CURVIER": SEXUALISED GIRLHOOD IN JAPANESE CARTOONS

*Damien Spry*

"You've got to make her skinnier! ... No, no! Curvier!"

– Naruto

## Introduction: Naruto's Dirty Trick

Imagine you are a bratty young teenage boy confronting an older man – your teacher – who has taken to scolding your insolence. What trick might you play on him? How might you be sure to get the better of him? Cheeky schoolboy and ninja-in-training Naruto Uzumaki knew how: He transformed into an alluring image of young, female sexuality. Confronted by such a picture of eroticism, his enemies are confounded and disarmed. Eyes pop out of heads, blood powerfully spurts from noses and men are – quite literally – knocked off their feet.

What kind of image would have such effect? What representations of sexuality would be so potent as to prompt instantaneous convulsions? Naruto's transformation – his "sexy jutsu" – is an embodiment of some of the typical representations of male heterosexual desire that are evident in many similar Japanese female cartoon characters. The defining shared characteristics – body shape, facial features and the way they relate to other characters, for example – function to make the characters look both highly sexualised and infantilised. From the neck up, they resemble young children; from the neck down, and in their clothing, they can look like teenage strippers.

Naruto apparently knows well that the way to disarm a mature man is to place such a sexualised image in front of him. The visual language, with which Naruto casts his spell, and its relation to other similar characters in contemporary Japanese cartoons and their historical precedents, is the topic of this chapter.

## The Method: Iconography and Its Application to Anime

In this chapter, popular children's cartoons produced in Japan (or inspired by Japanese aesthetics) and consumed worldwide are explored using iconographic visual analysis. Iconography is a form of visual analysis closely related to the visual semiotics pioneered by seminal French visual semiotician Roland Barthes (1973). Both approaches to visual analysis ask the same fundamental questions:

> The question of representation (what do images represent and how?) and the questions of the "hidden meanings" of images (what ideas and values do the people, places and things represented in the images stand for?). (Van Leeuwen, 2001, p. 92)

Visual analysis necessitates both close readings of the texts analysed and an awareness of the historical and contemporary cultural conditions that inform the production of those texts.

In undertaking this analysis, I hope to demonstrate the use of iconographic as a productive method with considerable explanatory power, and to suggest some ways in which the method can be further developed and applied to the study of gendered representation in children's television.

This report introduces and discusses a stereotypical character in Japanese and Japanese-inspired animation: The simultaneously infantilised and sexualised young female, typified – as will be shown – by the character of Sailor Moon, but prevalent in a variety of animated genres.

I address, first, the historical circumstances that led to the prevalence of highly sexualised animation in Japan, as opposed to the other global centre of production – the United States. Then, I share an analysis of a sample of television programmes that form part of the gender research project that begins with the expressed desires of creative designers who seek to present to viewers characters with specifically sexualised and fantasised characteristics. Such characteristics include the representations of the characters themselves (body shape, sexualised attire and nudity and positioning) as well as their position in relation to other characters and the reader/viewer; the latter relating to notions of the "gaze" common in (Western) feminist literature and its applicability to Japanese cartoon characters in children's television.

It must be acknowledged that the range of character types in children's anime is much wider than can be addressed here. This is not an attempt at a unified theory of gendered representation in anime. Nevertheless, as will become evident, these characters are fairly typically examples of how girls and young women are *commonly*, but not *always*, represented in popular children's television.

This chapter ends by discussing possible consequences of these types of characterisation, with the important caveat that analysing media *impact* might be better framed as exploring media *uses*, noting the fluid, highly contingent nature of media use, as well as the need for further research in this important area.

## History – Hokusai

Japanese animation is noted for the volume of production and its sheer variety. Many storylines employ the somewhat more standard fare that makes up the common stuff of narrative – romance, desire, conflict and discovery. Yet they are far from pedestrian, and Japanese animation can surprise newcomers to the genre. This is particularly so for anime related to matters associated with romanticisation and sexualisation of young characters. For example, there is an entire sub-genre of romances between beautiful androgenous young men (known as *bishonen* or *yaoi manga*) that is popular among women 25 to 35 years old. More explicit, and more infamous, is the large sub-genre of pornographic animation more commonly known within Japan as *porno anime/manga* or *ero anime/manga*, but sometimes referred to (especially outside Japan) as *hentai*. There are also stories featuring graphic and violent consensual and non-consensual sexual acts between aliens, tentacle-wielding monsters, trees, robots and – the focus of this report – children.

There are several explanations for why these graphic and disturbing images are so prevalent in Japan and more closely associated with Japanese animation than that generated elsewhere, particularly the other centre of the animation world – the United States of America. The most prevalent explanations focus on the cultural and political history of erotic and pornographic cultural production in Japan. Other answers emphasise the socio-cultural specificities of Japanese manga fans, while others include an analysis of the material forces of production particular and important in Japan. Each of these explanations is reviewed, briefly, below.

In a recent exploration of the influence and popularity of Japanese manga on American markets, readers and cultural producers, American writer and scholar Roland Kelts (2006) relates being taken by Hoshizaki – his guide – on a hentai shopping excursion.

> Hoshizaki spends some time finding me a representative selection of hentai manga. […]
> "Isn't this just a little disturbing?" I ask, pointing at the ferocity of a demon-tentacle/weeping schoolgirl rape scene.

"They're just pictures," he says. "And anyway, you've seen it before. Hokusai did a woodblock print of a pearl diver being raped by an octopus more than two hundred years ago. It's the same thing. And you people," he adds, "put Hokusai in art museums". (p. 133)

There are of course significant differences between the *ukiyo-e* illustrations of the past and the hentai of the present. The images are less violent, and – more significantly – do not feature young girls as participants or victims of sexual acts. But, as scholars of manga history note, there is much about Japan's historical animated art that resonates with the present. Scandalous, ribald and offensive drawings have been an aspect of Japanese cultural production for a great part of its history. At other times, a rather sniffy prudence dominated, in particular around the turn of the twentieth century when Victorian-Era squeamishness about matters considered indecent meant comics (as they had become known) became more modest. Animators became rigidly nationalistic or childish and flippant during the 1937-1945 wartime period, either willingly or through forms of coercion.

This changed in the post-war period. Osamu Tezuka's famous invention, *Astroboy*, heralded a renaissance and a confident renewal. This comic and its creator were immeasurably significant for later generations of Japanese animators, but, for the purposes of this report, another trajectory of production needs to be highlighted; namely the re-emergence of the risqué, the ribald, the sexual and the pornographic.

The 1950s also serve as a key moment in the history of animation with respect to the responses from audiences on both sides of the Pacific. Both American and Japanese animation – comic books, mostly – were enjoying increasing popularity as well as developing new directions: darker, more serious and freer in their explorations of violent themes, especially crime and horror (Hadju, 2008).

A new era of regulation ensued in the United States due to parental groups who were concerned about threats from ideological enemies and a perceived lapse in moral standards. This climate of suspicion led to increased levels of surveillance and control of risky and "at risk" behaviour, as well as a dramatic curtailing of comics. In short, both sex and especially violence were either removed or dramatically downplayed and obscured, becoming more suggestive and less literal or transformed from perceived threat and recast as heroic, patriotic and morally righteous. Although similar attempts were undertaken in Japan, they were not as successful and comics continued to explore and express adult themes, as well as to represent children and childhood in ways that some adults saw as a moral threat. While government regulation of comic books was introduced in Japan to restrict their capacity for "moral danger" (e.g., by banning representations of male or female genitalia), in effect, this has been circumvented by either illicit trade in comic books or use of rich (some might argue perverse) imaginations of animators who have replaced actual body parts with none-to-subtle metaphorical substitutes, such as a baseball bats, or tentacles. In summary, the history of comics in Japanese culture led to a situation in post-World War II cultural production in which sexualised characters – who were either comic, violent, pornographic or romantic – were part of the firmament.

This development in Japan had significant impact on other forms of animation, including on animated television programming for children, including for girls, and continues, as we shall see, in the programmes analysed from the research corpus. However, before presenting findings from the analysis of these programs, the following interpretation of Anne Allison's work on *Sailor Moon* (Toei Animation, Japan) will enable us to highlight some of the leading scholarship and research of contemporary Japanese children's popular culture.

### Anne Allison: Shojo Manga and the Schoolgirls' Fierce Flesh

Known as Usagi or Serena/Bunny in the English translations, Sailor Moon is a clumsy young schoolgirl who transforms into a super-heroine in order to protect the world and her friends from evil. Sailor Moon continued a trend of female characters known as bishōjo hīrō (beautiful girl heroes) that began in the 1960s and continued into the 1970s. She reflected a young, female consumer culture characterised by ideals of cuteness and an association with character fetishisation (Allison, 2006).

After some false starts, the series became very popular and developed a niche cult following in Japan and from there to wider mainstream audiences in international markets. Targeted at girls aged 2-10 years old, the series proved popular with boys and girls, as well as older viewers. Allison's suggestions for the appeal of Sailor Moon have wider implications for this report, and are worth presenting at length:

> This combination of action hero and "good style" is the reason she is so popular, according to an 8-year-old girl I spoke to in 1995. This is also the reason given for her fandom among *ojisan-tachi* (older men). With her leggy, slender body, long flowing blond hair, and the mini-skirted version of her outfit after morphing, *Seraa Muun* is also read as a sex icon – one that feeds and is fed by a general trend in Japanese toward the infantilization of female sex objects. The fact that Sailor Moon not only wears a sailor outfit but is also named for it is significant, given that this is the standard uniform worn by middle and upper school in Japan, as well as the clothing sexualized on young females (*shojo*) to project a nymphet effect. The uniformed schoolgirl is a dominant trope in

pornography, comics and sex culture in general in Japan, as witnessed by the new, frequently reported trend of *enjo kosai* – the practices of junior and senior high school students engaging in "assisted dating" with *sarariman*. (Allison, 2006, pp. 133/134)

The attractiveness of these young female characters, for young female viewers, is that they view Sailor Moon as cool, cute, and as a character who gets things done for her friends and manages to have both an ordinary life and a rich fantasy existence (including the boyfriend/husband and child from outer space and the future). As Allison noted, however, some aspects of the character that appeal to the target *shojo* market are also features that appeal to older, mostly but not exclusively male viewers who sexualise and fetishise Sailor Moon. It is very important to make this point quite clearly: Young girls, watching Sailor Moon, and perhaps inspired by her attitude, as well as her cool and cute appearance and costuming/sense of fashion, may seek to imitate and live out aspects of her character, but not necessarily in order to be or to appear sexual. Rather, Sailor Moon reinforces these young girls and teenagers' emerging sense of identity as they develop their own sense of style and dress and attitude. Their interest in Sailor Moon serves as a kind of solidarity amid the strong bond of schoolgirl friendship, where it serves as a motivator and source of esteem or pleasure.

This having been noted, we would be remiss if we glossed over another aspect of Sailor Moon's appeal: She is a sexual object, as she has been sexualised by older (mostly) men. Her appeal is based on somewhat formulaic but essential tropes of commonly understood sexual appeal – body shape, revealing clothing, coquettish eyes, and the like. However, it is her identity as a schoolgirl, symbolised by her school uniform, that is, I submit, the crucial aspect of Sailor Moon's fetishised sexuality. In this regard, we might ask the following question: To what extent is there a conscious attempt to both sexualise and infantilise characters like Sailor Moon? This is the subject of the next section.

### Creating Sexy Young Girls: Designers' Talk Compared with Examples from Current Children's Programming

What follows here are some indicative, not exhaustive, explanations offered by anime designers when speaking of their aims and motivations, as they relate to some aspects of the vocabularies and grammars of visual representation. Points made in these citations are discussed in relation to the programmes included in this survey of children's television.

## Babyface/The Eyes Have It

> The basic rule is to make the outline of the face an inverted triangle – the eyes large with large pupils, and the nose and mouth small. In other words, it is the face of an infant. There is a theory about why the infants of all animals look so cute. They say that if their parents die, another adult might raise the infant. Being cute is a weapon of survival. (Watanabe, 2004, p. 86)

One of the more easily recognisable defining characteristics of Japanese-style animation is the facial characteristics, especially the shape of the eyes. Eye shapes, of course, vary in Japanese animation, but the overly large and rounded shape is one that has become regarded as typical and characteristic. Large eyes continue to be favoured for their capacity for depicting emotional states – tears, fluttering eyelashes, narrowing pupils and so on. They are also, clearly, not realistic representations of Japanese eyes, and are often accompanied by markers of Westernisation – hair colour and body shape, in particular. Allison recounts designers insisting that "such Westernisation was simply a marker of fantasy" while noting that "it is telling that fantasy so typically takes a Western/Caucasian form" (2000, p. 146).

A number of the female characters analysed demonstrated this typically infantilised, fantasy face. One such character, and one to whom we will be returning, is Nami the Navigator from the programme *One Piece* (Toei Animation, Japan). Nami is an exemplar of these facial characteristics: Her large, dark eyes dominate her bright, roughly triangular face, framed by a short mop of girlishly cropped red hair. In the episode reviewed, we are introduced to Nami for the first time in the series. In one of the earliest shots, the screen is almost filled with her childish, excitable face with her wide-eyes matching her welcoming smile. The same shot also accentuates Nami's somewhat exaggerated cleavage, contained in a tight short-sleeved shirt. Nami's long and slender legs are barely covered by a micro-mini skirt, completing an ensemble that resembles that of some typical *hentai* fetishised characters: child from the neck up, sexualised teen/young adult from the neck down.

The fact that Nami is presented in this way, while looking directly at and making eye contact with the viewer, is significant: It demonstrates a form of visual grammar known as a "demand gaze" (see section below on visual discourses) that seeks to draw on and fix the viewers attention on that character. Thus, viewers are invited – or rather, the demand is made of them – to directly observe Nami while, at the same time, Nami's large, infant-like eyes seem to be directly observing the viewer. While viewers realise that they cannot actually be seen, the imagined and mediated connection between (fictional) Nami and the viewer generates possibilities for affective connections: "Look at me," Nami seems to be demanding, "and admire me, as I look at (and admire?) you."

## Dressed to Thrill

> After considering my style, what's [sic.] fashion and my personal taste, I decided
> to create a waitress character with a frilly costume. It's so embarrassing to even
> mention it. (Nekotom, 2004, p. 64)

A second characteristic of many of the female characters in the Japanese animation
reviewed is the stylised and sexualised clothing or costumes. Japanese costuming
is notable for particular use of elements that resemble, if not reflect, fetishised
costumes of some *hentai*. The schoolgirl sailor uniform worn by Sailor Moon is one
example. In *Legend of the Dragon* (BKN, USA), both main female characters are
transformed into their fighting alter egos. One is a dark, masked ninja. More directly
reflecting a prominent theme in Japanese pornography, the second is a scantily clad
tiger, complete with claws and stripes prominent on her long legs, arms and face.
The attribution of animalistic anatomical attributes and behavioural characteristics
is relatively common in both children's animation and in pornography, with female
characters often designed with cat-like ears and tail.

Elsewhere, female characters are dressed down, with their exaggerated adult
body shapes emphasised by skimpy clothing. Bulma, reviewed in an older episode
of the *Dragonball* (Toei Animation, Japan) series, exemplifies an earlier version of
the young, clearly childlike but overtly sexualised character as expressed in body
shape, and especially costuming. Even the name is both childish and immaturely
risqué, referring to the Japanese pronunciation for "bloomers", an older term for
women's underwear, but also a name for popular girls' gym shorts in Japan. In
fact, Bulma's entire family share this thematic nomenclature: her parents are Mr.
and Mrs. Briefs and, later, her children are named Trunks and Bra. In the episode
reviewed, Bulma, the short, busty figure, is barely contained in a brief red bikini
for much of the action. Indeed, Bulma is not much of a participant as she spends a
lot of the pivotal conflict scenes ensconced behind a rock, seeking a safe place to
observe the males as they engage in violent actions. While at times demonstrably
intelligent in ways that assist if not outsmart her male fellow protagonists as well
as antagonists, she is also represented as both sexy and helpless, a little spoiled and
prone to outbursts of screaming fear and anger; albeit such expressions are replaced
quickly with a more familiar coquettishness. Hiding, vulnerable and exposed in her
red bikini, she watches her men perform for her. As we, the viewers, watch her, we
are invited to consider her to be not only vulnerable, sexual and therefore desirable,
but also to see her as an admiring observer of male characters.

While in Nami's case "demand" was shown, another gaze is in effect in the
presentation of Bulma. Here an "offer" or invitation is issued: The character looks

away from the viewer and, so invites the viewer to look elsewhere. This signals to the viewer that the character is not the main protagonist; rather, the real action is elsewhere. Thus, they as well as the viewer are observers. The idea of watching and being watched is a trope in pornography; particularly, as Napier (2000) suggests, in Japanese pornography.

Bulma's main goal for the duration of the series is to gather enough of the magical dragon balls to achieve her primary goal: Namely, to find the perfect boyfriend. This is a commonly invoked motivation for female characters in the animations reviewed, particularly those aimed at younger viewers. Pucca, for example, the main character in the program of the same name (Studio B, South Korea) only wants Garu's love. Garu, in turn, demonstrates stereotypical male norms when he claims he is only interested in family honour and martial arts. In a similar coupling, Pucca's best friend, Ching, dreams of being a beautiful bride when she grows up. Abyo, her choice of future husband, is a self-described "super-handsome boy" and "future Kung Fu Star". Elsewhere, in *Sonic the Hedgehog*'s (Sega Corporation & Co, USA), the main female character in the episode viewed is Amy Rose (also known as Rosy the Rascal or Princess Sally), is young, cheerful and in love with the hero – Sonic.

This combination is quite characteristic and is composed of, first, male protagonists, who skilfully and either heroically or comically dominate the action and whose main motivation is to achieve victories over foes; and, second, female characters who are largely observers of male exploits, motivated by love and the hope of future reciprocal affection. In summary, a familiar if not problematic supposed truism is that, posed in one form or another, boys like to play at being the hero and girls like to play at the idea of being the princess to be rescued.

It is worth emphasising that not all anime or all cartoons contain the same types of characters and symbolic relationships. Indeed, there is such a rich eclecticism in Japanese animation that one could spend considerable time decoding the iconography and related symbolic meaning-making of most Japanese cartoons. However, our aim here is different: to identify a commonly-found gendered, sexualised and infantilised character type, and a relational visual grammar that places this character type in contextual and power relations with other characters and with the viewer.

This methodology is also appropriate for application to a single television programme or series for the purposes of providing an analytical reading of the characters, relations and narrative structures. In order to demonstrate how iconographic visual analysis can be used to explore the production of gendered and sexualised meanings, the following section uses exemplary excerpts from the popular children's television series *Naruto* (Studio Pierrot, Japan) as a case study to focus on the "key incidents": introductions, transformations and confrontations, in the flush of sexual or romantic desire.

## *Naruto: Detailed Iconographic Visual Analysis of Gender, Sexuality & Youth*

In the opening episode, the chief protagonist and namesake of the programme, Naruto Uzumaki, is introduced as a young ninja in training and secret possessor of great animistic power in the form of the life-force of a magical nine-tailed fox. An unruly, ill-disciplined brat when we first meet Naruto, he has few close friends in the small, hidden village where he lives and goes to Ninja pre-school. In fact, one of Naruto's only real talents, and one that sets him apart as a practitioner of the secret ninja magical arts, is his "sexy jutsu"[1], which he uses to annoy classmates and flaunt authority. Naruto's sexy jutsu is an important iconographic symbolic element for explorations of the representation of gender, sexuality and youth in *Naruto*. Naruto's sexy jutsu appears early in the series and serves as rich sources of symbolic and iconographic meaning. The following discussion begins by describing and then analysing two early examples of Naruto's sexy jutsu.

In the first example, Naruto is confronted by his instructor, Iruka Umino, during a standard classroom test. Naruto has been repeatedly unable to perform a standard, mandatory transformation into his instrustor Iruka; this despite the fact that many of the other students are able to do so with some ease. When asked to perform the transformation in front of the class, Naruto transforms instead into his sexy jutsu. A naked woman appears. She is young, slender and curvy with long blonde hair in girlish pigtails, typically large eyes and is reminiscent of the Sailor Moon character type discussed earlier. Clouds of smoke conceal her breasts and crotch. Coquettishly, she giggles and blows Iruka a kiss, a little pink love heart floating his way.

Iruka is initially literally stupefied. The background turns monochromatically deep blue and his face is drained of all colour. Then blood rushes out of his nose and he is thrown backwards off his feet by the force of the explosive nosebleed. Naruto returns to his normal self and announces with a laugh, "Gotcha! Ha ha ha. That's my sexy jutsu!" Not surprisingly, Iruka screams in anger at his petulant student.

In the second example, Naruto is hauled before Hiruzen Sarutobi – the Honorable Third Hokage – leader of the village and of its ninja protectors. The sagacious elderly gentleman has been called in to discipline Naruto by insisting he have his school photograph retaken. This is necessary because Naruto appeared with theatrical make-up and struck a fighting pose in his first picture. This was deemed to be unbefitting a wannabe member of the village's army of honourable and austere guardians. A battle of wills between Naruto and the Third Hokage ensues and Naruto duly transforms into his sexy jutsu. Despite his wisdom and experience, the Third Hokage succumbs to the power of the sexy jutsu. He is helpless as the blood erupts forcefully from his nose, knocking him out of his chair. In the aftermath, he is less angry and more sanguine than Iruka had been in the previous episode, and even admits admiration for the effectiveness of the jutsu. His young grandson, Konohamaru Sarutobi, then appears and confronts Naruto. Naruto defeats him easily without resorting to his transformation: He beats him up.

Konohamaru later seeks out Naruto and successfully persuades him to be his mentor and trainer in the ninja arts including, especially, the sexy jutsu. Naruto agrees and, after seeing some early unsuccessful attempts at producing a sexy jutsu, determines that the younger Konohamaru has little knowledge of what actually counts as sexy. Naruto decides that his first task as teacher and mentor is to introduce his young protégée to the sexualised female form in its most idealised and desirable forms. This is, in Naruto's words, to undertake "some research into female beauty".

Naruto begins Konohamaru's schooling with a trip to a local bookstore to peruse the magazines featuring young women in bikinis: typical *lollcon* fare. Next, the two boys transform into the female form (Konohamaru's jutsu is still well below the standard required to be classified as sexy, but it works as a disguise) and head into the girl's bathhouse for a peep show. Naruto's sexy jutsu being well-known and therefore easily recognised, the boys are quickly expelled. However, Naruto by now considers that Konohamaru's exposure to his idea of female beauty is sufficient for the work on the younger boy's sexy jutsu to resume. As the training progresses, we hear Naruto encouraging Konohamaru (both off camera) and offering improvements after each attempt; for example, "You've got to make her skinnier!" and, after a second attempt, "No, no! Curvier!" Thus continue Naruto's attempts to introduce Konohamaru into the world of fetishised female sexuality, the ability to manipulate the female form, and the power of pornographic iconography fantasy over helpless libidinous adult males.

### Analysis

These two excerpts from the first two episodes of the *Naruto* series display many of the features of sexualisation and infantilisation discussed earlier. The analysis that follows is structured according to the "key moments" in narrative classification system: introductions, confrontations, transformations, and displays of emotions.

## Introductions

Naruto's use of the sexy jutsu is the first example in the series of his unique mystical abilities and, as such, it has a special significance. By introducing Naruto in this manner, the young protagonist is characterised in two inter-related ways: First, he is a prankster who likes to make fun of his elders and those in authority over him; second, he chooses to do this by being sexually manipulative in ways that are both disarming to those he is challenging and funny for young boys (like Naruto himself) for whom this sort of juvenile sexual innuendo is a great source of amusement. These two characterisations – being anti-authoritarian and sexually manipulative – are closely related to one another: Naruto's ability to undermine authority is derived from his ability to understand male sexual fantasies about young women and to replicate the form so successfully. His sexy jutsu shares many of the characteristics of the sexualised and infantilised characters discussed earlier: Large eyes, small nose and mouth typify the *manga* style symbolic of childhood; long blonde hair, pulled back in pigtails, emulates many iconographic Sailor Moon-type and Lolita-type animated schoolgirls; albeit discretely covered in wisps of smoke left from the performing of the spell, the body is recognisably hyper-sexualised; gaze is directed at Iruka in the first instance, such that the viewer is presented with the "offer" to observe from the sidelines; in the second instance, the sexy jutsu's gaze is direct "to camera", such that the viewer is presented with the "demand" placed in the unenviable position of the Honourable Third Hokage.

Naruto's choice of models for this body type (soft porn magazines and girls in the bathhouse) and his directions to Konohamaru ("skinnier"; "curvier") make it quite explicit that he sought to produce a female image that conforms to the type outlined in the discussion above: the simultaneously infantilised and sexualised young woman. Importantly, he has produced this image of female sexuality because of the debilitating effect he deems it will have on mature, adult men.

## Confrontations

Naruto is shrewd enough to be aware of the sexual power of the image he produces and he is willing to use this power when he finds himself in confrontation with those in authority over him. These confrontations are not battles over life and limb. Rather, they are tests of strength and standing between a young boy and older men; between learner and masters; and between the governed and those in power. In these confrontations, Naruto is remarkably successful in disarming his older, more mature mentors and leaders. By rendering them incapacitated, if only temporarily, through sexual manipulation, he poses a direct threat to their sense of masculine honour, as it is understood in association with the traditional values expressed in the code of *bushido*. As Nitobe (1905/2001) indicates, the virtue of self-control was highly prized in Japan's masculine, militant past:

> It was considered unmanly for a samurai to betray his emotions on his face. [...] The most natural affections were kept under control. [...] Calmness of behaviour, composure of mind, should not be disturbed by passion of any kind (pp. 104/105).

Naruto's victory in these confrontations is due to youthful exuberance over mature dignity. It is a battle of masculinities: The juvenile masculinity of adolescent sexual innuendo is able to produce a male sexual fantasy. Hence, the mature masculinity of dignity and restraint is overwhelmed by the masculinity of unrestrained sexual lust.

## Transformations

It is only by changing into an object of male sexual fantasy that Naruto hopes to challenge (if only momentarily) the older men. This transformation – from ordinary student into super-powered alter ego – is reminiscent of the many types of identity transformations in Japanese anime and those of other cultures (e.g., *The Transformers* series is based on the concept; stories of super-heroes from outside Japan – Superman, Spiderman, Batman and so on; and, storytelling traditions that extend back to Ovid's *Metamorphoses*). This having been noted, a teenage school student transforming through a magical spell into an alter ego that is both sexual and powerful is iconically Japanese: The schoolgirl Usagi transforms into heroine Sailor Moon; near future heroine Cutie Honey transforms into one of her many alter egos as martial arts expert, rock singer, news reporter. In the transformation sequences, Cutie Honey gratuitously lingers over the stripping and then re-costuming of the heroines' bodies.

Naruto's transformation from 12-year-old brat into naked, blonde, sexy "lolita" is different again. His powerful alter ego is not an expression of his inner "girl power"; it is a manipulation of the female form for his own purposes. Such constructions seek, it seems consciously, to have pornographic power: An iconic image is produced with the intention of having a sexual affect on men and rendering them momentarily helpless through the manipulation of one of their base emotions – lust.

## Displays of Emotion

The representation of the sexualised female form causes older men to lose all control over their calm dignity. The nosebleeds depicting this reaction are possibly, for non-Japanese viewers, the most curious visual symbols of all those discussed in this analysis.

Powerful, mature men are represented, first, as transfixed through their facial expressions while being drained of colour. Then, they are overwhelmed by an uncontrollable ejaculation of fluid, simulating orgasm, brought about through the observation of naked young women. This signifies the humiliating emasculating effect of involuntary ejaculation and, more generally, the loss of stoicism and self-control. According to Nitobe (1905/2001), such values are important national values – especially, but not exclusively, for men.

Napier notes that, unlike actual live action pornography, in Japanese pornographic anime, male orgasm is depicted far less frequently than frustration or simply endless penetration. This may well be due to censorship limitations and also because orgasm might suggest a *vulnerable loss of control*. The sexual male's combination of frustration and desperate need for control underlines once again the paucity of sexual identities available to the Japanese male (2000, pp. 80/81; emphasis added).

The narrative juxtaposition of the sexy jutsu and the exploding nosebleed works as combined symbolic elements to represent relations between the gendered characters. As long as it meets the expectations of male sexual fantasies, female sexuality is powerful over male sexuality to the extent that even the most disciplined warrior-guardian is a helpless slave to his base sexual instincts. Female sexuality is a weapon to be used by men against other men; male sexuality is a weakness.

While these traits are observable, it is more difficult to ascertain, gauge or anticipate the consequences; that is, the impact or "effect" this form of children's media has upon its viewers.

## Conclusion

Some aspects of Japanese animation can be relatively easily accounted for by a basic understanding of its historical precedents and contemporary cultural circumstances. For example, it is clear that explicit sexual animation has been a part of Japanese cultural life for centuries. Then, as now, it was particularly popular among the middle-classes; from emerging merchant classes during the Edo period through 21st century salaried office workers and (relatively) affluent teenagers. It is also possible to understand how culturally and even politically significant Japanese animation has become commercially. Moreover, within Japanese animation, signifiers of young, even infantile, sexualisation of female characters are readily identifiable, and the similarity that they demonstrate to forms of explicitly erotic and pornographic animation (*hentai*) is apparent. It is clear that the combination of youth and sexuality, in an explicit fashion and with strong elements of fantasy that can blur the borders with fetish, is prevalent and popular.

Less certain is the way these images are consumed. How meanings are produced and shared. What are the consequences for individuals and societies where these animated characters appear and are admired or desired? Research to date (APA, 2007) suggests strongly that there are sufficient reasons for concern: Portrayals of distorted body images, sexuality and sexual relationships are among the most pressing of these concerns, as they may have, inter alia, consequences that range from reduced academic performance to increased incidents of childhood prostitution. These consequences are far from certain, and probably are highly contingent on factors, such as cultural specificities and individual capacity for resilience. Moreover, the responses to these concerns are not yet as clear as we deem them to be.

It is to these questions and concerns that future research and critical thinking must turn.

## APPENDIX

The sample was provided by IZI from the Children's Television Worldwide research project. It consisted of the following programmes:

Australia: Dragon Booster (ABC); Pokémon (Channel 10)
Kenya: Robotboy (Nation TV)
New Zealand: Transformers; Xiaolin Showdown; Mega Man; One Piece; Yu-Gi-Oh (TV2); American Dragon (Disney Channel)
South Africa: Double Dragon; Titan AE; Daigunder; Dragon Ball; Dragon Hunters; Legend of the Dragon (ETV/SABC); Megas XLR (SABC1)
USA East: Pucca; Digimon (Jetix/Toon Disney); Sonic X (Fox)

Additional material:

Naruto. (2002). Episodes 1 and 2. © Musashi Kishimoto (Published by Shueisha/Shonen Jump)

## REFERENCES

APA – Task Force on the Sexualization of Girls (2007). Report of the APA Task Force on the Sexualization of Girls. Washington, DC: American Psychological Association.

Allison, A. (2000). *Permitted and Prohibited Desires: Mothers, Comics and Censorship in Japan*. Berkeley, CA: University of California Press.

Allison, A. (2006). *Millennial Monsters: Japanese Toys and the Global Imagination*. Berkeley, CA: University of California Press.

Barthes, R. (1973). *Mythologies*. London, England: Paladin.

Hadju, D. (2008). *The Ten-Cent Plague: The Great Comic-Book Scare and How it Changed America*. New York, NY: Farrar, Straus and Giroux.

Kelts, R. (2006). *Japanamerica: How Japanese Pop Culture Has Invaded the U.S.* New York, NY: Palgrave Macmillan.

Napier, S. J. (2000). *Anime From Akira to Princess Mononoke: Experiencing Contemporary Japanese Animation*. New York, NY: Palgrave.

Nekotom. (2004). Bringing your Anime characters to life. In R. K. Agosto (Ed.), *How to create virtual beauties: Digital Manga characters*. New York, NY: Harper Design.

Nitobe, I. (1905/2001). *Bushido: The Soul of Japan*. Boston, MA: Turtle Publishing.

van Leeuwen, T. (2001). Semiotics and iconography. In T. Van Leeuwen & C. Jewitt (Eds.), *Handbook of visual analysis* (pp. 92-118). London, England: Sage.

Watanabe, T. (2004). Creating virtual beauties with the latest technology from lightwave 3D. In R. K. Agosto (Ed.), *How to create virtual beauties: Digital Manga characters*. New York, NY: Harper Design.

---

[1] A "jutsu" is a ninja technique that utilises the body's inner energy or life force. Other jutsu in the Naruto series include replication of other characters, the multiple replication of one's self, the ability to instantly memorise and replicate training techniques, and the ability to summon animals to one's aid.

# 5

# HEROES, PLANNERS AND FUNNY LOSERS: MASCULINITIES REPRESENTED IN MALE CHARACTERS IN CHILDREN'S TV

*Maya Götz, Gunter Neubauer and Reinhard Winter*

Research findings regarding gender representation in children's television are unequivocal: First, boy characters appear much more frequently than girl and women characters, both in television series for children and in films for children and families. Second, this has been the case for decades (Smith & Cook, 2008). Third, boys are more active, dominant, capable, and hold more responsible positions in the stories. They are more aggressive, louder; they laugh, insult and threaten more; and are more often rewarded within the storyline (Aubrey & Harrison, 2004; Barcus, 1983; Levinson, 1975; Sternglanz & Serbin, 1974; Streicher & Bonney, 1974; Thompson & Zerbinos, 1995).

While male aggression is mainly physical in nature, female protagonists tend more towards social violence, such as malicious gossip (Luther & Legg, 2010). If they are superheroes, males are much more numerous than female superheroes; more likely to be muscular, less emotional; more likely to be "tough"; and more inclined to make threats than ask questions. True, not all male characters are portrayed through stereotyped traditional gender roles, but a trend is nonetheless evident, particularly among the superheroes: Male heroes are shown to be more capable of holding positions of power and more able to save the world (Baker & Raney, 2007).

Media analyses in the 24 countries included in this study provide additional confirmation for these research findings. Males numbered 17,149 of the 26,342 main characters examined in children's television. Quantitative coding makes it clear that, on average, 32% of the main roles are assigned to women and girl characters, with 68% to men and boy characters. The males are more often the villains and lone fighters, and less often part of a team than female protagonists (see Götz & Lemish, chapter 1). The conclusion seems to be clear: Male characters dominate children's television.

Interestingly, gender-oriented research has undertaken surprisingly few investigations of boys and men. As Suzanne Enck-Wanzer and Scott Murray state: "There has been a bevy of research on construction of femininities across popular media; however, emphases on the construction of masculinities have, most often, been an afterthought or implied by default" (2011, p. 59).

In books about gender and media in general (e.g., Carter & Steiner, 2004; Gauntlett, 2002; Nayak & Kehily, 2008), there are individual chapters that discuss new forms of masculinity or the crisis of masculinity, largely in general terms (e.g., Connell, 1995; Frosh, 1994, 2000; Jukes, 1993; Segal, 1990; Seidler, 1989, 1994). However, few scholars have moved from the general to the specific. If there are separate analyses in this area, they are mainly quantitative in nature and organized to test hypotheses (e.g., Luther & Legg, 2010). Isolated qualitative studies have studied the portrayal and construction of masculinities and boyhood in the area of children's film and television, with particular reference to film (Pomerance & Gateward, 2005; Serrato, 2011; Stephens, 2002) or in individual areas such as an analysis of the image of boys in the news (Consalvo, 2003; Watts, 2011).

However, when it comes to a gender-sensitive, qualitative examination of boy characters, children's *television* has been largely neglected or is only mentioned in the introduction. Yet, as Carter and Steiner (2004) observed, there is no doubt of its significance:

> Not surprisingly, children's media – like their toys – are among the first contexts that each of us encounters for demonstrating how masculinity and femininity "ought" to be performed. Boys' action figures like "GI Joe" in the USA or "Action Man" in the UK depict muscles, tough and aggressive characters armed with the latest guns, missiles and explosives. Currently popular films such as *Gladiator, Lord of the Rings, Men in Black* and *Spiderman* indicate what are deemed to be "normal" or "appropriate". (2004, p. 12)

They continue to discuss other cartoons targeting boys, and argue that:

> On children's television, cartoons such as *Digimon Digital Monster* and *Yu-Gi-Oh* combine images primarily of boys and men who use their smarts, strength and superhuman monsters to exert their wills/superiority over others. Each week, the cast of characters must employ certain masculine skills and repertoires of exercise to defeat similarly inclined enemies and, finally, to confirm their superiority. (2004, p. 12)

Thus, aside from the studies undertaken by the authors (Winter & Neubauer, 2002, 2005, 2006, 2008, 2009; Götz, i.p.), which serve as the foundations for the study presented here, there is an acute absence of detailed examinations of the construction of masculinities in concrete media texts.[1]

Like femininity (discussed in detail in Götz & Herche, chapter 2; Prinsloo, chapter 3; Spry, chapter 4), we understand masculinity to be a social construction that is a configuration of gender praxis (Connell, 2000). Indeed, various versions of masculinities are produced in everyday discourse (e.g., Edley & Wetherell, 1997;

Mac an Ghaill, 1994). As gendered practice, these differences open up questions and opportunities for different ways for boys to act as masculine and perform masculine identities (Connell, 2000; Davis, 1997; Frosh, Phoenix, & Pattman, 2002; Millington & Wilson, 2010; Willis, 1977).

According to current social discourse, gender material is also performed by boys (Harris, 1995; Kimmel, 2008). If so, then we posit that children's television is often one of the key sources from which boys, as well as girls, derive symbolic material for defining themselves, and therefore find answers about what forms of boyhood enjoy social recognition. Accordingly, there is a good reason for investigations into the representations of masculinities constructed in children's television. The aim of this chapter is to contribute to such scholarly endeavors by shedding light onto the topic by presenting the research results from four different perspectives.

## Research Perspective 1:
## The Main Characters in Children's Television

The starting points for our studies were the analyses of main characters in children's television, as follows. First, we conducted a qualitative study based on 90 characters, followed by a quantitative analysis using a representative sample of German children's television (see Götz & Lemish, Inroduction). Following the principles of gender mainstreaming, we deliberately avoided examining girl versus boy characters. Instead, we sought to identify basic patterns in dramaturgic structures (e.g., how the main conflict is dealt with). Once these patterns were identified, we analyzed gender differences. Since this analysis was confined to children's television broadcast in Germany, we proceeded with a worldwide media analysis with the intent to understand these phenomena on an international scale.

## Result 1: Boys Are First and Foremost – ... More and More Diverse

The qualitative analysis of 90 main characters from children's television identified the following six narrative patterns in typification, according to similarities and differences in their manner of dealing with the main conflict of the story, and several sub-patterns: (1) "egocentrics", like SpongeBob; (2) "communicators", like the Bear from *The Bear in the Big Blue House* (Jim Henson, USA); (3) "responsible types", like Bob the Builder; (4) "resistant types", like Spiderman; (5) "clueless types", like Patrick (*SpongeBob*); and (6) "helpless types", like Bernd das Brot, (i.e., *Bernd*

*the Bread* in KiKA, Germany), the depressive German toast bread. These main
character typifications were categorized and counted in the subsequent quantitative
analysis of a representative sample for Germany. We found that the "resistant types"
and the "clueless types" were the most frequent characters (about a quarter of the
characters), followed by "egocentrics" (about a fifth), while the others played a
minor role, quantitatively. Within these six types, male characters occur three and
sometimes even four times more frequently than female characters. The exception
is the "helpless type", where male and female characters are nearly balanced.

These results clearly confirm, once again, that boys and men appear much
more frequently, and are seldom the "helpless" character in need of rescue. More
generally, these findings make it clear that producers employ a variety of boy and
men characters. Some are assigned superhero positions, while others serve as
communicators, act aggressively, or negotiate. While some characters are motivated
by responsibility towards others, egocentric motives drive other characters. Thus,
the first finding is that male characters are predominant in terms of number and
diversity.

### Research Perspective 2:
### Concentrating on Boys' – and Girls' – Favorite Characters

Since six typifications (with several subcategories) are too many for a detailed
analysis of the elements from which masculinity is constructed in the boy and
men characters in children's television, we decided to employ a sole criterion for
selection of characters – popularity among boys.

These data were collected in a representative study conducted by the IZI in
2007 and 2010 (see Table 5.1). In 716 face-to-face interviews conducted in Germany
in December 2007 and 2010, six- to 12-year-olds were asked about their favorite
characters. Based on these data, we created a ranking of the most popular characters
in Germany. These rankings were then used to identify the TV characters relevant
for boys.

Children are different and have different character preferences. Nonetheless,
certain characters are named with particular frequency every year, and are
correspondingly high on the charts. For example, SpongeBob has been the clear
winner *for boys* in several surveys. In 2007, he was followed by Bart Simpson,
Spiderman, Jimmy Neutron, and Andy, as well as female super-agent Kim Possible,
Homer Simpson, and Jerry. In 2010, SpongeBob and Ben 10 were followed by
characters including Bart Simpson, Batman, and Bob the Builder.

**Table 5.1.**
Boys' and girls' favorite characters 2007/2010

| Rank | Boys 2007 | | Boys 2010 | | Girls 2007 | | Girls 2010 | |
|---|---|---|---|---|---|---|---|---|
| 1. | SpongeBob | 22.8% | SpongeBob | 18.3% | Kim Possible | 14% | Hannah Montana | 28.4% |
| 2. | Bart Simpson | 9.5% | Ben 10 | 7.8% | SpongeBob | 8.9% | Barbie | 7.2% |
| 3. | Spiderman | 3.5% | Bart Simpson | 6.2% | Lilli the Witch | 3.4% | Kim Possible | 4.6% |
| 4. | Jimmy Neutron, Mickey Mouse, Andy (*What's with Andy?*) | 1.9% | Batman | 5.1% | Bart Simpson, Lisa Plenske (kind of Ugly Betty) | 2.9% | SpongeBob | 3.8% |
| 5. | Kim Possible, Pink Panther, Homer Simpson | 1.6% | Bob the Builder | 3.3% | John (*Good times, bad times*) | 2.3% | Bibi Blocksberg | 2.3% |
| 6. | Jerry (*Tom and Jerry*) | 1.4% | Homer Simpson | 2.7% | Zoey | 2.0% | Princess Lillifee | 2.0% |

For the girls, Kim Possible was right at the top of the list in 2007, followed by Spongebob, Lilli the Witch, Bart Simpson and Lisa Plenske and John, characters from a German soap. Hannah Montana topped the list by a clear margin in 2010, followed by Barbie in her various feature films (which were showing regularly in evening slots on Super RTL at the time of the survey), and witches or fairies such as Bibi Blocksberg and Princess Lillifee.

### What Characterizes Girls' Favorite Characters?

As many scholars in masculinity studies have noted (e.g., Connell, 2000; Harris, 1995; Kimmel, 2008), gender is a binary system. Therefore, in order to improve our understanding of one side, we begin our presentation by looking at the most popular girl characters.

Girls' favorite characters tend to be female. As with boys, this suggests a potential same-sex preference. All the characters in the episodes examined face challenges. While some respond to the spitefulness of the world around them or to problems that evolve from their own actions, all of the characters perform admirably in the face of these challenges. Kim Possible, as a superheroine, can combat every nasty villain with technology, action, and fighting. Hannah Montana is a superstar who performs brilliantly on stage despite her youth. As Miley, she has to deal with "normal" issues of failure, but in the end she always finds a cool, socially responsible way to handle these. Magical characters, such as Lilli the Witch, Bibi Blocksberg or Princess Lillifee, can prove themselves through their exceptional abilities. They make mistakes, but quickly realize them and, thanks to their magical powers, find ways to put everything to rights again. As indicated in the titles, Barbie re-enacts traditional fairy-tale material. But whether it is *Barbie of Swan Lake* (Mainframe & Mattel, USA) or *Barbie as Rapunzel* (Mainframe & Mattel, USA), she proves herself much more competent and self-determined in the face of challenges than the characters depicted by the original (male) authors. Soap characters popular with older girls, such as the telenovela character Lisa Plenske (a kind of Ugly Betty), also behave with striking social competence, pronounced sense of responsibility, and they are prepared to fight for love. This suggests that girls like strong girl characters. This strength is manifested in the extraordinary things they achieve, with the help of special talents (e.g., singing and dancing) or magical powers (see e.g., Götz, Lemish, Aidman, & Moon, 2005).

The few male characters selected by the girls have quite different characteristics. John from *GZSZ* (i.e., *Good times, bad times*) (Grundy UFA, Germany) may well serve the fantasy of the para-social erotic partner (Götz, 2002). Bart Simpson plays, consciously, with crossing boundaries, and is anything but a high achiever.

Overall, most girls like strong, successful girl characters who demonstrate social responsibility. One critical remark is needed: As elaborated in the chapters by Götz and Herche (chapter 2) and Prinsloo (chapter 3), all the strong, successful girls are stereotypically beautiful[2] and strikingly thin. Thus, the most popular girl characters are those who correspond to a modern ideal girl: They are intelligent, high-achieving, and able to cope with all problems and challenges; they act confidently, are popular and well-integrated, and have a sense of morality. They are "add-on characters". Being aware of this analysis, we turn to answer the question – what characterizes the most popular TV characters of boys?

### Result 2: Boy Characters Are... High Achievers – or Not

Based on the typification of the main characters of children's television (Götz, 2006), boys' favorite characters (like those of girls) mostly include the strong, combative characters (Batman, Yu-Gi-Oh), the "egocentrics" (SpongeBob, Bart Simpson) and the "responsible types" (at least one character: Bob the Builder). More specifically, two quite distinct types of characteristics were found among the most frequently mentioned boys' favorite TV characters. On the one hand, there are *superheroes* (e.g., Spiderman, Ben10 and Batman), whose special bodies or use of extraordinary technologies enable them to use force in the fight against evil. There are also characters, like Yu-Gi-Oh (called Yugi when he is a normal boy) who make their monsters fight to save the world according to particular rules of play. On the other hand, there are characters that just seem chaotically *naïve*, such as SpongeBob, or mean, destructive characters, such as Bart Simpon.

Not all the male characters are especially significant and suitable as favourite characters. For example, characters such as "mediators", "helpless types", or those who are down on their luck are important for the narrative, but probably serve as connecting characters. Thus, even though it would be very interesting to analyze how responsible, helpless, or mediating male characters were constructed, we are going to focus on the most frequently mentioned types for a closer analysis – at least in this study: the "combative" and the "egocentric characters".

### Research Perspective 3:
### Typification of the Most Popular Male Characters

We concluded that there are two fundamentally different types of protagonists among the most relevant television characters for boys – heroes and the humorous. Spiderman or Yu-Gi-Oh are examples of heroic characters. We assume heroes to be extraordinary people who bear the burden of an extraordinary destiny in an exemplary manner, and selflessly put their lives at the service of duty and their fellow men (Held, 1969). Accordingly, a hero overcomes the challenges that present themselves to him in a single bound, so to speak. The character's orientation is selfless and the hero's motivation is responsibility towards others. Other characters selected are mainly designed to be funny. They are strikingly egocentric and are really losers in respect to general moral and social attitudes (e.g., Bart and Homer Simpson or SpongeBob). This would suggest that there are anti-heroes as well as (super) heroes. Pursuing this line of argument, we propose that the characters attractive for boys can be roughly divided into two types. On the one hand the "surmounters" who leap over life's challenges. On the other hand, "subverters" wriggle their way through these challenges and obstacles.

In the next stage of analysis, the strategic points for analysis included the typical focal points for the construction of masculinity: the characters' motivation, their way of behaving, their status within the story, their way of dealing with failure, their communication and portrayal of emotions, their physical representation, their organization of their lives and everyday routines. The most frequently named male characters in 2007 and 2010 are the starting point (n.b., only places one to ten were analyzed).

### Male Protagonists Type 1: The "Surmounter Type"

Male "surmounters" manage what has to be done and act in a moral way, motivated by responsibility towards others. Two subtypes are employed as the adult hero who knows what has to be done: the "do-it type" (1a) and the "strategizer type" (1b).

### Type 1a: "Do-It Characters"

These characters are generally adults or at least young adults, such as the classic heroes – Batman, Superman, Spiderman, and X-Men. More recent additions to the market include characters like Ben 10, who, though just a boy, can use his watch from outer space to transform himself into ten different superhero-monsters. These characters are extraordinary people: They may have come from distant stars (Superman, Son Goku) and now use their abilities to protect humanity. Or, they have been different from birth (X-Men) or have been given special powers through a fateful accident (Batman, Spiderman, Ben 10). It is their bodies that enable them or even force them to become heroes.

"Do-it characters" are entirely focused on their action, their activity. They are doers. They carry out their missions more or less without being asked, and keep performing heroic deeds. Their effectiveness is predominantly manifest in their actions, and they do not seem to doubt that anything would impede their actions (i.e., no displays of ambivalence, doubt, reflection, obstacles). There is no evidence of problematizing or extensive reflection, no intellectualization. Interestingly, the "do-it type" repeatedly makes mistakes in the heat of the moment. He is deceived and outwitted, but does not allow this to change him. He simply tries to do better and to do the right thing at the next attempt (i.e., the trial and error principle).

As a character, "surmounters" promise and attain a kind of reduction of complexity: Simply put, they don't talk and think too much. The "surmounter's" motto seems to be: "Just do it, and everything will be simple." This *doing* is primarily action, action with a substantial component of violence. The "do-it" hits, shoots, or blows things up without reflection. He does not perceive nor, accordingly, take into account the consequences for other people, objects, buildings, or even himself. His violent action is self-evident; that is, it does not enter his frame of reference as something which might be reflected on (to use the concepts of Berger & Luckmann, 1965).

The "surmounter's" linguistic utterances are limited and condensed. He communicates mainly by means of action. Verbal communication mainly serves to communicate dominance or distance. Emotions are scarcely emitted by these characters, if at all; at most, following a serious accident they might elicit a groan. But, they do denigrate the abilities of the opponent through, for example, mockery or malice (Böhnisch & Winter, 1997).

The extrinsic motivation of the "do-it type" is the challenge posed by the immoral and wrong actions of others (clearly characterized as villains). Despite many crises and sometimes even the risk of utter failure, he always manages to triumph over them in the end. Under close consideration, the focus of these characters is not – as often supposed – the feat they want to perform or a constant desire for high achievement, but rather the manner with which they deal and cope with *external* expectations of their performance. Thus, "surmounter" heroes are constantly performing extraordinary feats, truly "heroic deeds", but receive no special, lasting recognition or any permanent acknowledgement of their better, higher status.

Within the story, the superhero often has a concealed double identity. He is just an inconspicuous character for most of the people around him, most of the time. It is only special challenges that turn the inconspicuous "ordinary guy" into a superhero (e.g., a villain's attack). As ordinary guys, these characters are often degraded or downgraded and lack status. However, in superhero mode, they are recognized and have a high status. For a short time, at least, they receive recognition. But, in some stories their real significance and motivation is misunderstood and they are subjected to hostility. However, the stories nearly all end with the misunderstanding or the special circumstances being cleared up, and the superhero's high status being recognized.

In terms of physical representation, these characters – at least in their superhero mode – are characterized by highly toned muscles and an exaggeratedly masculine body shape. As Baker and Raney found in their analysis of superheroes, these are often drawn with very pronounced muscles, especially in animations (Baker & Raney, 2007). In the superhero mode, this type symbolizes an idealized image of men, hegemonic masculinity, who are characterized by toughness, power and authority (Connell, 1995). On the other hand, in the "ordinary guy" mode, these characters are often portrayed with physical imperfections or inadequacies (i.e., devalorized masculinities; McDowell, 2003). They wear glasses, cannot express themselves adequately, particularly towards women, have acne or wear unsuitable clothing. They symbolize the devalorized man on a physical as well as psychological level.

The lifestyle of the "do-it character" is mainly shaped by his mission. His relational situation tends to be solitary, his everyday life ascetic. Some of these characters have reliable attendants (e.g., Batman's butler) or same-sex friends, in Batman's case Robin. However, explicit hints of a homosexual partnership are carefully avoided for characters of this type. In other words, only certain types of devalorized masculinity are represented. These are then presented as heroic, as their actions are motivated by responsibility for others.

Overall, these are all basic traits of what is described as a "heroic lifestyle", characterized by a high esteem for manly virtue, physical and moral challenges, and a reluctance to show emotion. The hero's life is completely focused on posterity and his highest moral attribute is self-discipline (Campell, 1949; Gesemann, 1943). He is, as it were, a victim of his excessive strength, which he has not chosen himself, but acquired accidentally. In this sense, his masculine body compels him to act in this way, to rescue the world by fighting. He must, as it were, deny himself a fulfilled, complete life. This idealizes, among others, perpetration and self-administered justice, devaluates communication and negotiation on the social level, and emphasizes the blocking of emotions, body awareness, or the wish for attachment as essential for maleness, for example. Thus, these characters seem to typify hegemonic masculinity (Connell, 1995) and an unhealthy self-concept (Böhnisch & Winter, 1997; Hinz, 2011).

## Type 1b: The "Strategizer Character"

The second type of "surmounter hero" is the "strategizer". This grouping includes characters such as Yu-Gi-Oh, Ash (*Pokémon*), Naruto or heroes from *Digimon* (Toei Animation, Japan). They tend to be younger, generally in early adolescence. It is usually by some mystical chance that they come to realize the mission imposed on them: They must save the world. In doing so, the "surmounter" employs the "understand and strategize" principle. In order to preserve or restore the threatened order, the focus is not on pure action, but first and foremost on understanding the rules and laws behind this order. Only then can actions be applied effectively and strategically.

This is also a kind of reduction of complexity strategy. It seems as though certain laws make it possible to handle the world. Yugi (as mentioned above, this is his name when he is a normal boy) has to prove himself in a scenario containing a latent threat. Yet life appears to be, largely, a predictable game governed by rules, with victory granted according to points. The burdens and challenges of life are simultaneously reduced and exaggerated in the form of a regulated duel: Engagements and attacks occur in an ordered sequence and are conveyed through the card game, without Yugi having to do any physical fighting. In the end, all the actors are subject to the rules, even if there are repeated attempts – especially among the "enemies" – to play tricks and ignore rules. Thus, there is a sense of law and order. Yugi is allowed to make mistakes, though there is a price to pay for these. Success, on the other hand, comes about partly through luck (with the cards), but mainly through perfect deployment of innate and acquired abilities in conjunction with appropriate strategy and optimal resource management. The process culminates in "playing one's cards right". But given the strength of the opponents, the ultimate triumph of good, "once and for all", remains an everlasting task, one that can never be entirely completed. Therefore, Yugi can and must face the fight again and again.

Male characters of this type are motivated by responsibility towards the world and their fellow humans, and their enthusiasm and special abilities in a competitive game or sport. Characters of this type grow with every battle, with every new challenge. They explicitly gain in recognition and status, as demonstrated visually by their progression to higher levels, the medals they win and so forth. In terms of lifestyle, boys are generally not yet integrated into working life, and school, too, plays a minor role if featured at all. The core content of their life is their mission. At the same time, they are integrated into a firm and reliable peer group, generally having one male and one female friend who share their mission but are usually not as skilful as the main character. The peer group recognizes the boy's achievements and responsibility, independent of his current performance.

"Strategizers'" communication with others is condensed. Their limited speech conveys essential information and contributes to reaching their goal. However, this character type also engages in offstage soliloquies. Employing reflective commentary in a parallel channel alongside explication of the plot, boy characters reflect on their own and others' behavior. Through this mechanism viewers come to understand what they think about their adversaries' planning, the strategies he may deploy, and, in turn, how such considerations influence the character's actions.

These characters have emotions, which, in typical anime fashion, are sometimes depicted in an overly obvious manner. For example, fear or joy is shown by a wide open mouth. When in contest mode, communication focuses on dominance and distance. While little emotion is expressed outwardly, at the same time emotions are articulated inside the character's mind.

As far as their physical representation is concerned, the depictions of the "understand and strategize type" resemble the average boy aged roughly 12 to 15. Different from girl characters, they are not characterized by an extreme low shoulder-to-waist ratio (see Götz & Herche, chapter 2), nor are they portrayed as overweight. They symbolize the normal, but "ideal" boy.

In summary, boys of this type have a trans-generational mission to save the people around them by means of strategic thinking. They usually learn about their special status and role around 12 years of age (as in the *Harry Potter* series), and then have to find a way to learn to fulfill the responsibility given them by nature.

The "strategizer" idealizes rules and employs one-dimensional ways of thinking as a basic way to deal with problems. Through it all, this character underlines the natural superiority of men through an absence or secondary role of female characters.

### "Surmounters": Portrayals of Strategizing, Combative Manhood/Boyhood

Thus, the "surmounter hero type" involves constructions of masculinity on various levels. In superhero mode, particularly as the "do-it" (type 1a), characterization employs various clichés of the dominant, hard man consistent with the stereotype of hegemonic masculinity. However, the stories told about the characters do not present their motivation as "exert[ing] their wills/superiority over others" (Carter & Steiner 2004, p. 12). From a critical, external point of view, it does appear that "each week, the cast of characters must employ certain masculine skills and repertoires of exercise to defeat similarly inclined enemies and, finally, to confirm their superiority" (Carter & Steiner 2004, p. 12). From the internal point of view of the story, the characters seem to be compelled into certain actions by their bodies and act – to the best of their ability – in a morally justifiable manner.

The fact that these are male bodies is not explicitly thematized and explicit dominance over or violence towards women is almost always omitted. Rather, the characters' emergence as dominant masculine characters is an alternative to their usual state of masculinity. Initially devalorized, these male characters only receive recognition by means of a physical transformation, a special (inherited) talent and/ or individual actions.

In both manifestations, as the "do-it" or "strategizer", the "surmounter" acts on the basis of an unalterable physical precondition (e.g., they have a body that does not belong on this earth [*Dragon Ball* series], has been changed through an accident [Spiderman], a generation-based predisposition located in the body [Naruto] or handed down as an object and a talent [Yu-Gi-Oh]). Such elements constitute their individuality. Thus, masculinity is constructed as something related to the body. However, different from the focus in female characters on attractiveness and hypersexuality (see Prinsloo, chapter 3), the boys' inner strength is employed to derive certain meanings, such as an unquestioned use of violence.

### Male Protagonists Type 2: The "Subverter Type"

The "subverter" includes characters such as Bart and Homer Simpson, SpongeBob, Patrick (*SpongeBob*) or Andy Larkin. These characters do not meet expectations, indeed their weaknesses are accentuated and celebrated, as is their capability to subvert and slip through obstacles. On first glance they do not fulfill the definition of hero, as they act in a self-centered way, often without consideration for others.

For the "subverter" protagonist, things that are actually embarrassing are emphasized and freed from their embarrassing effect. Thus, weakness becomes strength. For example, SpongeBob could not make it over the hurdle, so he redefines the hurdle by cultivating and celebrating the failing. This does not enable him to overcome the original hurdle, but he can now get over his "own" new hurdle and become the actual winner. He stands out through his active approach, pure doing. Such activity is devoid of reflection. He can also count on friendship and support. This insures ultimate success in his capacity as co-star. "Subverters" fail and they are proud of it. They enjoy eating, drinking and other bodily pleasures, without a hint of asceticism. Characters of this type are, in their own way, strong and capable. They bounce back from adversity; make jokes about any situation in life. They always think of something silly to do, and get out of awkward situations again and again. Their behavior does not conform to norms and does not conform to "masculinity" in the desired sense. Although measured by external standards, they are not "worth anything," they do make a difference – even if this just means causing chaos and disaster.

Thus, as hero, the "subverter" is more of an anti-hero, who undermines existing requirements (according to the principle of "going around the hurdle"). He is able to get by in this way, without ever quite meeting requirements. He cultivates failure. Actually, this is the one thing he is capable of doing "perfectly". His motto is: "Whatever I do – I'll get through!"

Such characters frequently cause chaos, tumult and confusion, thereby constantly challenging the order of the adult world and adult expectations of performance. This too gives rise to a kind of repetition compulsion: Characters of this type would bring about their own demise if they were able to escape, permanently, from this coping pattern. Therefore, they need a steady supply of new opportunities to demonstrate their ability to manoeuvre and sneak around obstacles. In this sense, they do not question pre-existing orders and rules or act with absolute destructiveness. Instead, they engage with these things in a thoroughly creative way. Their corresponding aggression is channeled and remains, in a broader sense, humorous.

The motivation of characters of this type is their own egocentric worldview, driven by desire. Their concerns are at the centre of the action. This leads them into confrontation with others, such as authorities or institutions. But they also accept and sometimes even embrace injury to others and disregard for moral or societal norms. While this is punished, sometimes, within the storyline, it does not alter such characters' fundamental motivation. Their potency consists in getting through and not giving up in the process. They do not allow themselves to be discouraged by repeated failures, chaos and disaster. This refusal to act in a manner that is appropriate and morally right gains them a certain recognition among their friends, a certain social status. This status is not diminished when authorities denigrate them. Nonetheless, their social status remains generally low. However, their social integration is absolutely reliable.

Although these characters act in a highly anti-social manner, they can ultimately rely on the goodwill of their family and friends. They generally live in a middle-class milieu and thus have ready access to normal status symbols such as a house, a car, adequate clothing, opportunities to visit theme parks etc.

"Subverters'" preferred form of communication is condensed and often shows no regard for others' feelings. Empathy is not a factor, at least not in their spontaneous actions. While it may feature in individual episodes, it has no lasting effect on their behavior. Feelings are sometimes expressed in various facets, and sometimes acted out and celebrated.

Physically, most of the characters are inconspicuous boys, somewhat small for their age. They symbolize the devalorized boy. Yet, Homer Simpson, as an adult version of the "subverter" is physically unattractive and often portrayed as dirty and unkempt. In their physical representation, these characters often symbolize the non-heroic man.

### Result 3:
### "Surmounter" and "Subverter" Constructions of Masculinities: Between Life as a Never-Ending Fight or Need to Cop Out

The following conclusions regarding constructions of masculinity are posited based on our analysis of some of boys' favorite television characters: Various forms of symbolization and exaggeration of masculinity are employed. Yet, there are different types and underlying facets of the portrayal of masculinities. Some are images of traditional, dominant masculinity, such as the superheroes (type 1a). These characters generally contain the devalorized forms of masculinities, often within the same character. Others learn to systematically deploy strategies and thus grow with every challenge (type 1b). Both types symbolize a way to simplify life as a fight: Challenges always endanger human existence and the only ways to overcome these challenges are physical exertion, techniques, or trained creatures which can be used as weapons.

To stand up to these threats, the boy characters analyzed either function through relatively one-dimensional rules or cultivate circumvention of authorities. In the case of the latter, they create new definitions that turn devalorization into gains in status (type 2). Frosh, Phoenix and Pattman (2002) refer to these strategies as versions of "popular masculinities" because it is closer to the discourse of boys aged 11 to 14 years.

Popular masculinities require attributes such as hardness, antagonism to school-based learning, sporting prowess and fashionable style (Frosh, Phoenix, & Pattman, 2002). Some of the points through which hegemonic masculinity is defined – heterosexuality, toughness, power and authority, competitiveness and subordination of gay men (Connell, 1995) – are experienced as problematic from the boys' perspectives if they are acted out in too extreme a manner (ibid). Neubauer and Winter (2001) claimed that many elements of traditional masculinity are not self-evident or attractive for boys, especially in their extreme forms. From the internal perspective of the boys in these stories, the point is not to formulate hegemonic masculinity, but to understand idealized ways to escape from a devalorized position. In this process, masculinity is shown to be a sort of fantasy of socially recognized boyhood or manhood of which certain facets are then depicted (see Table 5.2). By symbolizing life as a fight, by idealizing action and devaluating reflection, by emphasizing the necessity of the neglect of weakness and the blocking of emotions, characters reinforce the features they actually want to dismiss. This is a self-stabilizing system of hegemonic masculinities.

**Table 5.2.**

Types of manhood in children's television and their typical characteristics

| Type | "Surmounter type" (1) | | "Subverter type" (2) |
|---|---|---|---|
| | "Do-it type" (1a) | "Strategize type" (1b) | |
| Examples | Batman, Superman, Spiderman, X-Men, Son Goku (*Dragon Ball Z*), Ben 10 | Yu-Gi-Oh, Ash (*Pokémon*), Naruto, boy characters from *Digimon* | Bart and Homer Simpson, SpongeBob, Patrick (*SpongeBob*), Andy Larkin |
| Basic disposition | Special physical abilities acquired unintentionally (e.g., through an accident) "force" the character into an extraordinary position within society. He fights to save others and deprives himself of a normal human life. | Special gifts and responsibility handed down through generations lead to an extraordinary position: He saves the world around him by competing and gradually acquiring new knowledge. | Normal boys in their normal everyday lives secure recognition and friendship by their peer group, despite having limited abilities and performing socially unacceptable behavior. |
| Motivation | Immoral actions; threats to community from others | Immoral actions; threats to community from others | Own egocentric world view |
| Actions | Action-focused, no reflection, unquestioning use of violence | Contest shaped by rules. Character's own body has to survive the combat, but does so through an intermediary (being, technology), with input from a trainer/master | Pleasure is taken in undermining societal conventions and power structures, and breaking rules |
| Way of dealing with mistakes | Trial and error principle | Errors are impetus to learn new rules and strategies | Failure is celebrated and redefined as triumph |
| Body | Superhero mode: muscular; ordinary guy mode: physical "imperfections" | Average boy's body | Tend to be too small and slight for their age (symbolize devalorized boy) |
| Status | Superhero status: temporary recognition; everyday status: no recognition | Visible gain in status through increasingly high level, medals etc. | Denigrated by those in power, appreciated by friends |
| Emotions | Only internal | In part typical anime representation of fear, joy etc. In competition mode, usually only expressed internally | Various facets celebrated and acted out |
| Commun-ication | Communication of dominance or distance | Condensed, i.e., limited to few essential, goal-oriented words | Various forms, from communication of dominance and distance to condensed communication; distress also expressed |
| Lifestyle | Sometimes career; solitary family situation | Reliable peer group with whom they master challenges jointly | Generally middle-class milieu; firmly integrated into reliable network of family and friends |

But why do boys prefer these shows? In action-oriented reception research one of the key concepts is "theme". Underneath the storyline of a text, profound identity issues are told and negotiated. Preferences and interpretations of those texts are often driven by these themes which are highly relevant for the viewer. What are the themes behind the most popular characters of boys?

### Research Perspective 4:
### Looking for Ubiquitous Themes in the Boys' Favorite Shows

In the next stage of analysis, we took the most frequently named male characters of 2007 and 2010 (places one to ten) and watched at least one episode together, as a working group. Additional information was provided by "experts", who were commissioned especially to watch at least 20 episodes of the series' show. The aim of this investigation was to assess the extent to which the series presents thematic areas with the potential to assist boys in their own construction of masculinity. This discursive analysis drew upon two of the authors' research on boys and from experiences working with boys (Neubauer & Winter, 2001). The "boy themes" identified were presented visually by the characters and in the narratives.

### Result 4: Overarching Themes of Children's Television Heroes

In terms of narrative content, nearly all of the most popular stories involve aggression, both the problematic or threatening side of violence but also the "good" side, (i.e., being stuck in it; knowing what one wants; tackling things head-on; entering conflicts with gusto and so forth). They succeed when aggression comes from someone else and forces the characters to react. There are also stories of crisis and failure. Of course the hero does not become mired in failure, but always manages to cope with the crisis in the end, and to move on. Here, reversal of the theme of dominance is often present: The hero is small in stature, but superior.

Nearly all of the stories (except *New Spiderman*) are also about the hero's friendship with other characters. Such friendship endures and enables these characters to solve problems, especially in times of danger. Social relations are thematized: Group, clique, peers, team and system assist in achieving balance in group relations, as well as generational issues, particularly in the father-son dynamic.

These themes are solved in a manner that can be referred to as "super themes". They are not negotiated or dealt with overtly, but are presented in an indirect, covert manner. Strikingly, super-themes appear among all hero types and series with some degree of ubiquity.

Boy and men characters display a clear focus on action. Activity has clear priority over reflection. This is expressed in action that often also contains aggression. Long or profound conversations or the like are virtually non-existent. Male heroes are characterized by a focus on solutions. Among the characters attractive to boys, the main emphasis of the narrative or of the character's fundamental disposition is not – as in soap operas, for example – on discussing problems, but on solution-oriented action. Conversations serve to show ways to reach a solution. Problems do not lead to the exposure of the hero's weaknesses, but to the solution of the problem. The emphasis on action and solutions prevents discussion of problems (liberation from problematic elements). Evidently, boys want to see "problem-solvers" (and perhaps be problem-solvers themselves). This should not, however, be equated with victors, perpetrators or vanquishers.

Overall, the actions of the male characters are often characterized by a willingness to use aggression and violent actions. Acted out in physical or at least verbal violence but never discussed as a problem, action is used to attain goals. However, the consequences, in terms of physical and mental harm, are never mentioned (e.g., outcomes that might be the cause of injuries in real life).

Love, Eros and sexuality are frequently touched upon in conjunction with a spectrum of themes, but they always seem to be conspicuously frustrated or constrained. The sexual motto tends to be: "postponed, but not forever". Slight hints of sexuality are often expressed (e.g., crushes), but these are postponed for various reasons. In an episode of *Case Closed* (TMS Entertainment, Japan), for example, the story of a 17-year-old who is stuck in the body of a 7-year-old as a result of poison given to him by criminals, the desire for a specific girl is occasionally evoked as a brief glimmer of hope. However, he cannot act on this desire since it is his physical fate to be relegated to a childish phase of life.

### More Advanced Development of Girls of the Same Age

The more advanced development of girls is a theme involved in the narrative, as follows: Boy and men characters are friends with capable, sometimes exceptionally capable, and superior girl and women characters. This superiority is accepted by the male characters as self-evident, without any discussion of gender issues. Here, coexistence is possible without any humiliation or disgrace for the boys – in contrast to harsh reality. For example Sandy, SpongeBob's friend, is an action-focused "wild girl" whose affection for him can be depended on. She is superior to him in many ways, and sometimes overtaxes him with her actions – something he proves to be quite able to express for himself. However, she never denigrates him or hurts his feelings. In a second case, the superheroine Kim Possible is capable, can do anything, always wins but never denigrates her friend Ron Stoppable whose role in the team is that of the foolish but reliable friend. By devising characters like Kim Possible, the male creators Robert Schooley and Mark McCorkle have, by their own admission, portrayed their ideal of a female high school friend (Schlote, 2007). The ideal element is not the hypersexualization but rather the fact that the girl respects and does not humiliate the boy.

## Father-Related Masculinity

Finally, it is especially striking that the hero is presented with either a good-but-dead or a weak father. The dead father is held up as an ideal, and serves, implicitly, to motivate the hero in moral decision-making. Even more often, we find the partially disempowered father who is portrayed with clear and obvious weaknesses, and made to look ridiculous. This disempowered father figure may make it easier for boys to "conquer" their own fathers (Frosh, Phoenix, & Pattman, 2002); to become better, bigger or cleverer than them; and thus to accomplish one step towards adult status. A comparable separation from and positioning in relation to the mother occurs far less often.

## Summary

When genders are compared, male characters are quantitatively more numerous, more aggressive and more dominant. When analyzed qualitatively, they are in the first instance varied, though certain positions such as that of the victim who "only" needs rescuing occur much less frequently than among female characters. Upon closer consideration, the most popular television characters are the main characters who act combatively (Batman, Yu-Gi-Oh), egocentrically (SpongeBob, Bart Simpson), or who are motivated by responsibility for others (Bob the Builder).

In comparison to girls' favorite characters, this represents a greater breadth of symbolization of accepted gendered identities. All the most popular girl characters are "add-on characters". They are particularly pretty *and* slim *and* sporty *and* popular *and* intelligent *and* academically successful *and* socially responsible for their peer group and family *and* they save the world. Among the boy characters, there are some who are successful, but also others who take pleasure in circumventing the challenges of school and authority. Overall, these are generally reduced characters: They have isolated talents and simplified characteristics. Found on various levels, this reduction of complexity is typical of boys' themes. This is particularly the case in the "do-it character" who celebrates traditional symbols of masculinity. A close look at characters attractive to boys reveals that this tends to be the less important aspect. More striking is symbolization of different types of boy. On the one hand, there is the devalorized boy who secretly possesses extraordinary powers that he can harness when an appropriate challenge arises (type 1a). On the other hand, there is the devalorized boy who has cultivated his insufficiencies, so to speak, and who eludes life's challenges and in doing so gains recognition (type 2). In addition, there are types of boys who have been chosen to be given an exceptional passion and ability, and who engage in contests to achieve status.

When considered in light of the few studies on boys, many key criticisms of the characters take on a different contextualization. While these programs are about competition, they serve primarily to demonstrate that the male characters are capable of mastering the challenges facing boys, not to gain dominance or overcome others. They are about anti-social behavior, but this is behavior that does not primarily involve injury to others and breaking with social conventions. Rather, it is more about coping with demands that one cannot meet.

The perspective applied in this study seeks to understand underlying meanings. It also helps us reveal mechanisms by which masculinity is constituted and reinforced. While presented in an exaggerated manner, these heroic lifestyles are demonstrated to be natural and bound to the changed masculine body. This leads to the justified necessity for action, which is allowed to include aggression and physical violence. This in turn leads to a form of communication based on dominance and distance within which attempts to denigrate, for example, are justified. The boy and men characters in children's television are based on existing typical constructions of masculinity. This pre-existing orientation becomes even more firmly fixed with every exaggerated portrayal of the focus on action and solutions, paired with negation of the necessity for reflection (not just in the sense of strategic thought), for example.

What is reinforced here is closely related to the construction elements of "popular masculinities" (Frosh, Phoenix, & Pattman, 2002). It reflects typical boy themes, expands on them and tells stories of coping, but avoids anything unpleasant or that could become so.

## REFERENCES

Aubrey, J. S., & Harrison, K. (2004). The gender-role content of children's favorite television programs and its links to their gender-related perceptions. *Media psychology, 6*(2), 111-146.

Baker, K., & Raney, A. A. (2007). Equally super?: Gender-role stereotyping of superheroes in children's animated programs. *Mass Communication and Society, 10*(1), 25-41.

Barcus, E. F. (1983). *Images of Life on Children's Television: Sex Roles, Minorities and Families*. Westport, CT: Praeger Publishers.

Berger, P. L., & Luckmann, T. (1965). *The Social Construction of Reality*. New York, NY: Doubleday.

Böhnisch, L., & Winter, R. (1997). *Männliche Sozialisation. Bewältigungsprobleme männlicher Geschlechtsidentität im Lebenslauf* [Male socialization. Problems in overcoming male gender identities in CV]. Weinheim, Baden-Württemberg: Juventa.

Campell, A. (1949). Encomium Emmae Reginae. *Camden Third Series, 2*(15), 30-32.

Carter, C., & Steiner, L. (Eds.). (2004). *Critical Readings: Media and Gender*. Maidenhead, UK: Open University Press.

Connell, R. W. (1995). *Masculinities*. Oxford, UK: Polity Press.

Connell, R. W. (2000). *The Men and the Boys*. Cambridge, UK: Polity Press.

Consalvo, M. (2003). The monsters next door: Media constructions of boys and masculinity. *Feminist Media Studies, 3*(1), 27-45.

Davis, S. M. (1997). The second Annual Annenberg Public Policy Center's conference on children and television: A summary. Philadelphia, PA: The Annenberg Public Policy Center.

Edley, N., & Wetherell, M. (1997). Jockeying for position: The construction of masculine identities. *Discourse & Society, 8*(2), 203-217.

Enck-Wanzer, S. M, & Murray, S. A. (2011). How to hook a hottie: Teenage boys, hegemonic masculinity, and CosmoGirl! magazine. In A. Wannamaker (Ed.), *Mediated boyhoods. Boys, teens, and young men in popular media and culture* (pp. 57-77). New York, NY: Peter Lang.

Frosh, S. (1994). *Sexual Difference, Masculinity and Psychoanalysis*. London, England: Routledge.

Frosh, S. (2000). Intimacy, gender and abuse: The construction of masculinities. In U. McCluskey & C. Hopper (Eds.), *Psychodynamic perspectives on abuse: The cost of fear*. London, England: Jessica Kingsley.

Frosh, S., Phoenix, A., & Pattman, R. (2002). *Young Masculinities*. Basingstoke, England: Palgrave.

Gauntlett, D. (2002). *Media, Gender and Identity. An Introduction*. London, England: Routledge.

Gesemann, G. (1943). *Heroische Lebensform* [Heroic way of life]. Berlin, Berlin: Wiking.

Götz, M. (2002). Typische Aneignungsmuster der Soap [Typical appropriate paradigm of a daily soap]. In M. Götz (Ed.), *Alles Seifenblasen? Die Bedeutung von Daily Soaps im Alltag von Kindern und Jugendlichen* [All soap bubbles? The importance of daily soaps in everyday life of children and adolescents] (pp. 251-301). München, Bavaria: KoPäd.

Götz, M. (2006). "Ich war ein Raptor, ein riesiger Dinosaurier..." – Die Fantasien von Jungen und ihre Medienspuren ["I was a raptor, a huge dinosaur..." – The fantasies of boys and their traces of media]. In M. Götz (Ed.), *Mit Pokémon in Harry Potters Welt: Medien in den Fantasien von Kindern* [With Pokémon in Harry Potter's world: Media in children's fantacies] (pp. 207-230). München, Bavaria: KoPäd.

Götz, M., Lemish, D., Aidman, A., & Moon, H. (2005). *Media and the Make-Believe Worlds of Children: When Harry Potter Meets Pokémon in Disneyland*. Mahwah, NJ: Erlbaum.

Götz, M. (Ed.). (in press). Die FernsehheldInnen der Mädchen und Jungen: Geschlechterspezifische Studien zum Kinderfernsehen [Television hero/ines of girls and boys: Gender specific study on children's television]. München, Bavaria: KoPäd.

Harris, I. (1995). *Messages Men Hear: Constructing Masculinities*. Bristol, PA: Taylor & Francis.

Held [Hero]. (1969). In *Brockhaus [Encyclopedia], Vol. 8*, 17th ed. (pp. 346-347). Wiesbaden, Hesse: F.A. Brockhaus.

Hinz, A. (2011). Jungen und Gesundheit/Risikoverhalten [Boys and health/risk behavior]. In M. Matzner & W. Tischner (Eds.), *Handbuch Jungen-Pädagogik* [Guide to boys-education] (pp. 232-244). Weinheim, Baden-Württemberg: Beltz.

Jukes, A. E. (1993). *Violence, Helplessness, Vulnerability and Male Sexuality*. London, England: Free Association Books.

Kimmel, M. (2008). *Guyland: The Perilous World Where Boys Become Men*. New York, NY: HarperCollins.

Levinson R. M. (1975). From Olive Oyl to Sweet Poly Purebread: Sex-role stereotypes and televised cartoons. *Journal of Popular Culture, 9*(3), 561-572.

Luther, C. A., & Legg, J. R. (2010). Gender differences in depictions of social and physical aggression in children's television cartoons in the US. *Journal of Children and Media, 4*(2), 191-205.

Mac an Ghaill, M. (1994). *The Making of Men*. Maidenhead, UK: Open University Press.

McDowell, L. (2003). Redundant masculinities? Employment change and white working class youth. Oxford, UK: Blackwell.

Millington, B., & Wilson, B. (2010). Context masculinities: Media consumption, physical education, and youth identities. *American Behavioral Scientist, 53*(11), 1669-1688.

Nayak, A., & Kehily, M. J. (2008). *Gender, Youth and Culture. Young Masculinities and Femininities*. Basingstoke, England: Palgrave Macmillan.

Neubauer, G., & Winter, R. (2001). *So geht Jungenarbeit. Geschlechtsbezogene Entwicklung von Jugendhilfe* [This is how to work with boys: Gender-sensitive devepoment of boy-help]. Berlin, Berlin: Stiftung SPI.

Neubauer, G., & Winter, R. (2002). Da kannst du mal sehen ... Jungen und Soaps. [Here you see... Boys and soaps.] In M. Götz (Ed.), *Alles Seifenblasen? Die Bedeutung von Daily Soaps im Alltag von Kindern und Jugendlichen* [All soap bubbles? The importance of daily soaps in everyday life of children and adolescents] (pp. 319-344). München, Bavaria: KoPäd.

Neubauer, G., & Winter, R. (2005). So viel Sex soll's sein. Jungen und „ihre" Fernseh-Erotik. [This is how much sex should be. Boys and "their" television eroticism]. *TelevIZIon, 18*(1), 27-34.

Neubauer, G., & Winter, R. (2006). Oben drüber oder unten durch. Figurenqualitäten für 9- bis 11-jährige Jungen. [Over the top or going down. Qualities of figures for 9 to 11 year old boys.]. *TelevIZIon, 19*(1), 31-36.

Neubauer, G., & Winter, R. (2008). Cool heroes or funny freaks. Why certain programmes and TV characters appeal to boys. *TelevIZIon, 21*, 30-35.

Neubauer, G., & Winter, R. (2009). Quality from a boys' perspective. How boys perceive boy characters in prize-winning programmes. *TelevIZIon, 22*, 32-36.

Pomerance, M., & Gateward, F. (Eds.). (2005). *Where the Boys Are: Cinemas of Masculinity and Youth*. Detroit, MI: Wayne State University Press.

Schlote, E. (2008). "Kim Possible. She can do anything". A conversation with Robert Schooley and Mark McCorkle. *TelevIZIon, 21*,16-17.

Segal, T. (1990). *Slow Motion. Changing Masculinities, Changing Men*. Piscataway, NJ: Rutgers University Press.

Seidler, V. J. (1989). *Rediscovering Masculinity: Reason, Language and Sexuality*. London, England: Routledge.

Seidler, V. J. (1994). *Unreasonable Men: Masculinity and Social Theory*. London, England: Routledge.

Serrato. P. (2011). From "Booger Breath" to "The Guy": Juni Cortez grows up in Robert Rodriguez's Spy Kids trilogy. In A. Wannamaker (Ed.), *Mediated boyhoods. Boys, teens, and young men in popular media and culture* (pp. 81-95). New York, NY: Peter Lang.

Smith, S., & Cook, C. (2008, January). *Gender stereotypes: An analysis of popular films and TV*. Paper presented at the Conference on Children and Gender in Film and Media, Los Angeles.

Stephens, J. (Ed.). (2002). *Ways of Being Male: Representing Masculinities in Children's Literature and Film*. New York, NY: Routlage.

Sternglanz, S. H., & Serbin, L. A. (1974). Sex role stereotyping in children's television programs. *Developmental Psychology, 10*(5), 710-715.

Streicher, L. H., & Bonney, N. L. (1974). Children talk about television. *Journal of Communication, 24*(3), 54-61.

Thompson, T., & Zerbinos, E. (1995). Gender roles in animated cartoons. Has the picture changed in 20 years? *Sex roles, 32*(9/10), 651-673.

Watts, R. B. (2011). The lost boys of Sudan: Race, ethnicity, and perpetual boyhood in documentary film and television news. In A. Wannamaker (Ed.), *Mediated boyhoods. Boys, teens, and young men in popular media and culture* (pp. 165-180). New York, NY: Peter Lang.

Willis, P. (1977). *Learning to Labour: How Working Class Kids Get Working Class Jobs.* Farnborough, England: Saxon House.

Winter, R. (2011). *Jungen: Eine Gebrauchsanweisung. Jungen verstehen und unterstützen* [Boys: An instuction for use. Understanding and supporting boys.]. München, Bavaria: Kopäd.

---

[1] Joint studies: Boys as fans of daily soaps (2000-2002); What boys and girls consider as sexy in TV (2003-2004); The TV-hero(in)es of girls and boys (2002-2004-2009); Boys' interpretation of what adults think is good for them (2007-2008)

[2] Except the Ugly Betty character Lisa Plenske

# 6

# HOW DIVERSE ARE SUPERHEROINES? ETHNICALLY DIVERSE GIRL CHARACTERS IN GLOBALIZED CHILDREN'S TV

## Elke Schlote

According to a quantitative analysis of children's TV in 24 countries, fictional children's TV programs worldwide feature mostly "White", "Caucasian" main characters (see Figure 6.1; Götz & Lemish, chapter 1).

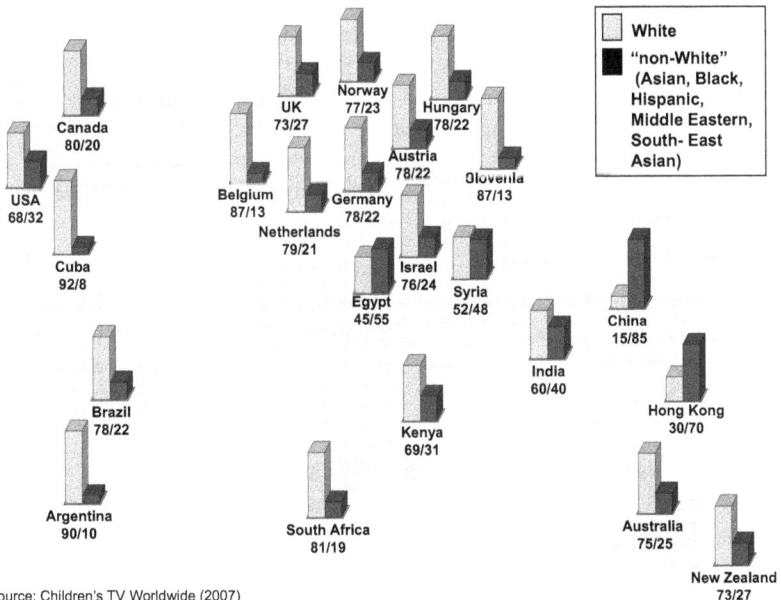

Source: Children's TV Worldwide (2007)

**Figure 6.1.**

Ethnic diversity in children's TV in 24 countries: skin color (in percent)

This finding is also true in parts of the world where people with fair complexion do not make up the majority of the population. Judging from the diversity in skin color of the protagonists, fictional TV programs are still not as diverse as the children watching them. This is because the majority of fictional children's TV programs in the countries participating in the study are imported mainly from North America.[1] Thus, there are few domestic productions in many countries tailored to the local situation and representing the nation's own ethnic diversity. Stated in a different way, children watching TV all over the world are likely to become familiar with the ethnic mix typical for the USA and Canada.

Recent media analyses show that children's TV in the United States does represent the ethnic diversity of this nation's different population groups (Akerman, Strauss, & Bryant, 2008; Götz et al., 2008). As far as external features go, representation in numbers is in proportion to social reality: According to the U.S. Census Bureau (2010), 36% of the population is "non-White". Götz and colleagues (2008) found that 32% of the main characters in U.S. children's TV were ethnically diverse. However, Akerman, Strauss, and Bryant (2008) analyzed 8,000 characters in U.S. children's programming and found 24% were "non-White": 14% Black, 5% Asian, and 5% Hispanic. The under-representation, by 12%, in comparison to reality (24% in children's TV programs versus 36% according to U.S. Census Bureau, 2010) can be explained by the low number of Hispanic protagonists in U.S. children's TV.

The aim of the investigation reported here was to determine if there is diversity in the appearance and characteristics of "ethnic" characters in the programs included in this larger international study. Fictional programs with global appeal that feature ethnically diverse main characters – most likely produced in North America or Europe – formed the basis for the qualitative media analysis whose results are reported here.

Analysis was limited to characters that appear in groups of the same gender. This research focus was selected for two reasons: First, groups potentially allow for greater diversity in members' external and internal characteristics; such as, skin tones, hair color, body features and talents. This tendency provides producers with the option of breaking with stereotypical depictions and, instead, to employ truly diverse portrayals of protagonists. Second, quantitative analyses found that girl characters are still a minority in children's TV (Baker & Raney, 2007) (see Götz & Lemish, chapter 1). Many groups in fictional programs in children's TV include a "token girl" character. When doing so, the producers continue to employ the stereotypical "girly girl" (see Prinsloo, chapter 3) who is either preoccupied with her external appearance and concerned about her attractiveness to boys or just the opposite – she is the strong, tough "tomboy" (see Götz, Neubauer, & Winter, chapter 5). However, it is the possibility that multiple character roles could be employed in one program or series as even pioneering representations that differ from the "standard fare" of the "girly girl" and "tomboy" character molds that led to advancing the in-depth qualitative analysis of fictional programs with ethnically diverse girls in groups presented here.[2]

Five programs from the corpus of the international study met these criteria: The animated series *Totally Spies!* (Marathon, France), *Bratz* (MGA Entertainment, USA), *Winx Club* (Rainbow S.p.A., Italy), *W.I.T.C.H.* (Saban International Paris, France), and *The Powerpuff Girls* (Cartoon Network Studio, USA) feature main girl characters with different skin tones and hair colors. Interestingly, these girl-only groups consist of "heroic" protagonists partly invested with superpowers.[3] These programs are also very successful brands in the global pre-teen market (e.g., Belloni & di Fiore, 2006; McAllister, 2007).

## *Previous Analyses*

A growing body of research maintains that representations of ethnic diversity are part of market-driven U.S. and global channels' strategies to cater to the wishes of diverse child audiences (Banet-Weiser, 2007; Lemish, 2010; Seiter & Mayer, 2004). Accordingly, the cast of characters in many shows is ethnically diverse. The inclusion of ethnically diverse individuals seems to be a cultural given in the new millennium. "Doing ethnicity" is performed as an individual characteristic of the protagonist and indicates a modern, "urban" style. Furthermore, what it means to be diverse is not an issue in the narrative, nor ever a problem in the shows that needs to be addressed and overcome (Banet-Weiser, 2007).

Analyses of commercials broadcast on different U.S. children's channels point to the use of the same typical characteristics associated with the Black, Asian, or Hispanic protagonists (Bramlet-Solomon & Roeder, 2008; Maher, Herbst, Childs, & Finn, 2008; Merskin, 2008). For example, athletic, singing and dancing abilities are emphasized in Black characters. More Black children in Nickelodeon commercials were shown playing basketball with friends or wearing sport jerseys than any other children (Bramlet-Solomon & Roeder, 2008). People in the U.S. associate American Asians with academic achievement, aptitude for business and electronic devices, bordering on the nerdy or left out (Zhang, 2010). This perception is reinforced by children's TV commercials: Asian American models are more often depicted using a computer or near a computer in a home or office background (Bramlet-Solomon & Roeder, 2008). Many more examples suggest that minorities are shown in lesser roles compared to Caucasian protagonists (Maher et al., 2008;

Merskin, 2008). For example, White children are dominant in relation to leadership; for example, when presenting attractive toys. This rendered Black and Hispanic protagonists comparatively less skilled and unimportant (Maher et al., 2008).

Another typical role of Black girls in popular culture is their depiction as wild and untamed, as in the case of the very commercially successful British pop group Spice Girls (Fuchs, 2002; Lemish, 2003). This all-girl group was formed in 1994 and then appropriated and publicized widely the term "Girl Power". The five group members assumed an easily recognizable role, expressed in their Spice names (Baby, Ginger, Posh, Scary and Sporty). They embodied typical models of female independence, strength and self-worth, thriving in a same-sex group.

> The one woman of color, Melanie B., is cast in the role of the "wild one": She is the one to break the rules, she is the one to expose large portions of her naked body, she is the one to wear animal skin, she is the one with the pierced tongue. The literature on the fascination of the White gaze with the Black body suggests that framing Melanie B. of all the Spices as the untamed wild creature cannot be dismissed as coincidental. (Lemish, 2003, p. 27)

This "arguably racist construction" (Fuchs, 2002, p. 348) of Mel B. as "Scary Spice" adds another dimension to images of young Black characters for teen audiences. In interviews with Israeli girls regarding their favorite pop group Spice Girls, Lemish (1998) found that Mel B.'s different skin color was downplayed. A 10-year-old girl said, "It doesn't matter [that she is Black]. The most important thing is that she is pretty" (Lemish, 1998, p. 162). On a deeper level, however, the strong focus on wild sensuality in her role resonated with the girls. Although all Spice Girls are constructed as sexually attractive and active, the interviewees only put Mel B. in a context with sexual assault and rape (Lemish, 2003) – the scary side of a sexuality that is constructed as dangerous, uncontrolled and "animal", and associated with being Black.

So far, few textual analyses of ethnicity in fictional series about girl groups have been undertaken. Most studies concentrate on selected TV series; for example *The Powerpuff Girls*, *W.I.T.C.H.* and *Bratz* (Baroody Corcoran, & Parker, 2004; Hains, 2007a; Valdivia, 2011). The critical readings presented claim that there are special roles or role expectations tied to the ethnicity of the protagonists.

> Close your eyes for a minute and just imagine that The Powerpuff Girls are black instead of white. What do you see? ... Instead of keeping the town of Townsville free of danger, they would be the danger – *baaad*-ass female gangstas on a crime spree in New Jill City. Unlike the negative portrayal of White, upper-middle-

class suburbanites as girls whose agency is presumably confined to shopping malls, Black girls do have real agency, not as a liberated choice but as a necessity for survival. Summoned as a strategy for successful resistance in a White man's world, it is not a characteristic that we would expect to be portrayed positively. (Baroody Corcoran, & Parker, 2004, p. 41)

In order to broaden this stereotypical black-white schema of protagonists, more and more "brown", mostly Latino/a, characters have been introduced recently into U.S. children's shows (Valdivia, 2011). These characters serve as a "bridge" by introducing "a subtle and ambiguous ethnicity that is palatable to the dominant culture while also appealing to ethnic audiences" (Valdivia, 2011, p. 94). The ambiguity in looks is a deliberate marketing strategy in, for example, the Bratz doll line that preceded the animated series and movie *Bratz*, as we see from the following statement by Isaac Larian, head of MGA Entertainment:

When we came out with these dolls, one of the things we did not want to do was just label them. Don't call them African-American. Don't call them Hispanic. Don't call them Middle Eastern. Don't call them White. Just convey difference. (Larian, quoted in Talbot, *The New Yorker*, 6 December 2006, p. 75)

The rule of thumb seems to be that if their background remains ethnically indeterminate, dolls in different shades of skin and hair color can be many things and hence they are marketable globally (McAllister, 2007). Thus, there are no references to specific cultures in their characterizations or actions. The focus is on bonding in the peer-group via shopping and enjoying popular culture, fashion, music and so forth. As a consequence, the Bratz universe is not about embracing multicultural difference. Rather, it seeks to create a unified look across ethnic borders (McAllister, 2007). The result is a "cartoonish hyperfemininity" (McAllister, 2007, p. 252) of big lips and eyes and a clothing style that earned the Bratz brand a negative notoriety as an example of the sexualization of girls, according to the American Psychological Association (APA, 2007).

Although the analysis of ethnic depictions was not the primary focus in a number of investigations, there are many studies on animated superhero series like *Kim Possible* (Disney, USA), *Sailor Moon* (Toei Animation, Japan), *The Powerpuff Girls*, *W.I.T.C.H.* or *Totally Spies!* that mark their strong girl protagonists as culturally valued (e.g., Baroody Corcoran, & Parker, 2004; Hains, 2007a; Lemish, 2010; Mazzarella & Pecora, 2007; Munford, 2007; Newsom, 2004).

In summary, based upon this body of research about girl protagonists in general, three critical aspects of these depictions stand out:

a. Girl protagonists may have extraordinary skills, but their looks still exhibit a narrow beauty ideal of a "girly girl" (Hains, 2007a) and/ or sexualized body shape (see Götz & Herche, chapter 2; Prinsloo, chapter 3).

b. Girl power protagonists act on values typically associated with femininity: helping, rescuing, healing others (e.g., Newsom, 2004), and often are instructed by men high in hierarchy (e.g., Professor Utonium and the Townsville mayor in *The Powerpuff Girls*, or middle-aged gentleman Jerry who assigns the Spies their missions in *Totally Spies!*). If girl protagonists are smarter and more skilled than those around them (like Kim Possible), they are characterized as extra nice to take off the edge (Hains, 2007b).

c. Enjoyment of all things girly with one's peers is channeled into being a good girl consumer who pursues beautification through consumption (e.g., Hains, 2007a; Lemish, 2003; McAllister, 2007).

Thus, the space of what it means to be a girl is broadened by the advent of the new generation of "girl power" performers like the Spice Girls and animated superheroines. At the same time, critical analyses show that the female protagonists' special powers and characteristics are harnessed to "feminine" appearances and prosocial achievements directed at others.

Focusing on the aspect of ethnic diversity in these groups, the goal of the study reported here is to add an important perspective on girl power narratives. These ethnic diverse representations of "super teens" in same-gender groups appeal to a global audience of diverse children who deserve to see themselves represented on the screen. This qualitative analysis investigates how diverse these characters really are, in looks, characteristics, and skills and discusses the findings from a perspective of quality in children's TV.

## Method

The "girl-group diversity corpus" was selected from the pool of children's TV programs collected for the international IZI study. Episodes from 5,932 fictional shows broadcast in 24 countries were coded by local research teams for, among other aspects, skin color and hair color of the main protagonists. A quantitative analysis of the data was undertaken using two main criteria: programs that had global appeal (i.e., they were broadcast in at least two countries at the time of the study) and they featured main protagonists with "diverse looks" (1.6% of all programs). Applying these criteria led to identification of episodes from 94 animated and live-action programs for six- to 13-year-olds, and from among those identified, five programs had girl-only groups, all from animated series.[4]

Qualitative analyses of episodes from each TV program were conducted in order to investigate how diversity is represented in the main characters.[5] The episodes were watched attentively with a focus on the outward appearance of the characters as well as on their behavior and interests. Broadcasters' websites in different countries were also consulted for pictures and characterizations of the main protagonists. Further information was obtained by consulting fan sites.

A report was compiled with all the information from the above-mentioned sources for each character. Thus, diversity could potentially appear in form of markers in three dimensions: external appearance (physiological dimension), inner life/character/interests (psychological dimension), and social context (i.e., the characters' family and friends). The reports were compared and the ethnic markers were clustered in order to determine if typical combinations of looks and characteristics occurred.

## Results

### White Characters Typically Outnumber Non-White Characters in the Girl Groups

Taking skin color and hair color as markers for – however ambiguous – ethnicity, then there are almost always more White characters (very fair-skinned with blonde, red or light brown hair) in the girl groups than characters with darker hair and skin combined. This finding includes *Totally Spies!* (group of three, White/non-White 2 to 1), *Winx Club* (group of six, 4 to 2) and *W.I.T.C.H.* (group of five, 3 to 2). Typically, there are only two shades of skin color – fair and dark. Only *Bratz* has an "ethnic" mix with four characters with four different skin tones. The majority of the group members in this series are not White.

Outward features of some of the characters do suggest possible ethnic association. For example, there is one girl with blonde hair and pink skin who is clearly Caucasian/White in all groups. A combination of fair skin and black hair points to an Asian background, such as, Hay Lin in W.I.T.C.H. who is distinctly characterized as of Chinese descent. However, most of the characters with dark skin have a relatively ambiguous look. Their ethnicity could be anything ranging from African, African-American, Middle Eastern or Hispanic. In the case of Bratz, for example, this seems to be what the creators intended. In The Powerpuff Girls, all three characters have the same pink skin and are differentiated only by hair and eye color – blonde, red and black.

## Most Characters' Ethnic Backgrounds Remain Ambiguous

The ethnic backgrounds of the protagonist are not specified in most shows. Jade from *Bratz*, for example, has green eyes, fair skin and jet-black hair. The *Bratz* website states her favorite food is Sushi, rendering her potentially Asian. But Sushi is not her favorite food because it is part of her culture or heritage, but "because it looks so cool on a plate!" (Jade, January 2012).

A singular counter-example is Hay Lin from *W.I.T.C.H.* Apart from her name and looks, there are quite a few markers that point to her Chinese descent: Her parents own a Chinese restaurant, her home is equipped with Chinese furniture and lamps, and her grandmother who has an important part in the storyline, wears traditional clothing and hairdo. This is a special case, as the parents and families of the girl heroes are seldom mentioned or shown in most of the series examined.

Thus, contributing to *look*-ambiguity, "non-White" characters can potentially represent different ethnicities. In most cases, their ethnic background is hinted at only in very few episodes or it is a presumed fantasy background, as is the case of *Winx Club* where the heroines are fairies from places such as Gardenia, Solaria, and Andros.

Another aspect in the characters' physiological dimension is that all girls in the group are given the same body size. With the exception of extremely tiny bodied Powerpuff Girls' girl characters have the same Barbie-like standardized body size with tiny waists, long legs and large, expressive eyes and follow a narrow Western beauty ideal (see Götz & Herche, chapter 1; Prinsloo, chapter 3; Spry, chapter 4). This is an extreme form in a series in which the girls are "transformed" to become heroines with superpowers. In *W.I.T.C.H.* and *Winx Club* the *look* of the heroine consists of a hypersexualized body shape dressed in scant clothes. While, on the one hand, this makes it appear that the different ethnic characters more equal on a superficial level, on the other hand, these depictions lack true diversity and promote unrealistic body images.

## There Is Typically Not Much Information about the Heroines' Social Context

The life of a teenage superheroine happens in one's clique as it battles evil in different universes (*W.I.T.C.H.*, *Winx Club*), in different places of the real world (*Totally Spies!*, *The Powerpuff Girls*) or from their favorite hangout (*Bratz*). Typical settings are high school, the shopping mall, or a resort. All the series include the shift from core family to peer group that takes place in the early teen years. This is why the girls' families are shown only as an exception, and there are few adults. This characteristic of the series supports the notion of ethnic ambiguity and furthers the perceived equality of the group members, as there is no information about the educational or economic backgrounds of the girls' families. A little more information can be found on the series' websites or fan wikis. For example, Taranee from *W.I.T.C.H.* has an Asian mother who is a judge and a Black father who works as a psychologist; this positions her firmly in the upper-Middle class (Taranee Cook, January 2012). Yet, her family association has no importance in most episodes. We see this relative lack of importance of family in inconsistencies in background stories: Alex's mother, Carmen, was first portrayed in the second season of *Totally Spies!* as Black (*Mommies Dearest* episode). Yet, in Season Four, she looked more like Alex, but somehow developed Asian (or Indian) features. Again, the Powerpuff Girls are exceptional among the programs investigated as they are not real girls with families but the result of a failed experiment.

### There Are Strikingly Typical Combinations of Traits Associated with Certain Looks across the Groups

Every girl in the group is created with character traits that make her special. These characteristics are reduced to a few exaggerated features and are mentioned frequently in the series in order to make them easy to notice during reception. Some of the features are traditionally feminine or "girly". They are acted out or mentioned by the protagonist herself or by a group member, as in the following example: Clover from *Totally Spies!* is frequently shown to be interested in nice clothes and to have crushes on boys. In talking about her in the first episode, Alex states, "Is it me or does Clover fall in love more often than Mandy maxes out her credit card?" Clover herself worries amidst an adventure to save civilization, "How am I going to try out the clothes for my date?" (*Shrinking* episode). Clover's characterization as a shopping addicted boy-crazy *fashionista* is a big part of almost every plot. It is what makes her unique and different from her group members, athletic Alex and rational Sam.

Some characters have not-so-traditional "girly" features. Aisha/Layla from *Winx Club* "is fearless, athletic and always looking for the next adventure" (Aisha, January 2012). In the series, she is shown acting according to this description. Aisha/Layla is introduced in the first episode of Season Two. She is a fairy with dark skin and long, wavy dark brown hair, as thin and hypersexualized as the other fairies. In a very dramatic plotline, she tries to save pixie babies from an evil lord all by herself. Exhausted, she arrives at the Winx fairies' school in Alfea. She is characterized as very headstrong by the headmistress, "My, what a wilful young lady"; and, the evil lord even calls her "stubborn" because she returns to his realm to complete the rescue mission, this time with her new friends (*The Shadow Phoenix* episode).

Interestingly, the skin color of the characters predicts whether a character is a "girly girl" or the "athletic girl": Clover is Caucasian-White blonde, while Aisha/ Layla has dark skin. This distinct pattern of how character traits and individual interests are distributed was found in all girl groups, despite the different group sizes, ranging from three main characters to a group of six. If the white-skinned, blonde protagonist of each group is compared to the main character with the darkest skin and hair color, the same combination of looks and characteristics appear across the groups. In each girl group, there is a fair-skinned, blond protagonist focused on her looks and shopping, who "has a thing" for boys and is overly dramatic about herself. Her dark-skinned, black-haired partner is always an athlete or hip hop dancer who is characterized as wild and courageous (see Figure 6.2).

| | Powerpuff Girls | Totally Spies! | Winx Club | W.I.T.C.H. | Bratz |
|---|---|---|---|---|---|
| B L O N D E | **Bubbles** <br> - "girly girl" <br> - babyish <br> - overemotional | **Clover** <br> - "girly girl" <br> - interested in boys <br> - fashion, shopping | **Stella** <br> - "girly girl" <br> - interested in boys <br> - fashion, shopping <br> - overemotional diva | **Cornelia** <br> - "girly girl" <br> - interested in boys <br> - fashion, shopping <br> - diva | **Cloe** <br> - "girly girl" <br> - interested in boys <br> - fashion, shopping <br> - overemotional diva |
| B L A C K | **Buttercup** <br> - athletic (strongest fighter) <br> - tough hothead <br> - "tomboy" | **Alex** <br> - athletic (soccer player) <br> - "tomboy" <br> - follower | **Layla/ Aisha** <br> - athletic (swimming) <br> - rebellious, wild <br> - feminine | **Taranee** <br> - athletic (dance, basketball) <br> - controls fire <br> - "tomboy"/ feminine | **Sasha** <br> - athletic (dance, choreography) <br> - attitude <br> - feminine <br> - leader |
| R E D | **Blossom** <br> - leader | **Sam** <br> - leader | **Bloom** <br> - leader | **Will** <br> - leader | |

**Figure 6.2.**
Girls' hair color and main characteristic traits in *The Powerpuff Girls, Totally Spies!, Winx Club, W.I.T.C.H.* and *Bratz*

The descriptions of blonde Clover match Stella's and Cornelia's characterizations, both of whom are also blonde and Caucasian. Their appearance is frequently mentioned in the series. Stella from *Winx Club* refers to her good looks quite often. For example, after an especially straining adventure in a cave, she says, "A little sunshine, and I am gorgeous again" (*Princess Améntia* episode). The German broadcaster's website comments on her obsession with her appearance:

> Stella is 17 years old and draws her energies from the sun and moon. She is very lively and kind and likes all things beautiful. She feels very confident about her own special beauty (sometimes a little bit too much) and it is extremely important to her that she always wears the latest fashion. ("Stella, nick.de", January 2012, translated from German)

However, this is not part of Stella's characterization in the U.S. ("Stella, nick.com", January 2012).

Cornelia's looks and interests are an issue when the girls talk about their upcoming fight against an evil snake: Cornelia, "I'm sorry, but I am far too pretty to end up as snake poo!". Further, in reference to the upcoming class picture day at high school, we learn that "Cornelia started shopping for it in kindergarten." Even during a rescue mission, team member Hay Lin asks the endangered male hero, "Do you have a girlfriend, because I think Cornelia likes you?" (*It resumes* episode).

For Cloe, the blonde character in *Bratz*, being fashionable is a given, because all the characters are interested in fashion and an urban lifestyle. She is depicted as being drawn to romance. For example, she is very excited when she reads in her horoscope: "I'm gonna meet a handsome prince who will carry me off on his horse". She is also very emotional, making a big thing out of everything that happens to her. For example, her group member, Sasha, looks in the horoscope and announces, "It also says you are a major drama queen" (*Pretty 'n' Punk* episode). However, Cloe has a practical side to her: On a camping trip she is able to distract a bear from attacking her friends with her honey and oatmeal facial mask she brought along (*Camping* episode). Thus, Cloe's preoccupation with her appearance is portrayed favorably as it happens to help in surviving in the wilderness.

Due to missing information about the specific ethnic and social backgrounds of the characters, the typical distribution in traits cannot be traced back to a specific ethnicity but is a matter of "Black" and "White"; a stereotypical Caucasian blonde girl versus a girl who is somehow, ambiguously Black. While there is a potentially greater diversity of roles for White characters, simply because there are more of them in the group, it is the blond girl who gets to be the extremely "girly girl" who is self-centered as well as obsessed with her appearance and how she comes across. The "other" Black girl is the one who has the part of the "strong" one, as she is physically fit and strong-willed (and sometimes hot-tempered). In *Totally Spies!* and

*W.I.T.C.H.*, she is depicted as "tomboy" with shorter hair than her friends. In *Winx Club* and *Bratz*, she is as feminine and sexualized as her peers.

However, in the context of superheroines, it is of little value to be strong and athletic – as all girls are slim, fit and capable of exerting their powers. Alex from *Totally Spies!* has short black hair and her skin tone is very tan. She is the most athletic of the group, but also the most clumsy and naive, breaking gadgets on their missions or letting the wrongdoers escape. Thus, she has aspects of a "tomboy", but is at the same time also interested in shopping and boys like Clover. She is the youngest of the group of three, and her role is best described as a "follower" to Sam and Clover.

Taranee from *W.I.T.C.H.* is exceptional in that she conforms to the stereotype only in her transformation. Taranee is the most heroic, wild and hot headed of the Guardians. She is in control of the fire element. Her outfit is deemed the most "athletic" of the group by her fans; "Taranee's Guardian uniform is the one that allows the most mobility out of the five, as most of her limbs are exposed for easy fighting." (Taranee Cook, January 2012). In her teen self, she is the opposite: fearful, shy, ambitious, and a good student (she is the only superheroine who wears glasses). However, she still is athletic, as playing basketball and dancing are her hobbies.

On the one hand, creating the Black character as "tomboy" sets a problematic example in the context of the "beautiful" feminine White characters. This could be easily mistaken as a statement on a "lesser" look in comparison. But making the "athletic" character as traditionally feminine produces its own contradictions. Aisha's/Layla's feminine appearance makes her more equal to the other beautiful fairies. However, her appearance never suffers during her missions. Commenting on the *Shadow Phoenix* episode on the Internet, a fan put her performance in relation to her looks: "No wonder she looks exhausted [sic.] from climbing that mountain, if I wore heels and climbed a mountain I would have probably fallen off [sic.]" ("Shadow Phoenix", January 2012).

The role of the group's leader is assigned to another White character, the one with red hair, in most of the series. This marginalizes girls with darker skin tones not only in number, but also in importance of role – except for *Bratz*. Here, Sasha takes the leader role in addition to being a dancer and choreographer with "attitude". The *Bratz* website characterizes her as "not afraid of confrontation, natural leader, street-smart" (Sasha, January 2012). In addition to being a dancer and choreographer, she is often seen taking the lead in putting together the girls' fashion and lifestyle magazine, keeping the schedule and calling her friends to order. Sometimes she oversteps and has to make up to her friends, "I apologize to everyone for my bad attitude ... my sizzlin' article yapping with the queen of cool scored big time. Another major scoop for *Bratz* magazine" (*Sasha's big interview* episode).

At first glance, Black protagonists seem to be more diverse in their looks and characteristics, compared to the standard blonde White "girly girl". However, different skin tones and shorter or longer hair cannot hide the fact that the "Black athletes" are marginalized in skills and importance of role in similar ways.

Another racial stereotype associated with Black characters is that they are constructed as wild or untamed, as is the case of Mel B. from the Spice Girls. Aspects of this are part of the characterization of the Black girls as especially "powerful fighters". *Winx Club*'s Aisha/Layla is outright characterized as restless, rebellious, and wild. "Athletic bookworm" Taranee gains her exceptional strength and courage not until her transformation to her Guardian role, but then she is the fiercest of the *W.I.T.C.H.* bunch and in control of fire. Although ranking behind her two Spies peers, Alex is the best fighter among the three. Sasha tries to keep her hot temper in check, and this makes her along with her claim to leadership a "control freak" in the eyes of her friends. However, from time to time her "attitude" results in emotional releases, causing conflict in the group.

Although the main protagonists in *The Powerpuff Girls* are differentiated only by hair color, Blossom, Bubbles and Buttercup fit the "red-head leader", "overemotional blonde" and "black-haired athlete/toughest fighter" character molds described above.

### Typically, Ethnic Diversity Is Not Part of the Plot

All groups share negotiations of their friendship and traditional girl-related issues in-between fights; such as, being self-conscious, caring for one's looks, or having trouble with boys. Thus, they are created in opposition to classical superheroes who act as loners and to classical groups of superheroes in which all actions and group-internal challenges are dedicated to winning a fight. The girl-only group serves as a space for mutual respect and mutual support, and equal value is placed on the member's different strengths they bring to the group, however typical and schematic they may be.

"Lesser" roles and attributions may well mirror what teenagers from ethnic minorities experience in their everyday lives. However, the above-mentioned attributions to Black and White girls are affirmed and not critically reflected by the protagonists in in-group discussions or in plot lines. There is one interesting exception: The Bratz girls fight against a world that is (literally) White and Pink, and dominated by an evil mother figure – Burdine Maxwell. Maxwell is the editor of a "teen magazine" who presents her world as the standard for teens. Accordingly, she chooses interns who conform to her ideas and advance her messages without questioning them. However, these standards require adjustments that are never possible for the Bratz girls because of their ethnicity. As a consequence, the Bratz girls start their own magazine. The originality and creativity that is needed for putting it together pays off, as the Bratz girls enjoy their project despite drawbacks and are frequently shown to outsmart Burdine and her crew with their ideas and sense of style. However, the Bratz model of self-efficacy is short-circuited to pop culture and consumerism. It suggests that it suffices to be "winning in style" against a hostile establishment, through participating in consuming the "right" commodities – which the Bratz brand readily puts on the market.

## Discussion

The qualitative analysis presented here focused on a new generation of superheroines who are making their way around the globe, in the form of animated series – *Totally Spies!*, *Bratz*, *Winx Club*, *W.I.T.C.H.* and *The Powerpuff Girls*. At the center of each program are ethnically diverse girls who band together with their friends to save the world, fight crime or battle against evil – be it in the form of alternative universes or the urban fashion business. Because of their strong, active female main characters, these series can be analysed in the context of girl power. The characters are designed to empower pre-teen girls, to model close-knit cliques, and give girls something to look forward to as they progress in their teen years. However, it is equally important to keep in mind that these "girl power" characters are part of intricate, highly effective marketing strategies, especially true for *Bratz* and the Disney universe.

It is a relatively recent phenomenon that the main characters in these group-programs feature diverse hair color and different skin tones. However, this qualitative media analysis found that the ethnic diversity of the supergirls is superficial. Characters are drawn with the stereotypical body size. Furthermore, these characters lack genuine diversity, since the same attributes are repeatedly linked with a certain stereotypical appearance. This is especially striking when comparing the "White" and "Black" characters of an ethnic diverse show: There is always a fair-skinned, blond protagonist who focuses on her looks and shopping, who is overly dramatic and may or may not be naive. Their dark-skinned/black-haired partner is of ambiguous ethnicity and always an athlete or dancer. In most cartoons, there is a White, red-head leader; except for *Bratz*, where this role is taken by the Black Sasha (who also happens to be a dancer).

Furthermore, ambiguously Black characters are the ones with lesser roles, as blonde and red-haired girls are always portrayed taking center-stage. This is because of their roles as "leader" and self-centered diva who receives all the attention through emotional outbursts. The special power of the ambiguously Black character is being a tough fighter and athlete. However such characteristics do not have high value in the context of superheroines, as every member is fit and strong in their fight against evil. Sometimes, the Black character is clearly in the role of a "follower" to the White girls, as in the case of *Totally Spies!* As a consequence, Black girls are marginalized in most groups, not only in number, but also in skills and importance of role. This conforms to findings in analyses of advertising in children's TV discussed above. It is important to note that in each series these characteristics are tied to individuals and not to a special cultural group, as the ethnic backgrounds of the protagonists are not specified. However, looking at the bigger picture across individual programs, the same characteristics are tied to the same outward features, reinforcing a racial stereotype.

This pop-cultural staple can be traced back to the very successfully marketed "girl power" band, the Spice Girls, who display different characteristics in their Spice names. *The Powerpuff Girls* main characters resemble the roles of three of the Spice Girls, blonde "Baby Spice", red-head leader "Ginger Spice", and dark-haired athletic "tomboy" "Sporty Spice". The new superheroines in *Totally Spies!*, *Winx Club*, *W.I.T.C.H.* and *Bratz* are combinations of the five Spice roles, including the two remaining Spice Girls, the fashion-conscious "Posh Spice" and Black "Scary Spice". Thus, the blond character is emotional and interested in her appearance (like "Baby" and "Posh Spice"), and the "Black character" is dark-skinned, wild and tough (like "Scary Spice") and athletic (like "Sporty Spice"). Looked at from a feminist perspective, these two character roles echo two trends in the girl power movement, the "girly", who puts value on certain aspects of traditional femininity, versus the self-empowering, strong "riot girl". But these femininities lose their progressive potential as subject positions for the diverse girls in the audience whenever they are tied to the same typical appearances.

Ethnic diversity is performed in the composition of the cast in every group of superheroines analyzed in this study. But the question remains: Is what it means to be diverse or to be part of an ethnic minority also part of the plot? In most of the series examined, the challenges faced by girl protagonists are tied to life-threatening fights of good versus evil. The girls have to stand together and fight against a variety of evil individuals holding power. This leaves space for individual interpretations, and could – among other things[6] – be viewed as referring to a personal experience of ethnic marginalization that needs to be opposed. The guidelines for action are provided by the protagonists, as they live up to the challenge and never stop fighting. However, the girls' agency is limited despite their superpowers, because they are positioned and have to react to challenges imposed on them. It is a model of apprenticeship that basically educates girl protagonists who are given privileges (their special powers) to function in their roles in the best possible ways.

In this regard, the series *Bratz* is different in two respects: First, the topic of ethnicity is part of the central conflict: The girl group acts and succeeds in a "pink and white world", as represented by their adult antagonist Burdine Maxwell who clings to her power to define standards. Second, challenges are picked by the girls themselves, for the most part, and acted upon with creativity and originality. Leaving aside the problematic body images of the characters and emphasis on consumerism, the concept driving this animated series is potentially empowering. But the pressing question of how to deal with experiences of marginalization in an unfair society is deflected towards joining in the consumption of the Bratz universe and acquiring symbolic power by buying Bratz products.

Questions concerning children's reception of these characters could not be addressed in this study, but are obviously very important in evaluating the quality of these representations. As an insight into this concern, we can cite one reception study undertaken with students on the perception of ethnicity in an animated series. Lu (2009) found that these viewers are prone to identify characters to be of their own racial group, at least in relatively ambiguous and stylized anime characters. Thus, it would be very interesting to investigate if and how girl viewers of different ethnic backgrounds see themselves in these depictions, and make meaning of the character roles and plot structures. While there is space for new representations of girls as superheroines in children's television, this media analysis indicates that there is still an absence of truly new roles and empowering stories for girls with different ethnicities.

## REFERENCES

Aisha. (2012, January). Retrieved January 11, 2012, from http://www.nick.com/shows/winx-club/characters/aisha.html

Akerman, A., Strauss, A., & Bryant, J. (2008). *About face: A story of gender and race in the kids' TV space.* A paper presented at the 94th Annual Convention of the National Communication Association, San Diego, CA. Retrieved March 11, 2010, from http://www.allacademic.com/meta/p258416_index.htm

APA – Task Force on the Sexualization of Girls. (2007). Report of the APA Task Force on the Sexualization of Girls. Washington, DC: American Psychological Association.

Baroody Corcoran, C., & Parker, J. A. (2004). The Powerpuff Girls: Fighting evil gender messages or postmodern paradox? In J. L. Chin (Ed.), Vol. 3, *The psychology of prejudice and discrimination* (pp. 27-60). Westport, CT: Praeger.

Baker, K., & Raney, A. A. (2007). Equally super?: Gender-role stereotyping of superheroes in children's animated programs. *Mass Communication & Society, 10*(1), 25-41.

Banet-Weiser, S. (2007). *Kids Rule! Nickelodeon and Consumer Citizenship*. Durham, NC: Duke University Press.

Belloni, A., & di Fiore, A. (2006). Genesis of W.I.T.C.H.: A global brand. *Harvard Business Review Italy, 1*, 10-17.

Bramlet-Solomon, S., & Roeder, Y. (2008). Looking at race in children's television: Analysis of Nickelodeon commercials. *Journal of Children and Media, 2*(1), 56-66.

Fuchs, C. (2002). Too much of something is bad enough: Success and excess in Spice world. In F. Gateward & M. Pomerance (Eds.), *Sugar, spice, and everything nice. Cinemas of girlhood* (pp. 343-359). Detroit, MI: Wayne State University Press.

Götz, M., Hofmann, O., Brosius, H.-B., Carter, C., Chan, K., Donald, S. H., ... Zhang, H. (2008). Gender in children's television worldwide: Results from a media analysis in 24 countries. *TelevIZIon, 21*, 4-9.

Hains, R. C. (2007a). "Pretty smart": Subversive intelligence in girl power cartoons. In S. A. Inness (Ed.), *Geek chic: Smart women in popular culture* (pp. 65-84). New York, NY: Palgrave McMillan.

Hains, R. C. (2007b). *Negotiating Girl Power: Girlhood on Screen and in Everyday Life*. Dissertation Temple University, Philadelhia, PA.

Jade. (2012, January). Retrieved January 11, 2012, from http://www.bratz.com/?section=bios

Lemish, D. (1998). Spice Girls' talk: A case study in the development of gendered identity. In S. A. Inness (Ed.), *Millennium girls: Today's girls and their cultures* (pp. 145-167). New York, NY: Rowman & Littlefield.

Lemish, D. (2003). Spice world. Constructing femininity the popular way. *Popular Music and Society, 26*(1), 17-29.

Lemish, D. (2010). *Screening Gender on Children's Television: The Views of Producers Around the World*. New York, NY: Routledge.

Lu, A. S. (2009). What race do they represent and does mine have anything to do with it? Perceived racial categories of anime characters. *Animation, 4*(2), 169-190.

Maher, J. K., Herbst, K. C., Childs, N. M., & Finn, S. (2008). Racial stereotypes in children's television commercials. *Journal of Advertising Research, 48*, 80-93.

Mazzarella, S. R., & Pecora, N. (2007). Revisiting girl's studies: Girls creating sites for connection and action. *Journal of Children and Media, 1*(2), 105-125.

McAllister, M. P. (2007). "Girls with a passion for fashion". The Bratz brand as integrated spectacular consumption. *Journal of Children and Media, 1*(3), 244-258.

Merskin, D. L. (2008). Race and gender representations in advertising in cable cartoon programming. *CLCWeb: Comparative Literature and Culture, 10*(2).

Munford, R. (2007). "Wake up and smell the lipgloss'": Gender, generation and the (a)politics of girl power. In S. Gillis, G. Howie, & R. Munford (Eds.), *Third-wave feminism. A critical exploration* (pp. 142-153). New York, NY: Palgrave Macmillan.

Newsom, V. A. (2004). Young females as super heroes: Superheroines in the animated Sailor Moon. *Femspec, 5*(2), 57-81.

Sasha. (2012, January). Retrieved January 11, 2012, from http://www.bratz.com/?section=bios

Seiter, E., & Mayer, V. (2004). Diversifying representation in children's TV. Nickelodeon's model: The history, politics, and economics of America's only TV channel for kids. In H. Hendershot (Ed.), *Nickelodeon nation* (pp. 120-133). New York, NY: New York University Press.

"Shadow Phoenix". (2012, January). Retrieved January 11, 2012, from http://www.youtube.com/all_comments?v=CCqE3qyQUlC

"Stella, nick.com". (2012, January). Retrieved January 11, 2012, from http://www.nick.com/shows/winx-club/characters/stella.html

"Stella, nick.de". (2012, January). Retrieved January 11, 2012, from http://www.nick.de/shows/601-winx-club

Talbot, M. (2006, December 6): Little hotties: Barbie's new rivals. *The New Yorker*, New York: Retrieved March 11, 2010, from http://www.newamerica.net/publications/articles/2006/little_hotties_4487

Taranee Cook. (2012, January). Retrieved January 11, 2012, from http://witch.wikia.com/wiki/Taranee_Cook

U.S. Census Bureau. (2010). State & country quickfacts. Available at http://quickfacts.census.gov/qfd/states/00000.html

Valdivia, A. N. (2011). This tween bridge over my Latina girl back: The U.S. mainstream negotiates ethnicity. In M. C. Kearney (Ed.), *Mediated girlhoods. New explorations of girls' media culture* (pp. 93-109). New York, NY: Peter Lang.

Zhang, Q. (2010). Asian Americans beyond the model minority stereotype: The nerdy and the left out. *Journal of International and Intercultural Communication, 3*(1), 20-37.

---

[1] Results of the international IZI study show that "the biggest export region of children's TV programs is North America with 60% of the worldwide production, followed by Europe with 27.9% and Asia with 9.3%" (Götz et al., 2008, p. 5).

[2] Because of the "token girl" character in many shows, there were only few global programs in the international children's TV sample that feature boy-only groups, and even less that have an ethnically diverse main cast (*B-Daman, What's with Andy?*).

[3] The groups' superpowers are very diverse. Only Blossom, Bubbles, and Buttercup from *The Powerpuff Girls* have "classical" superpowers like the comic book hero Superman. The *W.I.T.C.H.* guardians and *Winx Club* fairies are given magical powers over the elements. Sam, Clover and Alex from *Totally Spies!* have extraordinary fighting skills. Although their skills may be at least partly grounded in reality, they are never shown practicing them. Compared to the other groups, the Bratz girls' adventures in the international centers of the fashion and music business seem pretty normal. It will be argued below that their "superpowers" arise in connection to their ethnicities, because the central conflict they face is to stand up in a joyful and positive manner against the challenges of a world of White privilege.

[4] At the time of the international IZI study, *Totally Spies!* was broadcast in ten countries (Austria, Belgium, Brazil, Canada, Egypt, Germany, Hungary, Israel, The Netherlands,

Syria), *Winx Club* in ten countries (Austria, Brazil, Canada, Germany, India, Israel, The Netherlands, Norway, UK, USA), *The Powerpuff Girls* in nine countries (Brazil, Canada, Hong Kong, Hungary, Israel, India, Kenya, New Zealand, Slovenia), *Bratz* in four countries (Austria, Germany, Israel, The Netherlands), and *W.I.T.C.H.* in two countries (Australia and Hungary).

[5] *Totally Spies!*: Season 1, episodes 1-13; *Winx Club*: Season 1, episodes 1-6, and Season 2, episodes 1-7 (Aisha/Layla joins the team in the second Season); *W.I.T.C.H.*: Season 1, episodes 1-13; *Bratz*: Season 1, 13 episodes; *The Powerpuff Girls*: 6 episodes.

[6] As one reviewer remarked, the empowering girl protagonists could also be read as models for fighting patriarchy. The supergirls are firmly anchored in a system in which (White) men still hold positions of power. However, the Powerpuff Girls and the Spies fight evil under their supervision, the Bratz girls benefit from their privilege (e.g., the Bratz's male mentor Byron Powell). *W.I.T.C.H.* and *Winx Club* are more radical in that almost all powerful male adults are evil. The girls join forces with powerful older women against them, and co-operate with male protagonists of their age (who also act as love interests for the girls). Still, what does their hypersexualized appearance as heroines signify in this context? Do their long legs and short skirts additionally empower the protagonists (e.g., as an embodiment of beauty and self-determined sexuality to be enjoyed by the girls themselves), or are they manufactured for the male gaze, taking away from their autonomous supergirl power (see Prinsloo, chapter 3)?

# 7

# "WITHOUT A FAMILY[1]": REPRESENTATION OF FAMILIES IN CHILDREN'S TV AROUND THE WORLD

### Dafna Lemish

One of the main social trends characterizing late modernity is the transformation of the concept of family. Structured as two heterosexual parents raising their biological children, the nuclear, private family has been challenged by a variety of forms and structures: single parent families, divorced and second marriage families, uni-sex families, adaptive and foster families, multi-racial families, and the like. New bio-technologies are breaking the bond between the biological parent (the one who passes on the genes), the one conceiving and carrying of the pregnancy (e.g., surrogate mother) and the social parent (the person raising the child), allowing for new modes of parent-child relationships and family arrangements (Collins & Rodin, 1991).

One arena through which we learn about these changes is screen-representations of families. The media provide us with a host of images of diverse family forms and allow us to peek into their private and intimate lives. In doing so, we see, for example, how they handle the stresses often involved in raising children while maintaining the household; solve conflicts and negotiate agreements, survive hardships and crises. Through watching television programs and movies, we and our children compare ourselves to other families presented in dramas, comedies, newscasts and talk shows, advertising and reality shows. We also learn about the normative family by digressions from it, such as: new, non-conventional family structures and modes of behavior; those who experiment with more egalitarian parent-child relationships or those who breed domestic violence, sexual abuse, or infidelity. All of these representations provide us with clear messages regarding social expectations about what is permitted and prohibited, accepted and rejected, common and rare.

Since family images in the media are a construction, they are also capable of representing different structures and meaning in different places and times, and in a variety of contexts – political, cultural, social and economic. As a result, the analysis and discussion of family portrayals in the media can facilitate our understanding of the changes this institution is undergoing today. They also teach viewers to accept certain family models as "natural" and "taken for granted", others as "broken", "immoral" and dangerous to the stability of human society. At the same time, these images, as all images, are dynamic and ever-changing; and open to a multiplicity of interpretations, debate, opposition and resistance.

The theoretical departure point of this chapter assumes that all images are ground in ideological assumptions, beliefs and worldviews that exist in society. Applying critical analysis to them enables us to learn about the changing status of families in social reality, as well as the ways in which perceptions of the family are interwoven with dominate ideologies that preserve social inequalities. More specifically, the private sphere of family life remains a site of gender inequality quite resistant to social change, and thus is a central arena for ongoing feminist inquiry. Socialist-feminist theories regard the family in particular as a pact between capitalism and patriarchy:

> It made the market bearable for the male wage earning worker by placing the labor and sexuality of women at his service within the home. As the home became the sole focus of women's labor and creativity, women were socialized into accepting this role through the cult of domesticity, which raised being wife and mother to the level of a sacred duty. Children were placed at the heart of this family. In fact, children were given as the reason for its existence. (Kapur, 2004, p. 10)

Despite deep social and economic restructuring, changes in the responsibility for caring for the household as well as for raising children is still, mostly, in the hands of women, despite their growing presence in the public workforce in many societies.

### Family Representations in US Television

The images of families in programming viewed by children around the world is of particular importance, as it may serve a significant role in cultivating their perceptions of normative family life and convey messages to them about the roles and responsibilities adults assign to themselves as caregivers of children (Signorielli & Morgan, 2001).

Some of the main social trends in family structures in the real world have also found their way into television representations. For example, about 40% of screen-families in the US during the 1990s were composed of couples, in comparison to 70% in the 1950s, a significant decline. Similarly, the percentage of divorcees presented on American television jumped up from 3% in the 1970s to 15% in the 1990s (Robinson & Skill, 2001; Skill & Robinson, 1994). Another indication of this trend is the finding that, as fathers became more involved in the private sphere in the 1990s, the rate of women who were stay-at-home moms on television declined to 23% (Heintz-Knowles, 2001). Here, television can be claimed to be reacting to social changes in society as well as to the dynamics of the market and advertising pressures.

However, at the same time, many studies found that American television continues, for the most part, to present a conservative reality that tends to reinforce traditional family structures rather than encourage non-conventional ones. This is specifically the case in the analysis of children's programming, in contrast to family or adult programming. For example, a recent study found that there are significant gaps between family representations in children's programming and the reality of families in the Western world of the beginning of the third millennium (Callister, Robinson, & Clark, 2007). The traditional nuclear family arrangement of mother, father, and children was represented in 88% of the families (in comparison to 72% in the reality of the United States according to national census of 2004); single-parent families were represented in 12% of the cases (in comparison to 28% in that reality); and single mothers where presented in 10% of cases (in comparison to 23% in reality). Finally, 50% of the mothers in two-parent families on television were stay-at-home moms, while in reality only a quarter were the case.

In summary, television for children continues to glorify and perpetuate the traditional family order as the central and normative structure. Thus, presentation of alternative forms of families (like single parents or single-sex parents) is rare and deviant. This unrealistic representation of reality might be playing a role in the development of children who are living in quite diverse family constellations worldwide and not seeing themselves and their world reflected on the screens that play such a significant role in their socialization processes (Lemish, 2007). Since most of the television viewed by children around the world is imported, and over half of it originates in North America (see Götz & Lemish, chapter 1), these findings are relevant worldwide.

## The Study[2]

The purpose of this study was to provide a descriptive mapping of portrayals of families and adults in a sample of programs viewed by children around the world. In doing so, a family was operationalized as at least one adult and one child cohabiting on a permanent basis. Due to their central role as complementing family relationships in the lives of children in the programs studied, other adults who are not perceived as family members where studied as well. Two main research questions guided the research design and analysis of the data: How are families portrayed in children's TV around the world? How are adults portrayed in children's TV around the world?

In investigating both questions, we were most interested in three independent variables identified in the extant research literature that may be playing a role in determining the nature of those portrayals:

1. Gender differences in family life and adult world presented to children;
2. Differences in country of production (local versus imported programs);
3. Differences in the program's target audience (under school age versus school age children).

## Method

The sample of the programs included 431 randomly selected programs from broadcasts aired during spring 2007 in six English speaking countries included in the larger study: Australia, Canada, Kenya, New Zealand, South Africa, and the USA (UK was removed from the sample due to copy-right restrictions). In addition, Israel was added to the sample for reasons of convenience (author's language accessibility). The total hours of broadcasts analyzed was 144 hours of explicit children's television programming.

Each program was analyzed following a specially designed code book which included information about:

a. The program: name, genre, target audience, country of production, country of broadcast;
b. Significant adults (up to 3) who are not family members by gender, relationship to the child-characters, attitudes toward children, attitudes of children toward him/her;
c. Families (up to 2) by centrality of the family in the program, family structure; number of children; presence of grandparents and other family members; nature of family life; presence of physical and verbal violence; social-economical status of the family; family activities present; parental employment; division of labor in the household; presence of child-parent role-reversal (e.g., child taking care of parent).

Programs with dominate family life were subjected to a second stage of qualitative analysis that dealt with the major family-related themes presented.

The coding book was developed through several stages of piloting. At the final stage, approximately 15% of the coding was done by two trained graduate students (female and male) with a high degree of agreement (inter-coder reliability above 0.81 calculated by Cohen Kappa's was significant at $p<0.05$ level on most measures).

## Results: Images of Families in Children's Programming

The results of this analysis are presented in relation to selected central issues:

## 1. Family Structures and Activities

### Family Structure

The first major finding is that families are not very visible on children's television: 67% of the programs did not portray any family structures at all. It is particularly striking that only 25% of programs targeting pre-school children had families in them, in comparison to 42% of programs targeting school-age children. This finding seems counter-intuitive, as we might assume that the family is more central for the healthy development of younger children. Part of the explanation for this unexpected finding may be related to an associated finding: 85% of the dramatic programs for school-age children present families, in comparison to only 38% of animation programs for that age group. Since pre-school programming was almost entirely animated, this meant that there were lower rates of families being presented in them.

When present, family structures were quite conservative: Of the families presented in our sample, 47% were traditional two parent families, 22% presented only mothers, 19% presented only fathers, and only 2% made it explicit that it is a second marriage-type family. There were no occurrences of gay, foster or adaptive families in our sample.

Thus, the families portrayed were for the most part nuclear and centered around the immediate family. Only 3% of these families included both grandparents; 6% presented grandfathers and 8% grandmothers. Other family relatives appeared in only 8% of the families. Altogether, we can conclude that presentation of an extended family constellation was a rarity in most of programs for children.

A second striking finding was the fact that 85% of families portrayed in this sample were coded as living on a "good" socio-economic status (i.e., there were no visible or other signs of the absence of any material or unsatisfied needs in terms of housing, food, clothing, freedom to shop and travel, leisure culture, and the like). Additionally, 9% of the families were portrayed as clearly rich (i.e., they owned luxurious homes and vehicles and lived very luxurious lives); 2% as poor, and 4%

were coded as unknown. This clear misrepresentation of the living conditions of children around the world, including in the specific countries sampled, was also manifest in a variety of other findings. For example, 49% of the families had only one child; 36% had two children, and only 15% had three or more children. Thus, it can be concluded that there was a clear preference for middle and upper class lifestyle.

Not only was the family economic status idealized, but so was the nature of the family, too: 89% of the families were presented as positive in nature and around 99% had no evidence of physical or verbal violence involving adults and children (either directed towards children or directed from children towards adults). Very little information was conveyed about parental employment: It was completely unknown in 60% of the families; in 11% it was clear that a stay-at-home mother was present; there were two stay-at-home parents in 9%; and in 8% of the families it was clear that fathers were employed outside the home. Only 1% of programs presented mothers as clearly employed outside of the home, and only 3% of programs presented stay-at-home fathers. As noted above, these findings stand in sharp contrast to the realities of many children's lives.

The division of labor within the household was unknown in 81% of the families presented. When it was specified, it tended clearly to be traditional: 12% of families had a clear traditional gender-division; only 5% made a point of presenting an equal division of labor between mothers and fathers; and in only 2% of the families was there a clear role reversal with one parent taking the role traditionally associated with the other one (e.g., father washing dishes; mother mowing the lawn).

Interestingly, there were notable differences by country of origin. Note, that for several of the analyses we distinguished the US programming from the foreign-local ones and analyzed them separately. This was deemed to be necessary since what is coded as "local" for US constitutes *foreign* for the rest of the participating countries, and vice-versa. For example, there was a marginally significant difference ($\chi^2$ (1)=3.46, $p$=0.06) in the presence of mothers at home, according to the country of origin (excluding the US): There were more stay-at-home mothers in local productions (27%) in comparison to imported programs (12%). As we learned from the more general study, the latter originated mostly in North America and Europe. Similarly, there was a marginally significant difference ($\chi^2$ (1)=3.44, $p$=0.06) in the traditional division of labor according to the country of origin: Local productions tended to present the more traditional division of labor (32%) in comparison to imported programs (15%).

### Family Activities

What do families do together as families according to television programs that children view? As is evident in Figure 7.1, families mostly talk: 73% of their activities (multi-coding) included engagement in conversation of sorts (e.g., telling stories or talking about homework); and in 37% of their activities they were portrayed sitting around the table or engaging in food preparation.

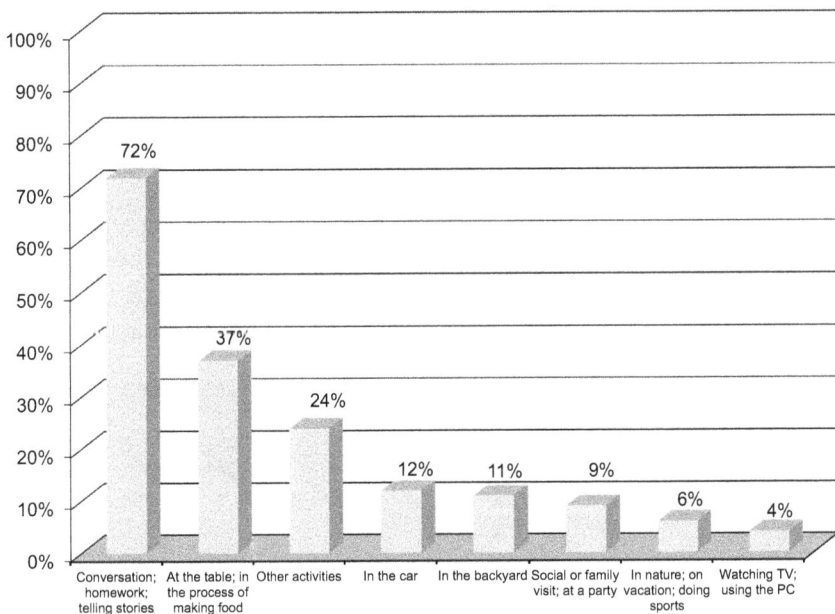

**Figure 7.1.**
Family activities

It is important to note that there were differences (only marginally significant statistically) in family activities according to the target audience of the programs. Figure 7.2 presents data that is quite in line with the reality of family life: Families with younger children spend more time in the backyard or talking and reading to their kids than those with older children, who tend to handle their interactions more around the family table.

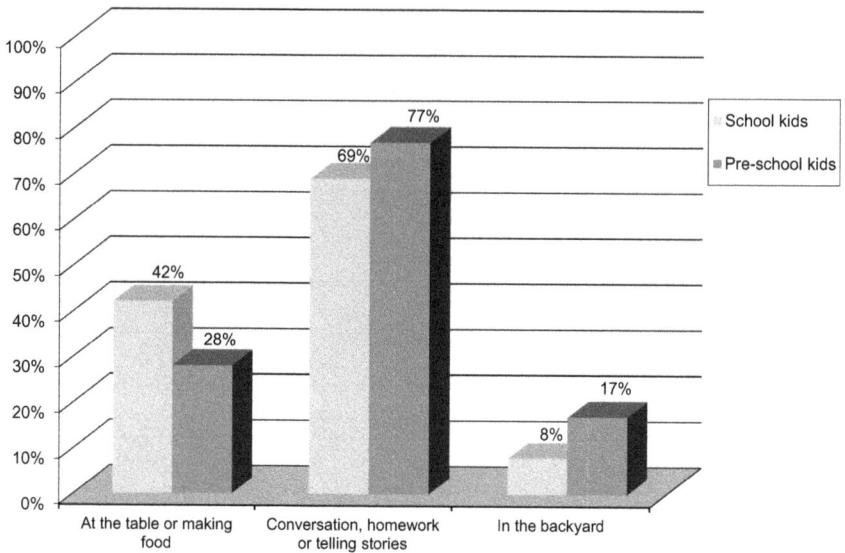

**Figure 7.2.**
Family activities by target audience

There were no significant differences between activities portrayed in programs produced locally or imported, except for marginally significant tendency toward more stay-at-home moms and a more traditional division of labor in the household and for women in the local productions.

In summary, the findings suggest that the way families are presented is consistent with the fact that there was an overriding domination of imported programs (77% in the entire sample of the larger study), mostly produced in North America and Europe (88% of programs in that sample). These are small nuclear families of middle-higher class lifestyle. There is little concern for employment or the challenges produced by competition and tensions created between managing work and home. The combination of the fact that the majority of children's television is animated (84% in the sample of the larger study and 77% in this study's sample) and that animation series present less family life than drama, contributes to the low rate of family presence altogether in children's television.

## Portrayal of Adults on Children's Television

In addition to families, we found that there were no adults present at all in children's lives in 34% of all programs. As presented in Figure 7.3, 39% of the adults present in the programs were general acquaintances of various kinds (e.g., family friends, neighbors, familiar professionals or service providers). There were as many adult enemies (18%) as educators (16%); the latter included teachers, counselors, educators, mentors, and coaches.

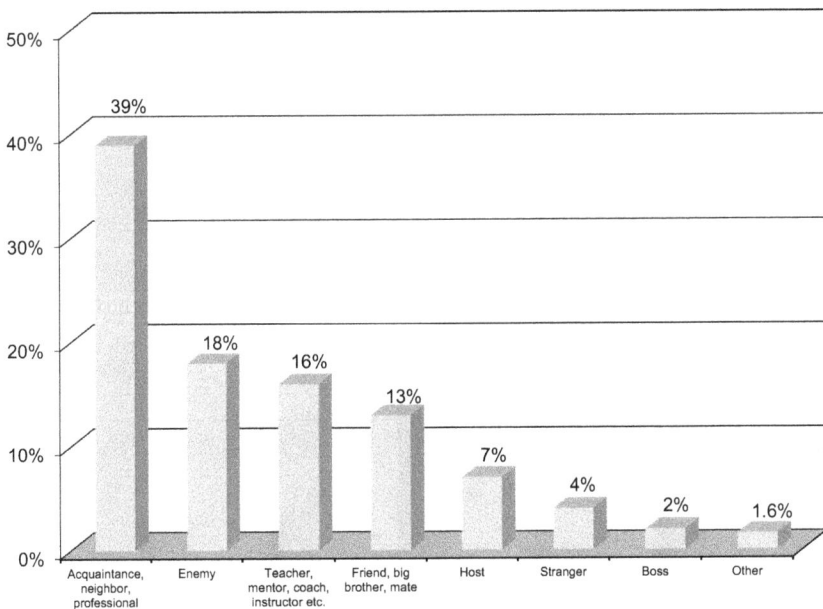

**Figure 7.3.**
Adult roles

## Gender Differences

The vast majority of the non-family related adults in children's lives were male (74%). This is more extreme than the 67% male population in our composed sample (family members as well as non-family members) as well as 68% of the general study sample. This suggests that the preference for male characters is even stronger outside of family based plots. Gender was found to be significantly associated with adult roles, in quite traditional ways. For example, as Figure 7.4 suggests, males appeared significantly more in enemy roles ($\chi^2$ (1)=14.45, $p$=0.001), while females appeared significantly more as educators ($\chi^2$ (1)=5.13, $p$=0.02), and hosts ($\chi^2$ (1)=10.06, $p$=0.02) of programs.

In a related finding, males exhibited significantly more negativism: 31% of males demonstrated negative attitudes and behaviors towards children in comparison to 15% of females ($\chi^2$ (1)=14.37, $p$=0.00). 28% of the children demonstrated negative attitudes and behaviors towards adult males, in comparison to 12% towards adult females ($\chi^2$ (1)=15.89, $p$=0.00). The same was found true for positive attitudes in both directions, with significantly (at $p$=0.00) more positive attitudes of women towards children and children towards women.

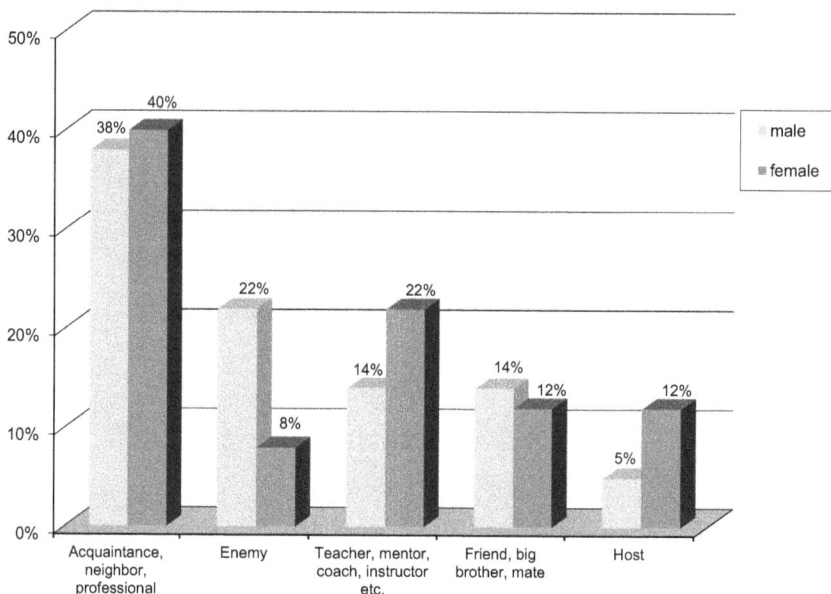

**Figure 7.4.**
Gender roles

## Target Audience Differences

The programs' target audience also played a role in character differences. As Figure 7.5 and Figure 7.6 suggest, these differences have two dimensions to them. First, negativism is a function of age: Significantly more negative attitudes and behaviors of both directions were exhibited in programs aimed at older children ($\chi^2$ (1)=44.64, $p$=0.00 towards kids; $\chi^2$ (1)=46.08, $p$=0.00 towards adults). Second, target audience effected the presentation of characters in the following ways: As expected, there were significantly more females in programs addressing young children ($\chi^2$ (1)=5.34, $p$=0.02); as well as significantly more friends and hosts in those programs ($\chi^2$ (1)=26.48, $p$=0.00 and $\chi^2$ (1)=13.81, $p$=0.00 respectively). At the same time, there were more enemy roles in programs addressing older children ($\chi^2$ (1)=28.56, $p$=0.00).

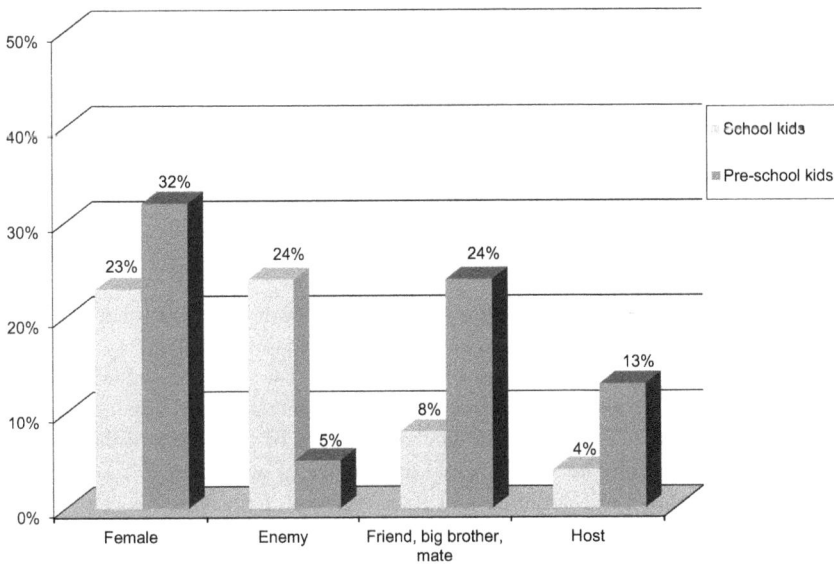

**Figure 7.5.**
Character roles by target audience

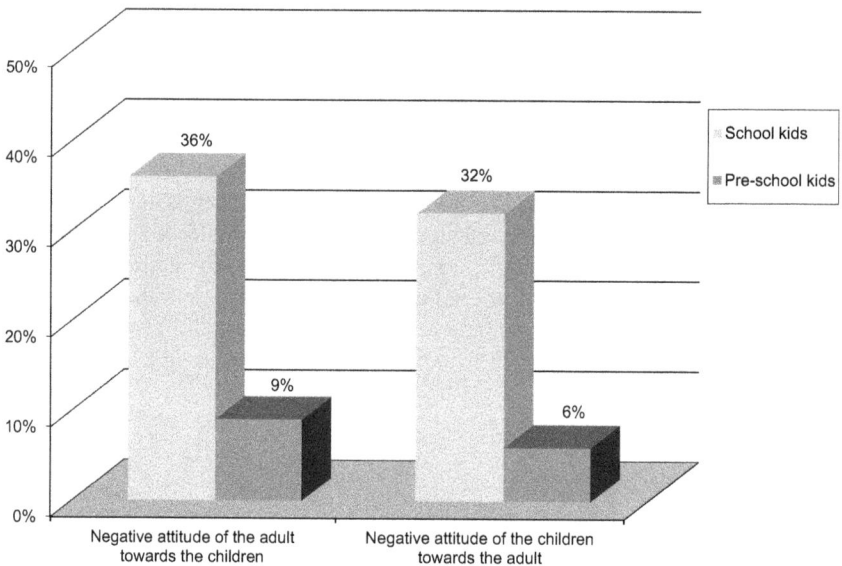

**Figure 7.6.**
Attitudes by target audience

## Country of Production Differences

Finally, Figure 7.7 presents two significant differences in character roles related to country of production: Many more characters assumed the role of enemy in foreign productions in comparison to local ones ($\chi^2$ (1)=21.84, $p=0.05$) and many more assumed the role of host in local productions in comparison to foreign ones ($\chi^2$ (1)=102.05, $p=0.01$). These findings can be explained by the nature of the genre of production: On the one hand, the heavy dominance of animation in the imported programming from Euro-America and Asia constitutes the vast majority of the "foreign" programming for the rest of the participating countries; and, on the other hand, there is a dominance of cheaper-to-produce, in-studio, host-style programs in the local fare of television for children. The high level of the presence of the enemy in the local-US column, suggests, for example, that American programming is a contributing factor in the presence of "enemy" roles in children's television.

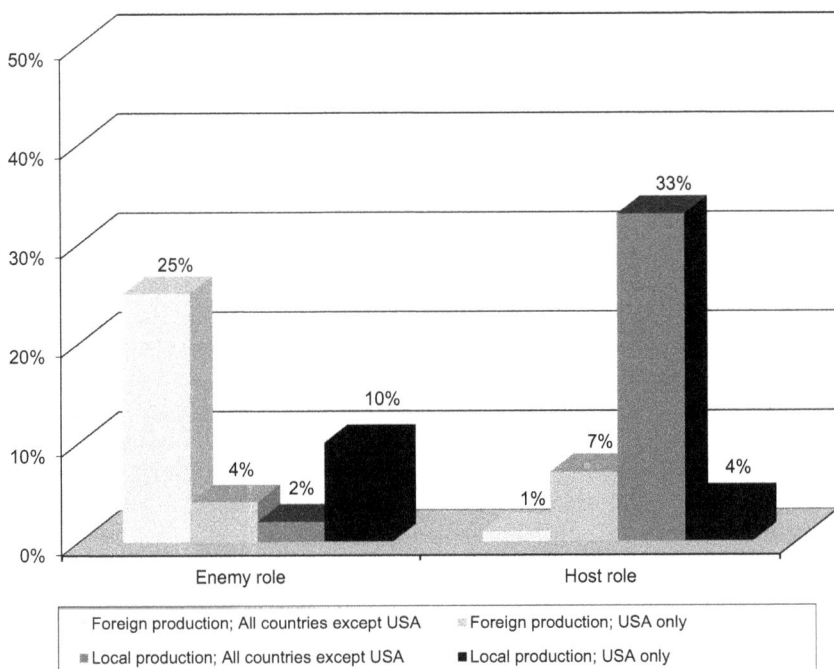

**Figure 7.7.**
Character roles by country of production

## Nature of Family Lives on Television for Children

According to the quantitative analysis, when families are, indeed, portrayed on television for children, they mostly appear in non-animated fiction; they are incidental to the story, and serve as a background feature of the narrative. Very little information is provided about the family, and the little that is there is conservative, positive, and non-violent.

However, an in-depth analysis of several prototype families in our sample enabled us to detect two types of families who are portrayed as playing a more central role in these programs. First is the "ideal" family appearing in animated pre-school series mostly based on early childhood books such as *The Berenstain Bears, Caillou* and *Arthur.* These series depict very supportive and loving two parent families in which children are treated with respect and warmth. Parents engage in educational activities with the children, and provide empowering experiences for their healthy emotional, physical and social development. The atmosphere in these programs is happy and optimistic, providing young viewers with a safe television viewing experience that may be concluded to be educational and beneficial.

*The Berenstain Bears* (Agogo Entertainment and Nelvana, Canada), for example, is a series based on books of the same title that depicts the life of a humanized nuclear family of bears living in their home in the woods. Family members are referred to by their family role – Papa, Mama, Brother, and Sister. The family is surrounded by a supportive and caring community of grandparents, friends, teachers, and neighbors. In an episode in our sample, family members collaborate in preparing a birthday surprise for Brother. Everyone is supportive and respectful of one another. The atmosphere at home, school, and on the school bus is peaceful, safe and friendly. Interactions between the characters are pleasant and warm. The home is neat and organized. Parents are in control of themselves, their children, and their surroundings. Everyone goes about their activities in a relaxed and happy manner. Life seems to be good in bear-country, and all small challenges are overcome with good will and well-thought intentions.

Another example in our sample, which is not book-based, is the animated American series *Jakers! The Adventures of Piggley Winks* (Parthenon Entertainment, UK). These programs relate the boyhood adventures of a pig from rural Ireland as he tells stories to his three grandchildren, as a grandfather in the present day. He is seen as a child, in flashbacks, playing with his friends and going to school. Most of the main characters are anthropomorphic animals, including Piggley and his family. In the episode from our sample, the child character is listened to carefully by the loving grandfather, who is respectful and happy to let him take his own seat on the "storytelling" armchair in order to share his experience with the rest of the attending family members. Language used is polite, loving and considerate, and the atmosphere is relaxed and supportive. The child appears to be empowered to feel secure and self-worthy by everyone present – grandfather, mother, and other siblings.

On the other hand, the rare instances of families in animations that target older children present far from ideal family situations. *Cramp Twins* (Loonland Animation, Hungary) is an illustration of such a case. The series deals with non-identical twin boys who live with their hygiene-obsessed mother and their westerns-obsessed father in the fictional town of Soap City. In the specific episode from our sample, a mean and aggressive baby-girl manipulates her incompetent parents to believe she is sweet and cute. The mother is easily led on, the father is entirely passive and voiceless, and the two twin boys who are the target of the baby's misbehaviors have no trust in their parents' abilities to resolve the unpleasant situation. The parents are unable to discipline or manage their children who get into various forms of mischief.

Another illustration of unpleasant portrayals of family life comes from a dramatic narrative – *Snobs* (Southern Star Group, Australia). This is a series on the friendship of a pre-teen girl from a wealthy middle-class family and a boy from a group of travelers, as well as several other peers – friends as well as bullies. The protagonist's mother goes to enormous lengths to try and stop her from befriending the boy, even threatening to send her to a boarding school. In the episode in our sample, the mother shows no respect for her daughter's wishes and independent thought, confronts and shames her in front of others, and is generally non-supportive of her. The daughter, on her part, takes independent action, disobeying her mother's instructions and manipulating the circumstances to her benefit.

These last two examples are illustrative of the criticism often raised against prime-time television; namely, inappropriate and dysfunctional models of family life styles are presented in which parents betray their responsibility of being positive and useful socializing agents (Comstock & Strzyzewski, 1990). Families in the 1990s, so the argument goes, were presented in a healthier manner: as united in emotional ties, engaged in functional communication styles, and capable of adjusting to a changing reality. This form of presentation has been declining gradually. There is a growing prevalence of televised families where children are undisciplined and behave in an uncontrolled manner, while the parents are either targets of ridicule or are absent all together, and thus not fulfilling their parental role (Douglas, 2001; Douglas, 2003). Fathers, in particular, are often presented as dysfunctional, childish and egocentric. Many mothers are not presented anymore as loving and protective characters, but as cynical, sarcastic women busy with their own lives (Reep & Dambrot, 1994; Scharrer, 2001). Many television families are presented as unstable, non-egalitarian in terms of gender as well as sibling relationships, and unsuccessful in appropriately socializing their children (Olsen & Douglas, 1997). More specifically, relationships between siblings have been found in one study to be non-positive in 40% of the cases: Television narratives did not present models of siblings who contribute significantly to the development of personal identity, support and mutual loyalty, and who help in dealing with parents – roles that the literature on the role of siblings in the family suggests are crucial for healthy development (Larson, 2001).

However, in contrast to these similarities between our study and studies of prime-time commercial television, we also found a major difference: While the frequency of representations of families in which behavior is blunt, vulgar, violent or sexual has been on the rise in prime-time television (Bryant, Braynt, Aust, & Venugopalan, 2001), such behaviors were completely absent in our sample of children's television.

## Summary

Based on this sample and the extant literature, we can conclude that children's television is not providing a realistic portrayal of family life as it tends to convey a quite conservative view of the two parents, nuclear, middle-class home, with mostly traditional gender roles. In doing so, programming for children continues to perpetuate a limited range of acceptable possibilities and does not serve children's needs to prepare for very diverse and complicated forms of family life, and by extension the realities of social life. The lack of variety and realistic portrayal of current social changes in family structure also denies children who live in non-traditional family constellations important resources of knowledge and experiences about lifestyles similar to their own. As was found in research dealing with other social issues, this may contribute to children and parents living in non-conventional family structures to perceive themselves as marginalized "others." Positive representations of alternative, loving family structures that provide a healthy environment for children would be an important step in changing this situation (Clark & Kitzinger, 2004).

Another major finding of the study is the relatively low presence of families in programming for children altogether. This absence has been framed as the "Home Alone" argument (following the hit-movie by this name) according to which children are now presented in popular culture as independent people (Kapur, 2004). According to this thesis, the construction of "childhood" is undergoing a major re-conceptualization as a result of the general profit-driven market and the commercialization of culture, as well as major technological changes. Children are perceived as independent consumers (rather than future citizens) and as the leaders of the technological revolution. The new technologies in particular have changed, drastically, the public-private division on which the family is based and contributed to the erosion of the authority of parents. Parents are portrayed as superfluous in this world: Children manipulate them and the entire adult world more generally. They overcome difficulties on their own and sustain themselves economically and socially. Indeed, in many of the programs in our sample, children are situated in the world on their own, fighting evil forces, going on adventures, getting in and out of trouble, fighting among themselves, and so forth – in a world that has no role for adults. While the need for independence and experimentation is clearly part of a healthy process of growing up, the absence of the stability of a family seems to be driven by more than succumbing to the naïve fantasies of children to be left "home alone." Following Kapur, we may argue that children's television is responding to and helping reinforce the reinvention of childhood, and as such, it is following in the footsteps of Hollywood productions.

At the same time, it is important to emphasize that programming for children is not uniform and there is a great variety in the way different television genres and programs within them present families in general (Chambers, 2001) and in our study more specifically, as the examples above demonstrate. We found differences between programs targeted at younger children in comparison to older ones, and in programs produced in different parts of the world. At the risk of over-generalizing, it is possible to summarize that programs for younger children and those produced locally outside North America are more conservative in terms of family structures and gender division of labor, yet they also portray family life in a much more positive light. A future study that examines a more representative sample of children's programming in a variety of societies and in all languages would provide a much more comprehensive and accurate picture of the validity of these findings and their implications for children watching television around the world.

## REFERENCES

Bryant, J., Braynt, J. A., Aust, C. F., & Venugoopalan, G. (2001). How psychologically healthy are America's prime-time television families? In J. A. Bryant & J. Bryant (Eds.), *Television and the American family* (2nd ed., pp. 247-269). Mahwah, NJ: Erlbaum.

Callister, M. A., Robinson, T., & Clark, B. R. (2007). Media portrayals of the family in children's television programming during the 2005-2006 season in the US. *Journal of Children and Media, 1*(2), 142-161.

Chambers, D. (2001). *Representing the Family*. Newbury, CA: Sage.

Clark, V., & Kitzinger, C. (2004). Lesbian and gay parents on talk shows: Resistance or Collusion in Heterosexism? *Qualitative Research Psychology, 1,* 195-217.

Collins, A., & Rodin, J. (1991). The new reproductive technologies: What have we learned? In J. Rodin & A. Collins (Eds.), *Women and new reproductive technologies: Medical, psychological, legal, and ethical dilemmas* (pp.153-161). Mahwah, NJ: Erlbaum.

Comstock, J., & Strzyzewski, K. (1990). Interpersonal interaction on television: Family conflict and jealousy on primetime. *Journal of Broadcasting & Electronic Media, 34* (3), 263-283.

Douglas, W. (2001). Subversion of the American television family. In J. Bryant & J. A. Bryant (Eds.), *Television and the American family* (2nd ed., pp. 229-246). Mahwah, NJ: Erlbaum.

Douglas, W. (2003). *Television Families. Is Something Wrong in Suburbia?* Mahwah, NJ: Erlbaum.

Heintz-Knowles, K. E. (2001). Balancing acts: Work-family issues on prime-time TV. In J. Bryant & J. A. Bryant (Eds.), *Television and the American family* (2nd ed., pp. 177-205). Mahwah, NJ: Erlbaum.

Kapur, J. (2004). *Coining, for Capital: Movies, Marketing, and the Transformation of Childhood.* New Brunswick, NJ: Rutgers University Press.

Larson, M. S. (2001). Sibling interaction in situation comedies over the years. In J. Bryant & J. A. Bryant (Eds.), *Television and the American family* (2nd ed., pp. 163-176). Mahwah, NJ: Erlbaum.

Lemish, D. (2007). *Children and Television: A Global Perspective.* Oxford: Blackwell.

Olsen, B. M., & Douglas, W. (1997). The family on T.V.: Evaluation of gender roles in situation comedy. *Sex Roles, 36,* 5-6, 409-427.

Reep, D., & Dambrot, F. H. (1994). TV parents: fathers (and now mother's) know best. *Journal of Popular Culture, 28*(2), 13-23.

Robinson, J. D., & Skill, T. (2001). Five decades of families on television: From the 1950s through the 1990s. In J. Bryant & J. A. Bryant (Eds.), *Television and the American family* (2nd ed., pp. 139-162). Mahwah, NJ: Erlbaum.

Scharrer, E. (2001). From wise to foolish: The portrayal of the sitcom father, 1950s-1990s. *Journal of Broadcasting & Electronic Media, 45*(1), 23-40.

Signorielli, N., & Morgan, M. (2001).Television and the family: The cultivation perspective. In J. Bryant & J. A. Bryant (Eds.), *Television and the American family* (2nd ed., pp. 333-351). Mahwah, NJ: Erlbaum.

Skill, T., & Robinson, J. D. (1994). Four decades of families on television: A demographic profile, 1950-1989. *Journal of Broadcasting & Electronic Media, 38,* 449-465.

---

[1] *Without a Family: "Sans Famille"* [Eng. *Nobody's Boy*] is a famous children's book written in 1878 by French author Hector Malot.

[2] I like to thank Rotem Alony of Tel Aviv University for her assistance in the coding, statistical analysis, and graphic presentation of findings.

# 8

# CONSUMERISM AND GENDER IN CHILDREN'S TELEVISION

## Kara Chan

A school bus carries a class of enthusiastic elementary school students to a nearby town. Mikan, a ten-year old girl growing up in rural Japan is making her first trip to an urban shopping venue. She finds the modern shopping mall amazing and incredible. She surveys all the cool stuff at the shops and exclaims, "Everything here just looks like so much fun!" Entitled *So Happy – Alice Academy in a Nearby Town*, this episode of a Japanese animated drama describes the shopping mall as a heaven where people can encounter all sorts of products that claim to make them happy.

This is just one of many scenes in children's television programs that communicate consumption values such as "possessions will make you happy".

Television is a major socializing agent in children's lives and often competes with other traditional socializing agents such as the family, school, peer groups, community, and religious institutions (Lemish, 2007). A popular view of socialization is that it enables children to fit into the society in which they live through learning socially appropriate behaviors. Through socialization, a child learns about the value system considered appropriate in his or her culture, and adopts the appropriate perceptions of the self and others (Lemish, 2007).

Television is an important socializing agent for children because, though they may not be aware of it, children rely heavily on the mass media to teach them about their environment and its social norms. For instance, young people's perceptions of social relationships are influenced by consumption images. A study asked children and adolescents to choose the pictures from a pool of typical advertising visuals that best depicted "the couple most in love", the most romantic scene, and the most romantic dinner. The findings indicated that romance was framed in consumer terms. While eating in a restaurant before going out for movie was considered as a typical date, eating in a high class restaurant and purchasing luxury goods were considered to be more romantic (Bachen & Illouz, 1996). Young consumers also express their interest in adult products. Teenage girls were keen to try out cosmetic surgery to enhance their eyes, lips, chins or ears in order to look like the women on television (Quart, 2003). Since the media feed the audience, constantly, with images of both sexes and messages about the consumption experience of men and women, it is very likely that these images impact the consumption values of the audience (Gauntlett, 2008).

The current study was conducted to investigate how consumption and consumption values are portrayed in children's television programs. The research project had the following objectives: First, to identify the types of products and services portrayed in children's television programs; second, to examine the gender differences, if any, of products and services portrayed in children's television programs; and, third, to examine how consumption is represented in the storytelling in children's television programs.

## Content Analysis

The research corpus consisted of 135.5 hours of children's television programming from Australia, Hong Kong, Kenya, New Zealand, South Africa and the United States of America taped in May and June 2007. These programs were part of a larger research project that investigated gender portrayals in children's television programs in 24 countries (see Götz & Lemish, chapter 1). Altogether, 123 of the hours recorded were English-language programs. The remaining 12.5 hours were children's programs in Cantonese (a Chinese dialect) broadcast in Hong Kong. Both quantitative and qualitative methods were applied in analyzing the sample.

The quantitative content analysis examined the consumption activities portrayed in this corpus of children's programs. Only dramatic content was included; that is, commercials and program trailers were excluded. The unit of analysis was each instance of consumption portrayed explicitly in the program. An instance of explicit consumption was defined to be a character in the program involved in purchasing, selling or consuming a consumer product (e.g., buying a package of candy) or a consumer service (e.g., riding a bus or visiting a theme park).

Consumption is embedded in many aspects of human activity. Therefore, often it is difficult to identify an instance of consumption. For example, all human characters in this sample of television programs are clothed. So, clothes are consumed. However, these activities were not coded as instances of consumption in the current study because of its implicit nature. The content analysis only covers those activities when consumption of goods and services is in the story's foreground. So, playing with friends in the garden is not considered as a consumption activity, but playing with a toy is considered to be a consumption activity. Activities that are usually free of charge were not coded as consumption activities. Industrial or business consumption (e.g., buying a computer for a company) were excluded in the current study.

Each consumption activity in the television program identified was coded per product category, age and sex profile of the product user, consumption context, presence of peers or family members, types of reward, and the appearance of brand name. The coding frame was based on a previous study of a Chinese cartoon program for children (Xia, Chan, & Chan, 2004). This study focused solely on the product category and users' gender profile.

The sample was coded by a research assistant recruited for the study. The author re-coded, independently, 25.25 hours of the programming (19% of the sample). The inter-coder reliability for each variable was quantified in terms of the percentage of agreement between these two judges. Discrepancies in coding were resolved through discussion and negotiation. The 0.85 minimum acceptable level of agreement suggested by Kassarjian (1977) was employed. Inter-coder reliability for all of the variables was in the range 0.85 to 0.89.

The six television programs with the highest number of consumption activities were analyzed further using qualitative methods. The aim of the qualitative content analysis was to examine how boys and girls are portrayed in various consumption activities. We also examined how consumption values are integrated in different types of children's television programs. Marshall and Rossman's (1999) method of comparative analysis was used to identify the dominant themes embedded in the text. This analysis involved constantly comparing and contrasting of statements (Strauss, 1987).

## Results

### Quantitative Content Analysis

Altogether 521 instances of consumption were portrayed in the 135.5 hours of children's programming studied. On average, there were 3.8 instances of consumption featured in each hour of children's programming (excluding advertising). The programs shown in the United States had the highest frequency, namely, 5.1 consumption activities per hour. The frequency was lowest in the programs from Kenya (2.7 consumption activities per hour).

Altogether there were 154 different television programs in the sample (two or more episodes of the same program were classified as one program). Consumption activities were unevenly distributed among the programs. Two-thirds of the programs portrayed one to three instances of consumption. These programs accounted for 34% of the consumption instances. The remaining one third of the programs (those with at least four instances of consumption) contained 66% of the consumption activities. *Alice Academy* (Group TAC, Aniplex, Japan), a Japanese cartoon program broadcast in Hong Kong, portrayed 22 instances of consumption.

Table 8.1 summarizes the characteristics of the 521 consumption activities. Consuming food and/or beverages was the activity most commonly featured. It contributed more than one third of the total activities. Other activities presented frequently were playing with toys (14%), entertainment consumption (9%), visiting retail shops (8%), and using household or personal goods (7%). These top four categories accounted for 61% of all consumption activities.

Food and beverages are probably the first product categories that children come to know about, as this product category fulfills their basic needs. Toys, as the second most frequently featured product category, indicated the importance of having fun in children's lives. Toys are often featured in pre-school educational programs as teaching and learning aids. For example, toy train cars were used to teach color patterns. As a train with alternating blue and yellow cars was presented, children were asked the color of the car that should go next.

Among the 521 consumption activities, 359 featured human characters as product users. Table 8.2 summarizes the types of product category of these 191 consumption activities by sex of the product users. Among the 359 consumption activities featuring human characters, a majority portrayed males and females consuming the product or the service together. Another 191 consumption activities featured males only or females only as product users. Chi-square statistical test indicated that males and females were portrayed differently in the types of product category they used ($\chi^2$=26.4, df=13, p=0.02). Males were more likely to consume food and beverages, computers, transport services, as well as personal services in the television programs than females. Females were more likely to consume clothing and toys in the television programs than males. None of the consumption activities only featured girls consuming computers or computer accessories.

**Table 8.1.**
Characteristics of the consumption activities (n=521)

| Characteristics | Frequency | % |
|---|---|---|
| *Product category* | | |
| Food and beverages | 155 | 30 |
| Toys | 72 | 14 |
| Entertainment (e.g. theme park) | 48 | 9 |
| Retail shops | 44 | 8 |
| Household and personal goods | 38 | 7 |
| Personal services (e.g. tuition, medication) | 37 | 7 |
| Traveling/airlines/transport | 34 | 7 |
| Media and media related products (e.g. watching movies) | 34 | 7 |
| Clothing | 31 | 6 |
| Computers and accessories | 10 | 2 |
| Telecommunications services | 8 | 2 |
| Animals or plants | 4 | 1 |
| Automobiles and fuel | 2 | 0 |
| Others | 4 | 1 |
| **Total** | 521 | 101* |
| *Sex of product users (for human characters)* | | |
| Males and females | 163 | 46 |
| Females only | 102 | 28 |
| Males only | 89 | 25 |
| Unidentified | 5 | 1 |
| **Total** | 359 | 100 |

* does not add up to 100% due to rounding

Table 8.2.

Product category by sex of product users (males only and females only)

| Product category | Males only (n=89) % | Females only (n=102) % |
|---|---|---|
| Food and beverages | 35 | 23 |
| Toys | 6 | 12 |
| Entertainment (e.g., theme park) | 7 | 7 |
| Retail shops | 5 | 9 |
| Household and personal goods | 6 | 7 |
| Personal services (e.g., tuition, medication) | 16 | 9 |
| Traveling/airlines/transport | 7 | 4 |
| Clothing | 3 | 18 |
| Media and media related products (e.g., watching movies) | 8 | 5 |
| Computers and accessories | 5 | 0 |
| Telecommunications services | 1 | 4 |
| Animals or plants | 2 | 2 |
| Automobiles and fuel | 1 | 0 |
| Others | 1 | 2 |
| **Total** | 103* | 102* |

* does not add up to 100% due to rounding

The types of product categories consumed by males and females showed a statistically significant difference. Girls and women were more likely to be portrayed as product users of clothes than boys and men. Boys and men were likely to be portrayed as product users of computers and accessories, as well as media products. The television programs sampled often featured females as users of clothing and accessories who bought these goods to enhance physical beauty. This finding supports the feminist criticism that women are portrayed as an object and consumable items are employed in a manner that adds to their desirability by association with the right set of products and lifestyles (Wilska, 2005). The absence of females as users of computers and accessories seems to undermine girls' interest and competence in use and purchase of technical products. This finding supports previous observations that consumption styles of young boys are characterized by an emphasis on technology and leisure time paraphernalia (Wilska, 2005). The gender difference in user profiles reported in this study is consistent with the finding from a study of store visits of urban Chinese children: Girls were more likely than boys to have visited clothing stores in the past month, and boys were more likely than girls to have visited computer stores and cybercafés in the past month (Chan, 2005).

## Qualitative Content Analysis

Six television programs in the sample portrayed 12 or more instances of consumption; namely, *Alice Academy, Max and Ruby* (Nelvana & Co, Canada), *Sesame Street* (Sesame Workshop, USA), *Cinderella* (Tatsunoko, Japan), *Hannah Montana* (Disney, USA), and *Blue's Clue* (Nick Jr., USA). The first three programs featured 22, 15 and 13 consumption activities, respectively. The next three programs each featured 12 consumption activities. This section contains story outlines and descriptions of how consumption values were portrayed in the programs.

*Alice Academy* is a Japanese cartoon series dubbed into Cantonese and broadcast in our sample in Hong Kong. The target audience is elementary school age children. Each episode of the program lasts about 28 minutes. Mikan is the protagonist of the story. She is a cute, energetic, and good-natured ten-year old with a magical power called Alice Power. She studies in the Alice Academy. The previously mentioned episode opens with narration explaining that students of the Alice Academy receive a variable monthly allowance linked to their school performance. Students often shop with the allowance in the nearby town where there are a variety of specialty shops, including a bakery, a stationery store, and shops selling clothing. Mikan wants desperately to go there. She says, "I am so excited to go shopping [...] I can't wait to get there". Mikan is fascinated by the products shown in the shops, such as a magic pillow that can produce romantic dreams. Her allowance of five rabbits is far from sufficient to get any of her dream products. A magical pillow costs 5,000 rabbits and a dress costs 300 rabbits. She keeps on saying, "I want this... It is so cute... I really want to get this... But it is too expensive." She becomes very upset after spending her money on an apple. She says, "I have no money, therefore, no hope." A classmate buys a box of candy that is described as the most popular snack in town. It is soft and tasty, and people feel happy when eating it. Mikan cannot wait for another month's allowance to try the product. She wants it right now. She offers to do a body massage or polish shoes in order to earn money for the candy. With the help of her classmates, she performs a skit of Danish author H. C. Andersen's story *The Little Match Girl*. The street show enables Mikan to earn enough money to buy the candy. She comments that the candy tastes superb because it was bought with her own effort. The program introduces a variety of products and services, including stationery, bedding, plants, snacks, clothing, matches, body massage, shoe-polishing, a clown performing on the street, and a dramatic performance. The content shows the prices of some of the products and compares the prices with Mikan's allowance.

"Glorification of consumption" was identified as a dominant theme in this program. Girls were portrayed as enthusiastic consumers fascinated by cute and fun stuff. Girls were also interested in products related to romance. The excitement of possessing the products and the frustration of not possessing them are expressed verbally. Materialistic values are communicated, as material possessions are linked with happiness, and possessions play a central role in the children's life in the television program (Richins & Dawson, 1992).

*Max and Ruby* is an animated cartoon series produced in the United States and broadcast in our sample in the USA. Max is a three-year-old bunny who lives with Ruby, a smart, goal-oriented seven-year-old. In the episode entitled *Ruby's Beach Party*, Ruby and her friends want to enjoy a beach party near a pile of sand in the backyard. As Max and his friend Morris play with toy dump trucks, Ruby tries to entice them away from the sand by offering them other toys, such as a screaming alien gorilla, a baseball and baseball glove, and a toss-a-ring toy. In another episode, *Super Max to the Rescue*, Max is portrayed playing with his toys at home; including a stuffed elephant, a train set, a toy bus, and blocks. As he plays, Max envisions himself as a super-hero, rescuing his toys when they are in trouble. Ruby and her friends take their toys to the backyard to set up a circus performance. Each of her toys has a role to play. The Jack-in-the-box is the clown, the doll Emily the star acrobat, the walkie-talkie bear the dancing bear, and the one-monkey band is the orchestra. Ruby tries to find a role for the stuffed elephant. Finally, the stuffed elephant saves the doll, Emily, when she accidentally falls out of a tree. Again, the dominant theme of "glorification of consumption" was communicated. Toys were portrayed as agents for excitement, empowerment, and exemption from boredom. Both boys and girls were portrayed as actively playing with toys in the program.

*Sesame Street* is an educational program for preschoolers and kindergarteners produced as well as broadcast in our sample in the United States. One episode features a special topic on food. It opens with Big Bird, Elmo and Telly visiting a restaurant. Elmo introduces the different types of food that children from different cultures eat, and how they eat it. A Chinese girl, for example, is shown eating a bowl of rice with chopsticks. The consumption activities serve as a backdrop to introduce the topic of food. No obvious theme on consumption values was communicated.

*Cinderella* is a Japanese cartoon series dubbed into Cantonese and broadcast, in our sample, in Hong Kong for elementary school children. In an episode entitled *Artist Jo*, Cinderella's two sisters hire professional artists to draw portraits that they plan to present to the prince. Since they are not satisfied with these portrayals, they send Cinderella to search for Jo, a famous artist to prepare other portraits. In another episode, entitled *Robbers*, Cinderella's mother goes to town and buys a beautiful hat. She boasts that one of her daughters will be selected to be the prince's bride. A number of tradesmen, including tailors and jewelry-makers, are eager to offer their services to Cinderella's family. The program introduces a dominant theme of the importance of consumer products and services to improve the physical appearance of girls in order to attract boys' attention.

*Hannah Montana* is an American television series for teenagers, broadcast in our sample in Australia. Miley Stewart, the program's main character, is a typical teenage school girl during the day and a famous pop singer named Hannah Montana at night. The episode sampled is titled *It's a Mannequin's World*. It is about Miley's father, Robbie, buying a childish outfit for Miley as a birthday present – a cute pink jumper with a mouse head in the front and a long tail at the back. Miley finds it embarrassing to wear the jumper at her birthday party. However, she does not want to tell her dad the truth as it would hurt his feelings. At the birthday party, two classmates attempt to get a picture of Miley in her cute outfit in order to disgrace her. Finally, she gains the courage to confront them, saying, "I love this sweater because it was given to me by someone that I care about very much." Altogether, 12 consumption activities were shown in the episode, seven of which involved buying clothes. Girls were featured shopping together at the mall for cool outfits and her dad was featured as a consumer shopping for clothing as presents.

A dominant theme that we identified in *Hannah Montana* was the conflict between the consumption values of adolescents and adults. Selecting cool products versus selecting cute products was the focus of a dramatic split between teenagers and adults. Studies have confirmed that clothing is used by teenagers to confer status to the owner, as well as to symbolize group identity and a sense of belonging to a certain group (Jamison, 1996). It has been shown in laboratory experiments that clothing brands were associated with self-identity for both third graders as well as seventh and eighth graders (Chaplin & John, 2005). The *Hannah Montana* episode supports this theme that clothing is an important consumer product for self-expression especially among teenager girls. The script suggests that clothing can enhance or exploit social relationships.

*Blue's Clue* is an American pre-school educational program broadcast in the United States in our sample. In the episode analyzed, toys such as a pail, shovel, and block are used as teaching and learning aids in introducing concepts of gravity. A bicycle, scooter, toy car, and skateboard introduce directional skills such as pushing a pedal and turning a steering wheel. The program also shows how to use a tape-recorder by pressing one button for recording and another button for play-back. Altogether 12 consumption activities were featured, most involving use of toys. No obvious theme on consumption values was communicated.

In summary, gender differences in consumption activities and consumption values are demonstrated in these qualitative analyses. Stories about purchase of clothing are the preserve of girls, only while boys are featured as product users of toys. Girls are concerned about social acceptance of their purchase while boys are concerned with hedonic aspects of the consumption. These results reinforced our arguments about gender differences observed from the quantitative content analysis.

## Conclusion

This study examined the portrayal of consumption and consumption values in children's television programs in a cross-cultural sample. The quantitative and qualitative content analyses generated three major findings.

First, the portrayal of consumption activities in children's television programs was distributed unevenly among the countries and programs sampled. Indicating the importance of basic needs and play in children's lives, consumption in children's programs most often featured food, toys and entertainment.

Second, there was no statistical difference in terms of the proportion of males or females featured as product users in television programs for children. However, there were significant differences in types of product categories by gender: There were products that were used only by females or only by males in television programs for children. Females were more likely to be associated with clothing and males were more likely to be associated with media and computers. Females may be seeking social acceptance in their purchases and consumption, while males seem to look for enjoyment and excitement in their purchases and consumption.

Third, consumption values were more likely to be featured in programs for older children. Consumption activities were mainly peripheral and served to support the story in programs for pre-school children. Here, consumption-related activities seemed to be used to teach certain concepts or skills, but consumption values were seldom featured explicitly. Consumption values did, though, make up a core part of the programs for older children and teenagers.

In conclusion, television programs in the countries represented in the research corpus engaged in different types of consumption-related activities.

While consumption of products and services were used as means in programs for younger children, consumption of products and services were embedded in the stories to communicate certain consumption values in programs for older children. Three dominant themes about consumption values were identified: glorification of consumption, conflict between children and adults in consumption values, and the importance of consumer products in enhancing physical beauty of females. Both qualitative and quantitative studies found gender difference in consumption activities and values portrayed in television programs for children.

Consumption and consumption values play an important role in children's television programs. Such programs presumably have a strong influence on consumer socialization through modeling and reinforcement. Gender differences demonstrated in the quantitative content analysis and qualitative theme analysis supported the feminist criticism of the frequent portrayal of women as objects, as well as, consumable items.

Of course, content analysis alone is limited as a research method because it generates no information about how the audience interprets the content. Future studies might profit from use of focus group interviews or personal interviews to investigate how children and their parents read the social and symbolic meanings of the consumption behavior portrayed in television programs for children.

## *REFERENCES*

Bachen, C., & Illouz, E. (1996). Imagining romance: Young people's cultural models of romance and love. *Critical Studies in Mass Communication, 13*(4), 279-308.

Chan, K. (2005). Store visits and information sources among urban Chinese children. *Journal of Consumer Marketing, 22*(4), 178-188.

Chaplin, L. N., & John, D. R. (2005). The development of self-brand connections in children and adolescents. *Journal of Consumer Research, 32*(1), 119-129.

Gauntlett, D. (2008). *Media, Gender and Identity: An Introduction* (2nd ed.). London, England: Routledge.

Jamison, D. J. (1996). *Idols of the tribe: Brand veneration and group identity among preadolescent consumers.* Working paper. Gainesville, FL: Department of Marketing, University of Florida.

Kassarjian, H. H. (1977). Content analysis in consumer research. *Journal of Consumer Research, 4*(1), 8-18.

Lemish, D. (2007). *Children and television: A global perspective.* Oxford, UK: Blackwell.

Marshall, C., & Rossman, G. (1999). *Designing Qualitative Research* (3rd ed.). Thousand Oaks, CA: Sage.

Quart, A. (2003). *Branded: The Buying and Selling of Teenagers.* New York, NY: Basic Books.

Richins, M. L., & Dawson, S. (1992). A consumer values orientation for materialism and its measurement: Scale development and validation. *Journal of Consumer Research, 19*(3), 303-316.

Strauss, A. L. (1987). *Qualitative Analysis for Social Scientists.* Cambridge, MA: Cambridge University Press.

Wilska, T. A. (2005). *Gender differences in the consumption of children and young people in Finland.* A paper presented at the 7th ESA conference Rethinking Inequalities, September 9-12, Torun, Poland. Available at http://sifo.no/files/Wilska.pdf.

Xia, W., Chan, K., & Chan, F. (2004). Consumer behavior reflected in a Chinese TV cartoon series: The big head son and the small head dad. *Xinwen Yu Chuanbo Yanjiu (Journalism and Communication Research), 11*(2), 21-26. [In Chinese]

# 9

# "WHAT REALLY ANNOYS ME ABOUT THE WAY GIRLS AND BOYS ARE PORTRAYED IN CHILDREN'S TELEVISION"
## Children from 21 Countries Write Illustrated Letters to TV Producers

*Maya Götz* and *Margit Herche*

To date, analyses of children's television programs are undertaken by adults. It is they who earn their living by creating and investigating media. They have tools at their disposal to conduct extensive analyses of media, they are capable of drawing theoretical connections, and they have the privilege of the time and resources to consider these matters. On the other hand, the target audience of children's television, children, are involved to a very limited extent in such studies. For example, children might be subjects of gender-related media reception research; asked to select and then label their favourite characters, according to their traits (e.g., Aubrey & Harrison, 2004; Calvert, Jordan, & Cocking, 2002; Thompson & Zerbinos, 1997), or, given the possibility to engage in a creative exercise and explain themselves (Götz, Lemish, Aidman & Moon, 2005). However, rarely do researchers ask them directly about their perceptions of a research category, such as gender. Those few studies that provided children with dedicated space to grapple with this category (e.g., Currie, Kelly, & Ponerantz, 2009; Hains, 2008; Kearney, 2011; Mazzarella, 2005; Zaslow, 2009) have shown how elucidating their feedback can be.

Following the lead of these studies with direct involvement of children, this project solicited their responses to representations of gender. Since the overall study is international in scope and seeks to provide an overview, we selected a method that enabled children from diverse countries to share their feedback with television producers. This process was guided by the following two research questions: What do children throughout the world criticize about the ways boys and girls are shown on children's television? What changes would they like to see?

## I. Method

### Sample

In total, 1131 children from ages 8-11 from 21 countries[1] and all major religions around the world took part in the study. There were 638 girls (56%) and 493 boys (44%). Where possible, the sample sought to account for diversity within individual countries. For example, in Germany and Hungary city children from Munich and Budapest, as well as, children from village schools in Altdöbern (Brandenburg, Germany) and Tótvázsony (Komitat Veszprém, Hungary) took part. In India and Ukraine, it was possible to involve children from New Delhi and Kiev, as well as, from other parts of the country (e.g., children of the Kol people in Uttar Pradesh, India, and children from the village Ulyanovka in Ukraine). Care was also taken to include children from well-off families, as well as, children from socially deprived backgrounds. In Argentina, for example, schools with a very diverse social intake were involved and their pupils interviewed. Several private schools (from Pakistan and Fiji) as well as orphanage schools (Déva, Romania) were involved. Additionally, many children with immigrant backgrounds from a range of schools in Munich, Budapest and Suva, for example, participated. But, let us be clear, we do not claim that this study is representative. Nonetheless, we do think that the variety of modes utilized reduces sampling errors to a certain degree.

### Procedure

A detailed procedure was developed so that it could be conducted locally with the help of teachers. The results produced by the children, directed by their teachers, are indicative that our directions were clear. Following an introductory discussion about the children's television shows they watched and/or were familiar, and TV characters they liked or disliked, each child was given a worksheet. The children filled in their personal data (age, name, gender, country, language), and then they were instructed to write and illustrate two letters addressed to television producers. The title on the page given to the children for their letters and illustrations stated: "What really bothers me about the way girls or boys are shown on children's television." Following completion of the two drawings, the children wrote one to two sentences about each of their pictures, stating what bothered them and why, as well as what they would like to change.

In order to effectively categorize the children's statements and the shows and characters they criticized, teachers conducted short individual interviews in which they asked each child to describe the extent to which the drawings referred to a specific show or character, and if so they were asked to name them. All of the children's responses were documented and subsequently translated into English, along with the sentences each child wrote about their pictures.

## Data Analysis

The analysis and evaluation of data was undertaken centrally by a small team in Germany (at the International Central Institute for Youth and Educational Television, IZI). The coordinators of the participating countries were available for consultation on individual details regarding the materials submitted. When evaluating the empirical data, the team attempted to take into account, as completely as possible, the full meaning of each individual student's statement or remark.[2] The focus of the analysis process was the children's individual statements and corresponding pictures. It was not possible to gain deeper insight into their life-world or even their family background. Thus, the possibility of reconstruction is limited. Similar statements were grouped together and coded accordingly. This allowed for a limited quantitative evaluation. This having been noted, we wish to emphasize that the main aim of this study was to give the girls and boys a voice of their own, in order to allow them to express through words and pictures what it is that annoys them about the representation of boys and girls. This was the basis for determining if this documentation complements the adult views present in academic and public discussion of this topic.

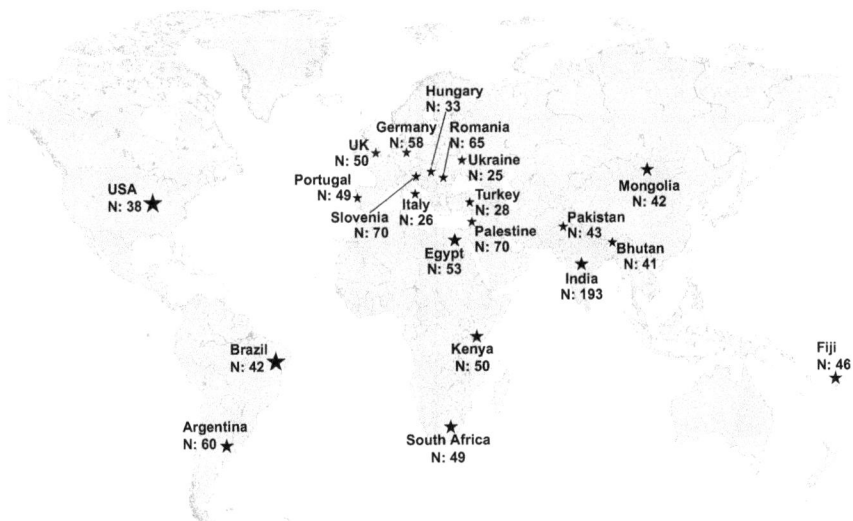

**Figure 9.1.**

Where the children's letters to TV producers came from (with numbers)

"I DON'T LIKE THAT BOYS BEAT UP ONE ANOTHER AND FREQUENTLY FIGHT ON TV."

MONGOLIA, BOY, 10

"MEN ARE TOO VIOLENT. I WOULD LIKE THEM MORE SENSITIVE."

BRAZIL, GIRL, 11

"I FIND ANNOYING THAT BOYS ARE SO VIOLENT – THEY SHOULD MAKE THEM LESS VIOLENT."

ARGENTINA, BOY, 9

"THEY FIGHT TOO MUCH! FIGHTING IS NOT GOOD!"

INDIA, GIRL, 8

## II. What Bothers Children about the Representation of Boy Characters

The children's criticisms are varied. Concrete shows and characters are referred to and formats on the global market (e.g., *Winx Club* [Rainbow S.p.A., Italy], *Bratz* [Mike Young Productions & Co, USA], *SpongeBob* [Nickelodeon Animation, USA], and *The Simpsons* [20th Century Fox, USA]) cited, as well as nationally produced and broadcast shows. Many children take a general stance on the representation of girls and boys on television, and occasionally (particularly in countries where there are limited offerings of children's TV), they criticize adult programs. In the following sections, we share their main criticisms of children's television and related exemplars of their comments and drawings.

### 1. They Are Always Fighting, and Are Aggressive and Violent

When girls and boys criticize the way boys are represented on television, they most frequently mention their aggressive behavior. Boys on TV are "only waging war" (boy, 10, Germany 114) and "fight with their friends" (boy, 10, Turkey 603). They are represented as "too aggressive" (boy, 10, Brazil 299) and "destructive" (boy, 10, Pakistan 310). Thus, many children conclude that "boys are shown as too cruel and angry" (Girl, 9, Mongolia 1124). Children know that "it is bad to fight" (girl, 8, Kenya 171), for "it brings violence into people's minds" (boy, 10, India 739) and "it persuades boys to fight" (girl, 10, UK 901).

The aggression of male television characters is also seen in the context of gender relations: "Men are too aggressive with women on TV" (boy, 10, Brazil 300). This includes sexual violence against girls and women, an act clearly rejected by children as wrong behavior: "They abuse us" (girl, 9, India 799) or "boys force girls to kiss them" (boy, 9, Kenya 156).

Suggestions for improvement offered to producers are simple and convincing: "Change violence into non-violence" (boy, 10, India 735); "make them more observant" (boy, 11, Pakistan 322). This does not mean they want to see only cowards, but "fearless boys" (boy, 9, Brazil 311). The boys, in particular, would rather learn how to control aggression than see violence represented: "I want him to control his anger" (boy, 10, India 773). Strength should be used for the right cause: "He should be good and should use his power against the bad forces" (boy, 10, Romania 540).

"HE HAS MANY TATTOOS AND MUSCLES (IN TV FILMS), OR HE IS TOO SHORT (IN FAIRY TALES)."

HUNGARY, GIRL, 10

"I DON'T LIKE THAT SPONGEBOB ONLY WEARS UNDERPANTS."

INDIA, BOY, 9

"BOYS ARE EITHER EXTREMELY STRONG AND POWERFUL OR VERY WEAK AND BEING TEASED BY EVERYBODY. I WOULD ALSO LIKE TO SEE SOME BOYS WHO ARE A LITTLE BIT MORE LIKE I AM."

UKRAINE, BOY, 11

"STUPID GUYS SHOWN ON TV MAKE ME ANGRY."

TURKEY, BOY, 12

"I DON'T LIKE BOYS CRYING ON TV. I WOULD CHANGE THAT HE IS HAPPY."

KENYA, BOY, 9

## 2. Not Just Stupid Losers and Wimps

However, boys' and girls' criticism of the representation of boys on television is also directed against their typical staging as "he's way too dumb" (girl, 9, Fiji 538). Boys who only have "jelly in their heads" (boy, 9, Germany 149) may be funny on occasion, but should not be characterized in such a manner constantly and exclusively: "He says rubbish" (boy, 11, Romania 520). The children's recommendation to TV producers for improvement is to "make him brainier by teaching him" (girl, 11, UK 903). This does not mean that girls and boys wish that the boys portrayed on television be "softer" or more feminine; on the contrary: "It bothers me when boys are too soft-hearted" (boy, 10, Hungary 23) and "boys are shown as weak and pathetic" (girl, 9, Mongolia 1117). "I think it's stupid that boys are sometimes small and weak" (girl, 9, Germany 124).

Children want to see clever, brave boys on television who are able to deal with their feelings: "They should be strong enough to do things in their way" (girl, 10, India 832), "fit and adventurous" (boy, 10, UK 919).

## 3. Normal Looks: Normal, Like Us

Children's criticism of the looks of boy characters is mentioned much less frequently. Sometimes the children think individual characters are "really fat and ugly" (girl, 9, UK 944) and find fault with scruffy hair: "He looks shabby" (girl, 10, India 822).

They did not approve of overly masculine styling with, for example, piercings, and earrings: "I don't like it when they wear many striking necklaces" (girl, 10, Hungary 24).

Clothing is criticized if it emphasizes the genitals too much: "I don't like that their trousers are so tight" (boy, 10, Romania 529); or, in an erotic manner: "I find it annoying when they open their T-shirt" (girl, 9, India 705). Children from non-Western cultures in particular are bothered when too much skin is shown: "I find it annoying that he is nearly naked" (girl, 10, Fiji 505). Even in a funny context this is the case, as with Bart Simpson who, for example, "was skating naked" (boy, 10, Fiji 517). SpongeBob, too, is criticized for being shown without trousers in some episodes.

Explicit criticism of the boys' body image tends to come more from girls, who find fault with characters as "too big" (girl, 8, Egypt 246) or stress that "I don't like big muscles" (girl, 10, Hungary 025). Children want television characters like themselves, both in terms of their physique and what they wear: "They should look exactly like [they do] in real life, with clothes they wear normally" (girl, 11, Brazil 330); "They should be like boys today, like me" (boy, 10, Argentina 214).

"GIRLS PUT ON GROWN UP'S CLOTHES AND ACT NOT ACCORDING THEIR AGE BUT TOO FLIRTATIOUS. THEY SHOULD BE NORMAL AND MODEST."

MONGOLIA, BOY, 9

"IT BOTHERS ME THAT GIRLS WEAR SHORT SKIRT AND PAINT THEIR FACES LIKE GROWN-UPS."

ARGENTINA, GIRL, 10

"IN CARTOONS THE GIRLS ARE SO THIN, IT'S NOT REALISTIC."

UK, GIRL, 10

"THEY HAVE STRANGE FIGURES."

SLOVENIA, GIRL, 8

## III. What Bothers Children about the Representation of Girl Characters

### 1. Girls with Sexy Clothes and a Lot of Make-up

Children's main starting point for criticism of girls on television was their appearance. Every second statement is directed explicitly at their clothes, particularly in what they regard as inappropriate sexualization. Clothing shows too much skin, turns the girls into sex objects and above all is inappropriate for their age: "Girls put on grown up's clothes and [do not] act their age, but [are] too flirtatious" (boy, 9, Mongolia 1119). Their styling is unsuitable and characters such as those in *Winx Club* or the Bratz girls "look like prostitutes" (girl, 9, Kenya 194).

Criticism of very short skirts and tight or cropped T-shirts was particularly strong in non-Western countries. For example, an Indian girl (10, 816) wrote: "They don't wear proper clothing; their stomach is shown like in Kim Possible". A girl (9, 535) from Romania criticizes the female protagonists of the US cartoon *Horseland* (DiC Entertainment, USA): "It bothers me that you can see their stomach". Children from non-Western cultural backgrounds, in particular, perceive there to be a divergence from their societies' socially accepted dress codes. Thus, an Indian girl (9, 814) states: "Girls wear short dresses and this is not allowed in some regions." Sexualized clothing is seen within the context of the threat of sexual violence: "Some girls are sometimes forced to wear short clothes which leads to rape" (girl, 9, Kenya 163).

Many children also criticized the heavy make-up worn by girl characters in conjunction with sexualizing clothing: "[It's] annoying that girls use too much make-up and always show off" (girl, 10, Fiji 506). Children recommend: "Do not let them put so much make-up on their face" (girl, 9, Romania 533), so that they look "younger and childlike" (boy, 12, Turkey 610).

### 2. Wasp Waists and Plastic Surgery

Besides sexualized clothing and make-up, children also found fault with the body image used in portraying girl characters on television. This starts with use of the wrong proportions of the female body – "when their legs are too long" (girl, 10, Hungary 25) – and escalates with hips that are often far too slender: "In cartoons the girls are so thin, it's not realistic" (girl, 10, UK 901). Children feel the pressure of "parents and the television telling them that thinner is prettier" (girl, 10, Argentina 226). Children prefer natural, healthier body images on TV shows: "I don't like dyed hair, their body shape and their mouth. They should have normal body and hair" (girl, 8, Slovenia 426). "I like natural beauty, not 'artificial beauties'" (girl, 12, Ukraine 1212). They do not want girls who are too thin. Instead, they prefer female characters with normal proportions that mirror reality.

"IT'S BAD THAT GIRLS CRY SO MUCH ON TV SHOWS."

UKRAINE, GIRL, 11

"THEY ALWAYS CRY AND HAVE A SQUEAKY VOICE."

BHUTAN, GIRL, 9

"SHOWS PORTRAY THAT BLONDES ARE DUMB. ALL BLONDES ARE NOT DUMB. I WOULD NOT MAKE ALL DUMB PEOPLE BLOND."

USA, GIRL, 10

"TV PEOPLE MAKE SMART GIRLS NERDS. ALWAYS! MAKE THE GIRLS COOL PEOPLE."

How tv people potray smart girls as NERDS !!

NERD

FIJI, GIRL, 10

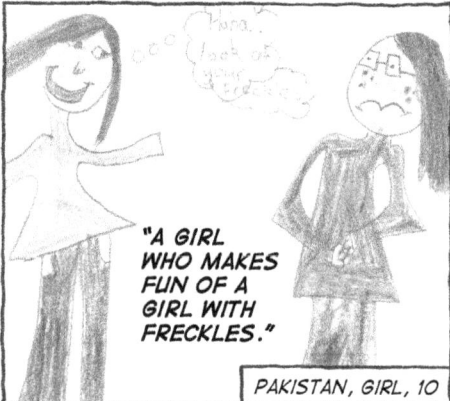

"A GIRL WHO MAKES FUN OF A GIRL WITH FRECKLES."

PAKISTAN, GIRL, 10

### 3. Why Always Blond and Stupid, or Clever and Ugly?

When hair color was mentioned by the children, it was usually for two reasons – use of unnatural hair coloring and showing blonde girls far too frequently. This was noted particularly in countries such as Egypt and India, where the majority of the population is not blond but dark-haired. Again, it seems to be the case that children want to see more natural hair colors that are like their own (girl, 10, India 734; girl, 9, Egypt 243; girl, 10, Egypt 274; girl, 10, Egypt 267).

In countries where blond hair occurs naturally, children criticized use of wrongful and clichéd stereotypes: "Shows portray that blondes are dumb. All blondes are not dumb" (girl, 10, USA 1027). Her suggestion for improvement: "I would not make all dumb people blond. Make them brunettes" (girl, 10, USA 1027). This girl does not ask the basic question of whether girls should be shown as less intellectually capable in some marginal cases. But she does criticize repeated stereotyping. A 9-year-old boy (242) from Argentina observes that when particularly clever characters are typified the girls are purposely shown with "braces, glasses and ugly plaits"; or "they always make smart people have glasses" (boy, 11, Fiji 528). Recommendations for change: "Make the smart girls cool people" (girl, 10, Fiji 507).

### 4. Why Always Bitchy, Competitive and Completely Overreacting Emotionally?

Girls and boys are also bothered by clichéd representations of character traits in television characters. For example, it annoys them "that girls are shown as so bitchy" (girl, 9, Germany 124) and "rude and bossy" (girl, 9, UK 949). The Bratz girls or Sam, Alex and Clover from *Totally Spies!* (Marathon, France) "always quarrel with each other" (girl, 10, Romania 516). Also, "girls are shown as too intimidating and bossy and they make fun of others" (boy, 10, Mongolia 1105). Instead of showing over and over how bitchy girls can be, the children demand more socially appropriate and friendly behavior, and more friendly contact between characters: "Girls should be nicer to each other" (girl, 10, Germany 126). This can set a good example for the viewer: "All the girl TV stars should set good examples" (boy, 11, USA 1038).

But it is not only bitchiness that children perceive as an unpleasant and exaggerated cliché in the representation of girls, as excessive emotionality of girl characters also bothers them, as in: "She always cries so much [that] everything is flooded" (boy, 10, Germany 131).

## IV. Criticism of Girl and Boy Characters in Comparison

It is exceptionally hard to quantify the qualitative data gathered, particularly from 1131 children from so many different cultural and personal backgrounds. Though the same set of instructions were used, fundamentally these are qualitative statements gathered in different locations, under different cultural conditions, and with different people. This important qualification having been noted, we did try to devolve categories from individual statements and to group many of them under general categories. This enabled us to order and quantify certain basic elements, and then, on this basis, to compare the most general points of criticism offered by the children regarding girl and boy characters. Acting, again, with great caution, we were able to clearly code 951 comments of criticisms relating to girl characters and 880 comments of criticisms of boy characters on television (see Figure 9.1).

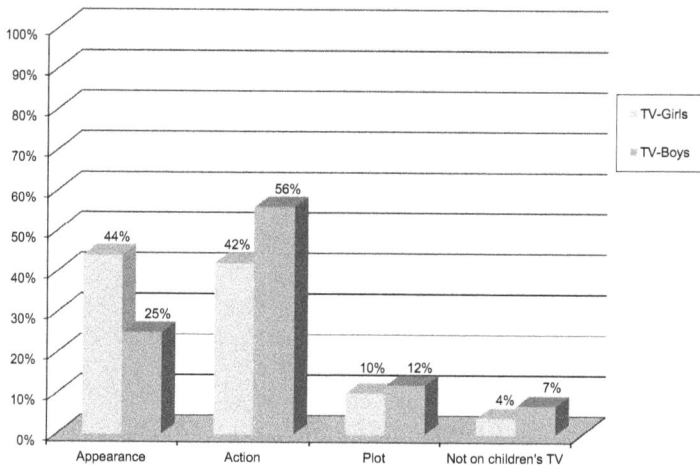

**Figure 9.1.**
What girls and boys in 21 countries criticized on TV-girls/boys

Criticism of girl television characters was most frequently directed at their appearance. 44% (n=426) of the illustrated letters make statements of this kind. Fault is found with clothing (n=223; 52% of criticisms of appearance), which is perceived as too sexy, simply ugly, too girly or too adult. If criticism is directed explicitly at the body, (n=65; 16% of criticisms of appearance), the body is thought to be lacking in proportion, too thin or sometimes overweight (see Figure 9.2).

The second main point of criticism relates to the characters' behavior and how their character traits are constructed. This criticism appears in 42% of all illustrated letters (see Figure 9.3).

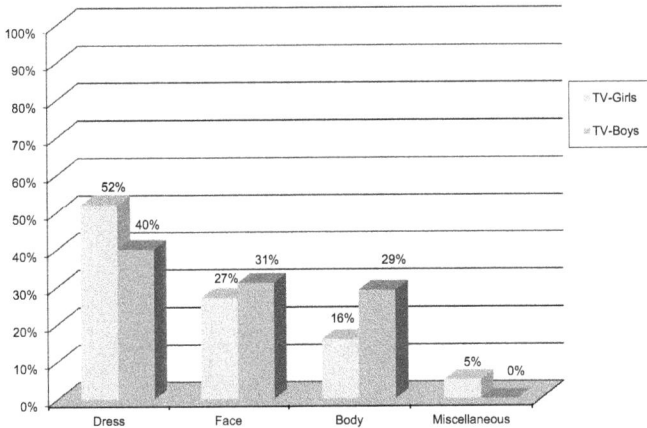

**Figure 9.2.**
What girls and boys criticized on the appearance of TV-girls/boys

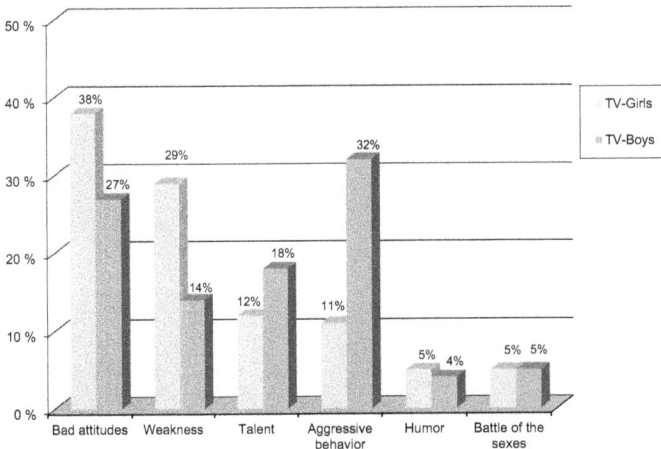

**Figure 9.3.**
What girls and boys criticized on the behavior of TV-girls/boys

Criticism of the representation of boys was dominated by their behavior and character traits (56%). Criticisms of their appearance make up only a quarter of statements. This is far lower than criticism of representation of girls. Indeed, only one in every fourth statement in the entire sample refers to the boys' appearance, unlike nearly half in regard to girl characters. Clothing, too, seems to play a less important role here.

"SHE DOES NOT WEAR A NATIONAL DRESS."

INDIA, GIRL, 10

"IT ANNOYS ME WHEN BOYS ARE PRESENTED AS STUPID AND BORING. I WOULD LIKE THEM SMARTER AND I WOULD CHANGE THEIR CLOTHES."

BRAZIL, BOY, 10

"I DON'T LIKE HER YELLOW HAIR. SHE SHOULD HAVE LONG AND DARK HAIR."

EGYPT, GIRL, 9

"THE PRESENTER DOESN'T WEAR SCARF 'HEADCOVER', HIJAB. SHE IS NOT BEAUTIFUL AND THE PLACE IS FULL OF MEN AND CARS."

PALESTINE, BOY, 9

"PERFECT PETER IS SO NICE AND CLEVER AND HE ALWAYS CRIES. HE SHOULD BE NASTY."

UK, BOY, 8

"BOYS SMOKE AND QUARREL WITH ONE ANOTHER. SMOKING ENDANGERS HEALTH."

UKRAINE, GIRL, 10

## V. National Tendencies

Though the children's statements vary from country to country, we might expect there to be some similarity. While there are such themes, these are individual statements and cannot be seen as representative of all the children of these countries. Nonetheless, they do raise points that are often deeply intertwined with the respective discourses of everyday culture and media agendas, or even simply with particular preferences.

Some of the criticisms raised by children from India can be seen as culturally specific, as in the case when children miss seeing typically Indian clothing; when a female TV presenter in Pakistan was criticized several times for not wearing legal clothing or a veil; or as was the case in other Muslim societies as the case of a Palestinian boy (9, 1207): "[She] doesn't wear scarf [as head cover] and the place is full of men and cars."

Similarly, we recall the matter of children portrayed dressed in clothing that is different from local custom. This was the case of criticism made in Egypt related to the predominance of blonde girls, something that clearly differs from the hair color of most children there.

In South Africa, one of the particular themes was that girls and boys were presented as "machos" (they use the word "nigger" in this context) and in a too positive light.

In Argentina children complained that boys were dressed like adults and behaved in a rude way like stealing something from other people or drinking a lot of alcohol.

One of the most commonly mentioned criticisms in Brazil was that boys on children's television are portrayed as excessively stupid. Disapproval was also often directed to girl's clothing, like: "They sould wear normal clothes not looking like a flamboyant woman but clothes they like, with not much exaggeration." (girl, 10, 331).

While children in Brazil referred to presenters in studio productions, children in Fiji expressed similar criticisms, for example in regard to cartoon characters.

One focus of criticism in Mongolia was the bad behavior and unkindness of boys. The depiction of obviously wrong behavior on the part of boys was also frequently criticized in the Ukraine (e.g., when it came to smoking).

"I DON'T LIKE THAT SHE IS SHOWN POOR AND HER DRESS IS RICHLY PATCHED."

ROMANIA, BOY, 11

"SOME GIRLS ARE SOMETIMES FORCED TO WEAR SHORT CLOTHES WHICH LEADS TO RAPE. WEARING SHORT CLOTHES IS BAD. I WOULD CHANGE THE DRESSING BY WEARING THE RIGHT CLOTHES."

KENYA, GIRL, 9

"THAT THE SLEEPING BEAUTY HAD TO SLEEP FOR 100 YEARS... BECAUSE SHE MISSES SO MUCH IN LIFE."

GERMANY, GIRL, 11

"IT ANNOYS ME THAT GIRLS ARE SHOWN NAKED. FASHIONABLE GIRLS SHOULD BE SHOWN ON TV!"

HUNGARY, GIRL, 9

"IT ANNOYS ME THAT GIRLS ALWAYS COOK ON TV."

HUNGARY, GIRL, 8

"GIRLS LOOK PERFECT ON TV."

USA, BOY, 11

In the United Kingdom, on the other hand, there was criticism that certain boy characters like "Perfect Peter" were too "nice and clever" and that it would not hurt if they were a bit "nasty" occasionally. Also the girl characters received strong disapproval for being too skinny. So appeal to the producers was: "Make the girls a tiny bit fatter." (girl, 10, UK 901).

The inappropriate, erroneous portrayal of boys as too strong and too brave was bemoaned by children in Bhutan and elsewhere.

In Germany, the behavior of girls on television was a particularly frequent object of criticism. They stated that they were portrayed as too aggressive in some programs or as too passive in traditional stories.

Children in Hungary frequently criticized the depiction of too many stereotypically gender-specific jobs.

In Kenya, the sexualization of girls was linked to sexual violence several times. This is a major concern given the HIV/AIDS epidemic and associated sexual violence.

A frequent criticism from Portugal was that girls were portrayed as too self-centered, trendy, and obsessed with their appearance.

In the United States, children raised the point several times that the girls were too perfect.

Thanks to the current debate in the media, several Italian children criticized plastic surgery for girls and women. In Hungary, the theme of explicit sex videos and nudity was touched on several times, as a particular concern of girls there.

Only in Romania was there an appeal not to show girls so explicitly in impoverished clothes. The main criticism made by children from Argentina was the excessive emphasis on crime among boy characters.

Interpreting the comments within the varied specific cultural contexts is of immense importance but is beyond the scope of this descriptive chapter (e.g., Lemish, 2010).

"BOYS ARE ALWAYS MORE SPORTY AND STRONGER THAN GIRLS. SOME GIRLS (LIKE ME) ARE EXTREMELY STRONG AND SPORTY BUT ON TV SHOWS THEY MAKE GIRLS FRILLY AND PRISSY."

USA, GIRL, 11

"BOYS ARE ALWAYS THE BAD GUYS. I WOULD MAKE GIRLS AND BOYS THE GOOD GUYS AND THE BAD GUYS."

PAKISTAN, BOY, 10

"BOYS TRY TO SHOW OFF THEIR SPORT SKILLS. GIRLS CAN DO THINGS, TOO."

PAKISTAN, GIRL, 8

"GIRLS ARE SHOWN ON TV MORE AT HOME AS HOUSEWIVES. SHOW THEM AS SPORTS PEOPLE."

PAKISTAN, BOY, 11

"GIRLS ARE GIRLY AND NEVER PLAY SPORTS OR BE THE HERO. THEY SHOULD NOT BE SO MUCH LIKE GIRLS, ALL ABOUT PRETTY THINGS, AND BE THE HERO!"

Girls should be shown better on TV!!!
Girls Hot!!

PAKISTAN, GIRL, 10

"THERE ARE MORE BOY SMURFS THAN GIRL SMURFS. THERE IS ONLY ONE GIRL SMURF. I WOULD ADD MORE SMURFS THAT ARE GIRLS."

USA, BOY, 11

## VI. Children Recognize Gender Stereotypes

The children's observations and criticisms demonstrate, clearly, in our view, how capable girls and boys can be as critical viewers. When given the opportunity to share their views about the programs aimed at them (as this exploratory study attempted to do), they are definitely capable of identifying clichés and gender relations. This includes quantification, as in the assessment: "There are more boy smurfs than girl smurfs. There is only one girl smurf" (boy, 11, USA 1006); statements about their favorite characters, with penetrating observations such as – only male heroes have the main roles: "I don't like that SpongeBob doesn't have a girlfriend. He should have one and her name should be Bettina!" (girl, 9, Germany 109).

Children also detect gender stereotypes such as a Pakistani boy (11, Pakistan 323), who shared, first an observation: "Girls are shown on TV more at home as housewives" and, then, a recommendation: "Show them as sports people". Children also recognize inequality: "Girls are girly and never play sports or be the hero" (girl, 10, Pakistan 314). A Romanian girl (8, 515) recommends changing this situation: "It annoys me that girls are not boys' equals. Girls should be stronger, too". "Girls are shown as weaklings", according to a Pakistani boy's (10, 310) description of the female characters.

Children notice gender differences in role constellations, and are bothered by them: "Boys are always the bad guys. I would make girls and boys the good guys and the bad guys" (boy, 10, Pakistan 309). Thus, they explicitly demand gender equality in the distribution of both good and bad characters. "The girls are defenseless and they are never the heroine" (girl, 10, Brazil 332). They notice these gender-specific tendencies precisely because they experience themselves as competent: "Boys are always more sporty and stronger than girls. Some girls (like me) are extremely strong and sporty but on TV shows they make girls frilly and prissy" (girl, 11, USA 1016). As this is not shown on television, a girl (10, 1102) from Mongolia for example supposes that "TV people prefer boys over girls and show only boys on their programs". She suggests: "Girls and boys should be equally shown on TV", and a Brazilian girl (11, 302) adds: "Boys and girls have the same right to be protagonists".

## Conclusion

Children from all over the world take note of and criticize certain aspects of the ways in which girls and boys are represented. However, this does not mean that those aspects criticized are not influential. Even if noted and criticized, in some way or another they probably will become part of the children's mental images of what it means to be a "real" woman, a "real" girl or a "real" man or boy. However, if given the opportunity to offer criticism and make recommendations, the children's views shared in this study simply contradict the statement employed all too often, and it seems quite inaccurately, by producers: "But they want it that way, that is just what makes it attractive".

Stated simply and directly, it is our conclusion that children take exception to many typical aspects of gender representation, and gender-specific tendencies noted here.

Girl characters' stereotypical, hypersexualized appearance is seen, in particular, as unpleasant and diverging from everyday experience. Children certainly notice that girls on television are strongly made-up and dressed in a much more adult manner than they are themselves. Actually, they would prefer to see girls represented as they really are – maybe idealized slightly, but not (or not exclusively) in terms of hypersexualization.

Thus, the critical analyses of the body (see Götz & Herche, chapter 2) and its staging (see Prinsloo, chapter 3) by both "scholars and children" are remarkably consistent. Children criticize stereotypes, constantly rehearsing certain combinations of traits. While academic research identifies some of these in statistical terms (see Götz & Lemish, chapter 1), the children seem to employ a sharper, more critical view. Today's girls and boys know very well, for example, that intelligence and looks are not necessarily related. Accordingly, they object to the stereotypical depiction of clever girls as ugly. The clichéd representation of female stereotypes in TV girls, who are shown as "bitchy" and "emotionally overact", diverges from their multifaceted everyday experience of girls and the ways girls communicate and express their emotions. This is the variety they would like to see mirrored in TV characters. They would also like to see their own appearance, skin and hair color, and culturally specific way of dressing represented among other aspects. However, as the international media analysis (see Götz & Lemish, chapter 1) or the qualitative analysis of the "exotic TV-girls" (see Spry, chapter 4) have shown, girls on TV are mainly white and from a Western industrial cultural background.

Male television characters' portrayal as constant, often purely aggressive fighting and "violent behavior" forms the main point of criticism of the representation of boys and men on TV. Children, like their academic counterparts (see Götz & Lemish, chapter 1), recognize that boy characters are more differentiated than female TV characters, but nonetheless their appearance is clichéd. The children in this study see them as appearing either as successful fighters or competitors, or as "stupid losers" who just muddle their way through. Children's everyday experience of boys is much more varied and multi-faceted. This is the variety they would like to see in their television heroes, as well as more positive perspectives above all, such as strategies for managing conflict and everyday life.

Altogether, the present study and its various analyses can be summarized as showing a fairly clear and consistent picture of stereotypical representations of gender, none of which correspond to reality. The underlying reasons for use of these portrayals are varied and complex. But, in the interest of promoting quality and supporting girls and boys in negotiating their identity, it should be stated: In an increasingly globalized and diverse world, it would certainly do children's television good to take note of these critical voices and analyses, and to consider them in a self-critical manner.

The global children's TV market is clearly dominated by North America as it holds 60% of the market share in over 24 countries. Most of these programs are created by men. Of 531 programs offered internationally, 86% are directed by men.[3] Only some of these appear sensitive towards gender issues (Lemish, 2010). Thus, it is all the more important to collaborate closely when developing the symbolic material used by children across the globe in forming their ideas and perspectives of the world and what it means to be a girl or woman, or a boy or man. For, as Spiderman says so fittingly, "With great power comes great responsibility".

# REFERENCES

Aubrey, J. S., & Harrison, K. (2004). The gender-role content of children's favorite television programs and its links to their gender-related perceptions. *Media Psychology*, 6(2), 111-146.

Calvert, S. L., Jordan, A. B., & Cocking, R. R. (2002). *Children in the Digital Age: Influences of Electronic Media on Development.* Westport, CT: Praeger.

Currie, D., Kelly, D., & Ponerantz, S. (2009). *'Girl Power': Girls Reinventing Girlhood.* New York, NY: Peter Lang.

Götz, M., Lemish, D., Aidman, A., & Moon, H. (2005). *Media and the Make-Believe Worlds of Children: When Harry Potter Meets Pokémon in Disneyland.* Mahwah, NJ: Erlbaum.

Hains, R. C. (2008). Are super girls super for girls? The negotiation of beauty ideals in girl power cartoons. *TelevIZIon*, 21, 10-15.

Kearney, M. C. (2011). *Mediated Girlhoods: New Explorations of Girls' Media Culture.* New York, NY: Peter Lang.

Lemish, D. (2010). *Screening Gender on Children's Television: The View of Producers around the World.* New York, NY: Routledge.

Mazzarella, S. (2010). *Girl Wide Web: Revisiting Girls, the Internet and the Negotiation of Identity.* New York, NY: Peter Lang.

Thompson, T., & Zerbinos, E. (1997). Television Cartoons: Do Children Notice It's a Boy's World? *Sex roles*, 37, 415-432.

Zaslow, E. (2009). *Feminism, Inc.: Coming of Age in Girl Power Media Culture.* New York, NY: Palgrave MacMillan.

[1] The following countries took part in the study: Egypt, Argentina, Bhutan, Brazil, Germany, Fiji, India, Italy, Kenya, Pakistan, Palestine, Portugal, Romania, Slovenia, South Africa, Turkey, Ukraine, Hungary, UK, Mongolia, USA.

[2] Some of the data gathered could not be used, as the children only completed one illustrated letter, did not object to the representation, or because their handwriting, sentence structure or statements were indecipherable.

[3] According to the evaluation of the IZI of the female and male producers of the cartoons listed in: Cannes Catalogue 2010: The MIPCON Junior Catalogue/Guide; published by Reed MIDEM. Paris, France.

# About the Authors and Their Own Favorite Character When They Were a Child

## Kara Chan

Kara Chan (Ph.D., City University of Hong Kong) is Professor and Chair of the Department of Communication Studies at Hong Kong Baptist University. Her research focuses on children, youth, advertising, media discourse as well as consumer behavior. She is the author and co-author of several books, including *Advertising to Children in China* (Chinese University Press, 2004) and *Youth and Consumption* (City University of Hong Kong Press, 2010). She worked for more than ten years in the advertising and public relations industry and as a statistician for the Hong Kong Government. She has published over 100 journal articles and book chapters on advertising, consumer studies, and gender studies.

Kara was raised in Hong Kong. Her favorite children's magazine as a child was the weekly *Children's Paradise.* It resembled a child version of *Readers' Digest* and published stories from all over the world that always fascinated her. Her favorite movie character was Oliver Twist.

## Maya Götz

Maya Götz is Head of the International Central Institute for Youth and Educational Television (IZI) at the Bayerischer Rundfunk (i.e., Bavarian Broadcasting Corp.) in Munich, Germany. She is also head of the PRIX JEUNESSE Foundation. She graduated from the Pädagogische Hochschule in Kiel (Germany) with the state examination as well as a Master of Arts degree in education. In 1998 she was granted a Ph.D. degree by the University of Kassel in Germany. The title of her doctoral thesis was *Girls and Television*. Her main fields of research are children/youth and television and gender-specific reception research. Her publications include the books *Children and Media in Times of War and Conflict* (co-edited with Lemish, Hampton Press, 2007); *Media and the Make-Believe Worlds of Children: When Harry Potter Meets Pokémon in Disneyland* (with Lemish, Aidman, & Moon; Lawrence Erlbaum, 2005); *Only Soap Bubbles? The Significance of Daily Soaps for the Everyday Life of Children and Adolescents* (KoPaed, 2002, in German) and the upcoming *The TV-Hero(in)es of Girls and Boys* (in German).

In childhood, her favorite TV characters were Maya the Bee, a character with a waist-to-hip ratio (WHR) of 1.3, and Vicky from the series *Vicky the Viking*. Vicky is actually a boy, but he is depicted in a gender-neutral way so that Maya unquestioningly considered him a girl.

## Margit Herche

Margit Herche graduated from the University of Regensburg with a Master of Arts degree in English and German Literatures as well as Gender Studies. She worked at the IZI at the Bavarian Broadcasting Corp. in Munich, Germany, as a free-lancer. She was responsible for the research projects – *The body of the "global" girl and boy in animated children's programs* and *What annoys children around the world about the portrayal of girls and boys on TV?*. Currently, she works at a secondary modern school in Regensburg (Germany) and will be finishing her teacher's degree in 2013.

When she was a young girl, she was fascinated by the adventures of a miniature boy called Nils Holgersson, who became great friends with animals and traveled with them on a fantastic journey. She always imagined how awesome it must be to experience the world from a bird's view, flying on a staunch friend's back.

## Dafna Lemish

Dafna Lemish (Ph.D., The Ohio State University 1982) is Professor of Communication and Chair of the Department of Radio-TV at Southern Illinois University Carbondale, and founding editor of the *Journal of Children and Media*. Previously, she was Professor of Communication and Chair of the Department of Communication at Tel Aviv University in Israel. She is author of numerous books on children, media and gender representations including most recently: *Screening Gender on Children's Television: The Views of Producers Around the World* (Routledge, 2010); *Children and Television: A Global Perspective* (Blackwell, 2007); *Children and Media in Times of War and Conflict* (co-edited with Götz, Hampton Press, 2007); *Media and the Make-Believe Worlds of Children: When Harry Potter Meets Pokémon in Disneyland* (with Götz, Aidman, & Moon; Lawrence Erlbaum, 2005). In addition she has published over 120 academic articles and book chapters in these areas in several languages.

Dafna was raised in Israel before the introduction of TV but while visiting the US as a child she adored a brave and loyal dog named Rin Tin Tin, of the TV show with the same name, and always dreamed of having such a friend. And, then, when she was the mother of three children, the family raised a dog they called Rinti.

## Gunter Neubauer

Gunter Neubauer is a managing partner in the Tübingen Institute of Social Sciences (SOWIT) in Tübingen (Germany) and works as a social scientist, organizational consultant and group dynamics coach. He certified in the areas of education, theology and child-care/youth work. Today, he teaches at the Evangelische Hochschule (i.e., Protestant University of Applied Sciences) in Ludwigsburg (Germany). His current main areas of work are boys' and men's health (e.g., he is a collaborator in the first German report on men's health), gender competence and gender education (such as the topic "boys and men in children's day-care centers") and social work with boys. He has authored numerous expert's reports and articles in textbooks and journals in these fields (see www.sowit.de). He and Reinhard Winter have produced studies for the IZI on the qualities of characters and heroes for boys, on boys' interest in soaps, and in the representation of sexuality and eroticism on television.

Gunter Neubauer grew up in an environment with a skeptical attitude towards television and counted himself lucky to at least occasionally catch a glimpse of the heroes of *Bonanza, Daktari* and *Star Trek*. However, there was never a danger of him falling under the spell of a favorite character ...

## Jeanne Prinsloo

Jeanne Prinsloo (Ph.D., University of the Witwatersrand 2002) is an independent researcher/consultant in the broad fields of media, gender and education. Now, as Professor Emeritus, she remains affiliated with the School of Journalism and Media Studies at Rhodes University where she worked for eight years prior to relocating to Durban. She is also affiliated with the Centre for Communication, Media and Society at the University of KwaZulu-Natal, as an honorary professor. She continues to lecture postgraduate students and supervise research. Prior to working at Rhodes, she taught media studies and media education at the University of KwaZulu-Natal. Her research has been concerned broadly with media issues of representation and identities, notably gender, race and children in the postcolonial space of South Africa. She has published widely both in the form of academic journals and book chapters.

Jeanne grew up in South Africa prior to the arrival of television in the 1970s and in a household that eschewed American comics as trashy. Popular culture came in the form of imported British girl's magazines and Enid Blyton's *Famous Five*.

## Elke Schlote

Elke Schlote earned her Ph.D. in sociolinguistics at the University of Konstanz (Germany). She has been a researcher and scientific editor at IZI since 2005. Here, she is involved in publishing the review *TelevIZIon*. So far, she designed and conducted eleven extensive media analyses and qualitative reception research projects, mostly on topics of educational television and migration/diversity. She has published diverse book chapters on her work and authored many articles in *TelevIZIon*.

Nine-year-old Elke's favorite TV character was Sci-Fi superhero Captain Future. Captain Future and his team experienced thrilling adventures on strange planets and always emerged victorious because of their joint efforts as well as their intelligence and strength. However, Elke did not relate much to female crew member Joan – which isn't surprising given that she had a very limited role in the series. In this sense, Elke's interest in superheroes and gender stereotypes is quite long-standing!

## Damien Spry

Damien Spry was recently awarded his Ph.D. in Media and Communications from the University of Sydney. His thesis is titled *Mobile Media, Childhood and Politics in Australia and Japan*. His research into media use by children and young people has been presented in Germany, the United States, Japan, South Korea, and Australia. He is a co-editor of *Youth, Society and Mobile Media in Asia* (Routledge, 2010) and the author of numerous chapters on mobile media and the politics of childhood.

Growing up, Damien loved *Monkey*, the Japanese TV show (based on the Chinese classic tale *Journey to the West*). Monkey's weapon, a powerfully magical staff, was a favorite toy among the boys in the small town where he grew up in outback Australia. How he longed for Monkey's thick, bushy sideburns and magical powers: such insolence, what fighting skills!

## Reinhard Winter

Reinhard Winter (Ed.D.) is a psychodrama director who, together with Gunter Neubauer, heads the Tübingen Institute of Social Sciences (SOWIT) in Tübingen (Germany). At present, his main areas of work are boys (as in boys' education, health, boys at school, social work relating to boys) and project evaluation (in the area of intercultural openness and right-wing extremism). He has regular teaching assignments at the University of Tübingen, the University of Applied Sciences and Arts, Northwestern Switzerland and at the St. Gallen University of Applied Sciences. His latest publications are *Boys: An Instructional Manual. Understanding and Supporting Boys* (Beltz, 2011, in German) and *Boys and Health. An Interdisciplinary Handbook for Medicine, Psychology and Education* (co-edited with Stier, anticipated date of publication 2012, in German).

Growing up, one of his favorite television characters in his youth was Zebedee from the series *The Magic Roundabout*. Zebedee bounces on a spring and can do magic with his distinctive moustache.

Peter Lang · Internationaler Verlag der Wissenschaften

Kathleen Arendt / Patrick Rössler / Anja Kalch /
Franziska Spitzner

# Children's Film in Europe

**A Literature Review**

Frankfurt am Main, Berlin, Bern, Bruxelles, New York, Oxford, Wien, 2010.
XII, 164 pp., 1 fig., 3 graph.

ISBN 978-3-631-60454-0 · hardback € 34,80*

This book provides a comprehensive overview of the scientific literature
on children's film in Europe since the year 2000. An intensive research
using online sources, library catalogues, websites complemented by expert
interviews was conducted as basis for this literature review. The analysis
covers 42 European countries investigating three dimensions: children's film
funding, children's film production and distribution and children's film culture,
and systematizes the sources on a European, transnational and national level.
The distribution of available sources varies strongly depending on the region,
country, and dimension analyzed. In addition, recommendations for future
research and collaborative efforts are provided.

*Content:* Literature search and review on live-action feature films for children
in 42 European countries · Systematization on European, transnational
and national level · Analysis of three dimensions: funding, production and
distribution, culture · Recommendations for future research and collaboration

*The e-price includes German tax rate. Prices are subject to change without notice

Frankfurt am Main · Berlin · Bern · Bruxelles · New York · Oxford · Wien
Distribution: Verlag Peter Lang AG
Moosstr. 1, CH-2542 Pieterlen
Telefax 0041 (0)32/3761727
E-Mail info@peterlang.com

**40 Years of Academic Publishing**
**Homepage http://www.peterlang.com**